GONE WITH THE WHIM

Leaving the Bible Belt for Sin City

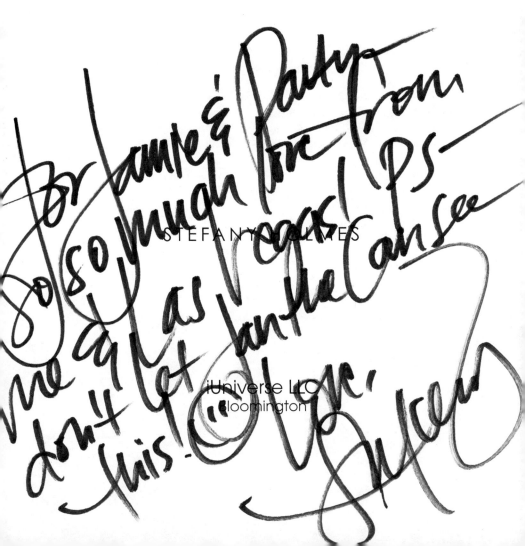

STEFANY HOLMES

iUniverse LLC
Bloomington

GONE WITH THE WHIM
LEAVING THE BIBLE BELT FOR SIN CITY

iUniverse books may be ordered through booksellers or by contacting:

iUniverse
1663 Liberty Drive
Bloomington, IN 47403
www.iuniverse.com
1-800-Authors (1-800-288-4677)

Because of the dynamic nature of the Internet, any web addresses or links contained in this book may have changed since publication and may no longer be valid. The views expressed in this work are solely those of the author and do not necessarily reflect the views of the publisher, and the publisher hereby disclaims any responsibility for them.

Any people depicted in stock imagery provided by Thinkstock are models, and such images are being used for illustrative purposes only. Certain stock imagery © Thinkstock.

ISBN: 978-1-4917-3031-7 (sc)
ISBN: 978-1-4917-3033-1 (hc)
ISBN: 978-1-4917-3032-4 (e)

Library of Congress Control Number: 2014906008

Printed in the United States of America.

iUniverse rev. date: 04/25/2014

Aria®, Bellagio®, Budweiser®,Beer Pong ™, Caesar's Palace®, Encore®, Foundation Room®, Ghostbar®, Jack Daniels®, Lavo®. Luxor®, NASCAR®, Mandalay Bay®, MGM Grand®, Paris®, Palms®, Planet Hollywood®, Rio®, Surrender®, The Cosmopolitan™ of Las Vegas, The Mirage®, The Pallazo®, The Venetian®, Tryst®, Wynn® Las Vegas,XS® Nightclub

8 1/2 Ultra Lounge & Piranha Nightclub. Information obtained from http:// www.piranhavegas.com/. Copyright 2013 Piranha Nightclub.

Boulder City. Information obtained from www.visitbouldercity. com. Copyright 2013 Boulder City, NV.

Cannery Casino Resorts Endorses Responsible Gaming. Las Vegas: Cannery Casino Resorts, LLC, 2011. Print.

Chateau Nightclub and Gardens. Information obtained from http://www. parislasvegas.com/things-to-do/chateau-nightclub-and-gardens.html. Copyright 2014 Caesars License Company, LLC.

City of Las Vegas. Information obtained from www.lasvegasnevada. gov. Copyright 2013, City of Las Vegas, NV.

Crown Nightclub. Information was obtained from http://www. thecrownvegas.com/nightclub/. Copyright 2010.

Fremont Street Experience (2013). Information obtained from www. vegasexperience.com.Copyright unknown. Stefany Holmes claims no copyright to information obtained from this website.

Ghostbar. Information was obtained from https://www.google.com/search?sourceid=n avclient&aq=&oq=the+palms+las+vegas+Ghostbar&ie=UTF-8&rlz=1T4MXGB_ enUS563US563&q=the+palms+las+vegas+Ghostbar. Copyright 2013 Palms Casino Resort.

Gilley's Saloon. Information was obtained from http://www.gilleyslasvegas. com/saloon. Copyright 2014 Treasure Island, LLC.

Hakkasan at MGM Grand. Information was obtained from http://hakkasanlv.com/. Copyright unknown.

Haze Nightclub. Information obtained from http://hazelasvegas.com/ home. Copyright 2014 Haze Nightclub – Las Vegas Nightclubs.

House of Blues Foundation Room. Information was obtained from http:// www.houseofblues.com/venues/clubvenues/foundationroom.php. Copyright 2014 House of Blues Entertainment, LLC, a Live Nation® company.

Hyde. Information obtained from http://vegasseven.com/channel/nightlife/. Copyright Unknown.

Las Vegas Weekly Magazine (2013). Information obtained from www.lasvegasweekly.com/magazine/. Copyright and Trademark property of Las Vegas Weekly.

Marquee Nightclub & Dayclub at the Cosmopolitan of Las Vegas. Information obtained from http://vegasseven.com/channel/nightlife/. Copyright unknown.

PBR Rock Bar. Information obtained from http://www.pbrrockbar. com/bar/. Copyright information unknown.

Responsible Gaming Means: Knowing When to Stop. Las Vegas: Caesars License, LLC, 2013. Print.

Rhumbar. Information obtained from http://rhumbarlv.com/index.php/about-us. *Copyright 2014 Rhumbar.*

Savile Row. Information obtained from http://www.luxor.com/nightlife/savile_row.aspx. *Copyright 2014 MGM Resorts International.*

Springs Preserve. Information obtained from www.springspreserve.org. *Copyright and Trademark 2013 property of Springs Preserve, Las Vegas, NV.*

Stratosphere. Information obtained from www.stratospherehotel.com. *Copyright and Trademark 2013 property of American Casino & Entertainment Properties.*

The Bank Nightclub. Information was obtained from http://thebanklasvegas.com/home, *copyright 2014.*

The Golden Nugget. Information obtained from www.goldennugget.com ,*copyright 2011 Golden Nugget Hotels & Casinos.*

Vanity Nightclub. Information obtained from http://www.hardrockhotel.com/party/vanity- nightclub-las-vegas. *Copyright 2014 Hard Rock Hotel & Casino.*

Vegas Seven (2013). Information obtained from www.vegasseven/digital/. *Author and Copyright unknown. Stefany Holmes claims no copyright to information obtained from this website.*

When The Fun Stops. Las Vegas: Nevada Council on Problem Gaming, 2012. Print.

For Driver and my mom

AUTHOR'S NOTE

In the interest of privacy, some names have been changed. But not many. If they were changed, it was probably because they'd expect me to pay them, or something. No one mentioned is a composite because the people I know and meet and adore are all colorful enough. The landmarks and venues within are also real and lovely and typically wonderful. All included or referenced product names and establishments are trade names, trademarks, or registered trademarks of their respective owners. Any copyrighted material belongs to respective owners and this work makes no claim to previous copyrights. All information researched was drawn from various websites (2011-2014), as cited in the appropriate section, and are not original products of my gigantic brain. Some timelines have been compressed because this book would have been way too long to read otherwise. The events and accounts within have indeed happened, so this is definitely a work of nonfiction. And like all of life, this compilation is based on and derived by my own memory, for better or worse.

CONTENTS

Day Trips: Have Driver, Will Travel

PREFACE/DISCLAIMER

If a shattered tailbone—the result of an exotic dance routine—and a hefty collection of unflattering photos in a fat suit weren't enough to seal the perfect farewell party, then pinch me. I'd never even *been* to Las Vegas, not even the airport, so the first time I pulled into Sin City would be to begin a new venture in a house taken site unseen.

I was physically transported to Las Vegas by "Driver," a pet name for the other half, who was offered a transfer for work. From Atlanta, we drove for five days with a cranky array of heavily sedated animals, spending four consecutive nights in KOA one-room Kabins. Each wooden wigwam provided a scavenger hunt map that routed the restroom facilities and every morning, we'd create the same embarrassing scene of canine-feline-avian management and cumbersome novice reloading. All because I still wanted to have the camping experience once we decided to forgo the week-long Winnebago rental and bought what BMW refers to as an S<u>A</u>V. Activity, not utility. Which would explain the three days it took for them to scratch their heads and their balls trying to install the Class III hitch that would safely lug the mini U-Haul trailer outfitted with all necessary rations to sustain our 2,000-mile westward expedition.

***

I had trouble deciding from what perspective I should pen this memoir, but then I read somewhere that 40 percent of books are most likely to become bestsellers if they have a female protagonist. So that did it; I would protagonize. Sounds important, and like a lot of responsibility.

Please know this isn't a foolproof roadmap or blueprint for Las Vegas. It doesn't even have GPS, and besides, Vegas is *always* changing. I'm neither a historian nor a librarian, and the world is a better place for both of those courteous decisions. I'm not here to offend anyone; I'm just here to dispel a few myths, perpetuate a few truths, and fill in a few blanks. The rest is all about me, my protagonism.

That reminds me, I sometimes make up words. I also blissfully emphasize with italics as if we were having an actual animated conversation. And I like fragment sentences. A lot. As well, my structural and stylistic preferences have been known to set off a few standard grammatical alarms according to the manuals. But I cannot sing or read music, that's why this is a book and not a marching band or concert tour.

Before we get too far, you should probably know I'm not your typical Southerner. In fact, I'm not Southern at all. I'm a product of Sarasota, Florida, who semi-accidentally spent a dozen years living in metro Atlanta. By nature, I speak seashell, map hurricanes, slow for manatees, and escape alligators. The rest I had to learn, all by myself. Prior to the Peach State and its surrounding region, I had never heard of scuppernong jelly, tick jars, or had ever walked a country mile. Just as I didn't know my way around a parlay card, creosote bush, or slot canyon when we landed in Vegas. Likewise, I would have never argued if you told me a one-armed bandit was a handicapped bank robber.

What's worse, college grad and everything, I was under the erroneous impression that Las Vegas was the state capital and was convinced I would have to live in a hotel or brothel once we arrived. I also never imagined I'd need to tell my parents it's where I'd be moving, presumably running away with my gigolo and doing something for profit with my boobs. And maybe tassels.

So this is my story. A true story fueled with personal opinions, active observations, dorky letters to friends, and a handful of low-rate limericks. A real page-turner conveniently crafted from my own perspective and completely biased outlook. Upon completion, you will emerge a better person. Probably even smarter, too, because you're going to learn stuff. But most importantly, it will make you prettier than you already are.

You're welcome. *To Fabulous Las Vegas.*

INTRODUCTION

Most folks associate the South with people who sound like Paula Deen and sink uneven loads of saccharin into their hospitable tendencies. A place where everything is battered with bread crumbs and bookended by mint juleps. Many think it's all barnyards and square-dancing, homemade spittoon cups and hand-rolled tobacco. A land of banjos and Skoal rings, a backdrop for *Deliverance* in the Heart of Dixie where everyone has hay in their teeth and is addressed by a hyphenated (or sounds-hyphenated) name. All females are born Daughters of the American Revolution and write best-selling books about the Civil War as they rock back and forth on the rambling front porches of their plantation homes, permanently shaded by weighty, thick-rooted magnolia trees. Most presume the South is just one big brick estate with solid oak hardwood floors and ornate Corinthian columns fashioned for antebellum belles who twirl around *ad nauseam* in muted hoopskirts and extra-wide, semi-sheer horsehair cartwheel hats, chasing their shrimp and grits with all beverages entitled and pronounced "Coke."

Assumptions abound that the South is quite simply a high cholesterol hash house of cornbread and hominy all balled up into collard greens, fried chicken, and Baptists. A humid territory full of renowned barbeque stands, confederate flags, and more churches per capita than anywhere else in the world. A region where the women speak from behind compact mirrors and the boys are bred to be "good ole." These presumptions are both musty stereotypes and beautiful truths.

And Atlanta is its headquarters, its control center, the heart of its entire operation—a revered metropolis of sophistication, progression, and evolution—one that proudly and successfully refuses to omit high fashion, fine dining, and rampant diversity from its sweeping, suburban-sprawling, 29-county demographic.

Atlanta not only touts its Ted Turner empire and perfect periwinkle hydrangeas, it also consists of lingering day-long brunches and anticipates more precipitation than Seattle annually. A mecca for millions linked by all sixty-five roads named Peachtree, this older city courts a younger crowd for its optimistic business opportunities, while the majority of the still-soaring population steers clear of the limited public transportation system even when traffic is at a maximum. Cars often have no choice but to unanimously stack up like magnetic Legos, both in town and outside the perimeter. Atlanta is known as a haven for hip-hop, rapture for the sports fan, and a hotbed for antiques. It's also a welcome mat for mosquitoes, a playground for tornadoes, and a sleeper hit for ice storms.

And two thousand miles to its west, Las Vegas prevails as one of the most frequented destinations on the planet—for vacation, escape, and boring business conventions that demand a more grown-up and distorted mascot than Orlando's Mickey Mouse. It's a place without opossums and skunks; a world with few mold spores, flyswatters, or umbrellas. It's a land where the heat only gets hotter, the casinos only get fancier, and the people only get more interesting.

It's a runaway backdrop for last-minute, hassle-free, unplanned, or carefree nuptials and the quintessential setting for anyone who wants (or needs) to let it all hang out and then dump it on the nightstand just prior to checkout. It's a service-driven town that breaks records in number of hotel rooms, wedding chapels, starred restaurants, construction dollars, foreign travelers, animated attractions, and marketable nudity. Many only associate Vegas with showgirls, prostitutes, Mormons, and mobsters—all of whom ride unicycles, dress like Liberace, and live huddled together in casinos on a 4.2-mile National Scenic Byway stretch of pavement labeled Las Vegas Boulevard. Or, more commonly referred to as "the Strip."

There's no babysitter, no curfew, no guilt, and no black-out dates in Sin City. Only blackouts, bachelorettes, and very bright lights. It's likely the shot glass capital of the souvenir world and a place that's been accused of using "Las Vegas culture" as an oxymoron in its bio. (Please welcome The Smith Center and Downtown Container Park.)

While Atlanta is rich with battle markers and pivotal American history, Vegas is rife with magicians and fire-breathing acrobats. More than a quarter of Atlanta is covered by trees, and Vegas is discouraged to lay sod. The South means pimiento cheese, seersucker, and college football. Vegas means elopements, potential payouts, and hookah lounges.

But now these two cities have one serendipitous thing in common: gigantic Ferris wheels. Forever bonded by entities as neutralizing and as universal as sweatpants. No one saw it coming—it's brilliant.

Contrary to popular belief, Vegas is much more than a fondue pot of adult sensations, an incubator for self-gratification, and an airy caricature of its embellished persona. It's a world-renowned retreat, a bucket list triumph, and an overly typecast vacuum-like state of mind. It's also a military town. Vegas is more than just a clockless interior where time, temperature, and brain activity are all held on a provisionally numbed plane. It's a multifarious prism of forethought and splendor, an underrated spectrum of unconventional glory, a peerless identity far from being in crisis.

Yet few who make it to Las Vegas know this, or see anything beyond their cocoon-like casino lining and the neighboring resorts that cast magnificent shadows over the assorted application of guests. Most folks don't even consider there is anything outside of the farfetched woolgathering layer anyway, other than the Grand Canyon, which looks a lot closer on a map and on the incoming flight over. Even fewer know there is actually an operative city to all sides of the Strip's vitality and jubilation, though some visitors do take the entire lane by the horns and tread the complete distance along both sides of the Boulevard.

And finally, there's the set who've never been to Las Vegas, toting around all the very same . utty, dirty, trashy assumptions I once did.

I went straight from a naïve and fully-petaled flower to putting my dishes away in a Clark County kitchen. I lost the ill-fitting southern drawl and befriended the mayor. (Well, sorta—*Hey, girl!*) I've eaten my way through restaurants, fallen for the timeshare sales pitch, spent an entire third shift learning keno, and seriously contemplated dealer school enrollment. It's a different world with different traditions; one that I've embraced like it was my job.

Because I needed one of those.

DEAL ME IN: ORIENTATION

JAMES

James was the first fellow I met—in the driveway—immediately upon our trailered arrival.

There he was, with a smile as broad as the horizon, ambassador of our new subdivision, glowing like a jack-o-lantern at dusk on Halloween. This guy had all the makings to be president, and not just because he is black and black presidents are in. He simply has that bumper sticker-cliché charisma and charm needed to dazzle the hot pants off any ally or foe, home or abroad. And I dare not put it past him that, in forty-two years when he is almost fifty, he may just be leading our fine country.

James zoomed past as we were unloading that first day and circled back around by the time I had pulled out one of the cat carriers from deep inside our U-Haul dangler.

"What's that?" he asked, not really exposing his bright side.

When I explained we had a cat he was curious if it was as big as he was. I asked if he weighed about forty-five pounds and when he agreed, I told him, "No, the cat's bigger."

He seemed impressed with my candor and asked to meet "it" sometime. Which will never happen.

Color me jaded: I am. After more than a decade of suffering through ungrateful rugrats, I wasn't used to nice children ringing the doorbell and respectfully offering to weed the front rocks (an HOA requirement) for ten dollars. I had almost forgotten what a doorbell even sounded like. My history in some of Atlanta's transitional neighborhoods regarding any such encounter would have included indiscernible howls from the street, with an entitled demand for cash or the ransom from what went missing the day before. Solely a request for monies tendered, but no services rendered. Makes complete sense, I must be an idiot. Even the UPS man would just hurl packages over the low picket fence and zip away for fear of having his rig unattended for too long.

James drives a Razor scooter when he's not campaigning on his BMX dirt bike. Or, he's on a lavender girlie banana-seated bike trying to ride with no hands, begging me to watch. I only look in case he falls, which would be hilarious. He is often spotted with his vice president—a taller, somewhat older, white version with glasses—named Oscar. Which is a rather adult name for a kid, but I had other things to judge. I thanked them dearly when they showed up, but let them know I had planned to take care of my landscaping in the morning, when I could spray weed killer and the twisting winds wouldn't blow it back into my mouth. They pleaded for me to wait until they got home from school so we could all "do it together." So as a compromise, I did it in the middle of the night by the glare of sporadic headlights from the neighbors on the graveyard shift.

Later that afternoon, James returned solo, reswizzling his offer to weed and then asked once more when we were out walking the dogs. He was riding in circles with the less pesty Veep who finally piped in, "James, she said no. Let's go build a fort."

At that point, James was unaware that I, too, have a foot-propelled Razor scooter, Driver has three hundred bicycles, and Sedona (the 105-pound Mastiff mix) is nearly suited to wear a saddle. One roll around the block on any of those and I may just be able to confirm that he is, or should be, involved with the Democratic Party some day.

I will continue to weed at odd hours to avoid unnecessary interaction, but I'm definitely considering having James put together a brief PowerPoint that outlines the entire HOA handbook so I don't have to read it. For ten dollars.

Twenty, if he nails a faceplant.

LV DMV

I held out for seven years before I finally gave in to becoming an official Georgia resident. I still had a Florida plate, Florida driver's license, Florida insurance, and I even went back to Florida to visit the dentist, the dermatologist, and to vote. I was much happier with Florida's mascot, the Sunshine, than anything involved with Georgia's fuzzy piece of fruit. That's why there was nothing more liberating than racing down to the Nevada DMV with two wheels in the air to exchange my southern plate for the Silver State. Besides, I *love* jewelry.

Me: [entering the building] "I don't care what it costs, I'm getting the cute tag. You know, the one with the Vegas sign. It's commemorative, I think."

Driver: "That's fine. Get whatever you want. I'm gonna get the veteran one since we're in a military town."

Me: "Should I get a veteran tag, too?"

Driver: "Were you in the armed forces?"

Me: "Do they check?"

Driver: [no response, just a glance]

Intercom: [inside a beautiful building that did not smell like Doritos and marijuana, despite the fact it features a huge snack bar and fully-operational restroom facility] "Ticket number G787. BEEP."

Lady: "Hi."

Lady, again: "You can sit."

5

Me: "Okay. HI! [all caps, all enthusiasm] Just moved here from Georgia, guess I need the works. What do you need to see first?"

Lady: "Everything you've got. Hopefully, it's everything you need."

Me: "Here." [pushing a pile of papers in her direction]

Me, again: "I think I want the cute plate with the Vegas sign."

Lady: "Okay. That will be sixty more."

Me: "Sixty more than what?"

Lady: "Sixty more than your registration."

Lady, again: "Or, you can have the standard plate everybody gets for just a dollar more."

Me: "A dollar more than what?"

Lady: "Your registration fee."

Me: "How much is that? I just moved here [*like I said*] so I don't know what you're talking about."

Lady: "Well, let me get you an estimate."

Me: "An estimate? Are you going to *paint* my car?"

Lady: "You're at about eight-forty."

Me: "Eight-forty. Eight dollars and forty cents? That's a weird number. Is that with tax?"

Lady: "No. Eight hundred and forty."

Me: "Um. [craning my neck in search of Driver's whereabouts] For a new plate and a new license?"

Lady: "It's how we make up for not having a state tax. And you actually get two plates, front and back."

Me: "Eight *hundred* and forty dollars? Like, that's what I pay right now?"

Lady: "Yes."

Me: *"EIGHT HUNDRED AND FORTY DOLLARS?"*

Lady: "Yes. And with the specialty plate, about nine."

Me: "Nine."

Me, again: "I don't think I'm going to get the Vegas plate today."

Lady: "Yeah, your vehicle is new. The system works on how much you can spend, not how much you make. Oh [looking at her screen], you're actually at eight fifty-eight."

Me (in my head): What a relief, considering I make nothing.

Lady: "Really, who looks at their plate anyway? You just so happen to be in line for the 'extremely hot female' series." [finding a jingle for the plate's alphanumeric acronym as she yanked it from an ordered stack]

Lady, again: "What are you doing in Vegas anyway?"

Me: "I didn't bring my checkbook. Do you take credit cards? It was a transfer."

Lady: "No, *really*. Why did you come here?"

Me: "Are you from here?" [diverting]

Lady: "Been here about four years. Hate it. Loved going to Atlanta. Stayed at that Marriott twice. The one where you can look all the way down to the lobby."

Me: "Oh, yeah. Downtown."

Lady: "So what kind of transfer?"

Me: "For work."

Lady: "Wow, rare for here. Especially nowadays. I'm dying to get outta here."

Me: "Well, I *love it*."

Lady: "Give it time."

Lady, again: "What kind of work?"

Me: "Stuff my Driver does. Mainly driving." [still reeling at my near 900 dollar afternoon]

Lady: "Is that your Driver?"

Me: "Huh?" [Driver approaching from behind]

Me (to Driver): "Eight something."

Driver: "Huh?"

Me: "Eight hundred and fifty dollars."

Driver: "For?"

SMITH'S

I LOVE SMITH'S.

I want a bumper sticker that reads: "I get my kicks at Smith's," or "Follow me to Smith's." But people probably would, and then I'd have to go to Smith's every time I got in the car. And that's ultimately taking on too much responsibility for the brand, especially before Mr. Smith endorses me as their unofficial spokesperson and I formally annul my role as such with other national brands.

I never cared much for Kroger because it sounds like an anthropomorphic animal's name, though I have learned the two grocers are affiliated. I stopped going to Publix years ago when I lived in Buckhead because you had to valet park. And for me, that was not "a pleasure." It made no sense to wait for some teenager to bring my car around when I was palming no more than a six-pack of Lender's pumpernickel bagels and some smoked salmon. The whole process sucked up way too much time and back then I was convinced groceries just made you fat anyway.

Even if you're a loyal and devoted resident of Atlanta's east side, you'd still agree the parking lot at Edgewood Shopping Center—Kroger and beyond—is, by all means, no place for cars. Or grocery carts. Or baby strollers. Or shoppers. Or even stores, when all is said and done. It's a mine field for anyone but Superman or Inspector Gadget who can't seamlessly swing in from the tilted telephone poles that are stapled to death by yard sale signs and CD release posters. I'm positive that entire complex was designed by elves who aren't aware of a car's actual dimensions and inabilities to maneuver around the footprint of a Twister game mat—all in oncoming, impatient, bottlenecking traffic.

Upon moving, I made a conscious effort to interrogate every grocery store (and parking lot) within the confines of my cheery 5-mile sphere of influence. My requirements were plenty, but the categories and choices were different once actually on the ground. Albertson's is a retailer here, too, one that I, quite frankly, have always associated with powdered donuts at 3 a.m. I can explain, but probably won't.

Before I even crossed the threshold of the electric sliding doors at Smith's, I heard Sherrill conducting both business and pleasure from her festively-adorned folding table and chair. You had no choice but to walk smack dab into her overactive sign-up stand because it was pretty much blocking the entrance. Fanned out across its surface were rewards cards in every color and pens anchored by things too big to steal. All items were scattered across her station like miniature pencils at a lottery stall. Clipboards snapping like Hungry Hippos and an audience so thick I thought someone was giving birth. I weaved my way in and stepped up closer, ducking around the balloons and banners that shot out of all four sides to confirm this was indeed where I needed to register my new life at my new food bazaar.

I told Sherrill we had just moved to Vegas from Atlanta. And like everyone who learns this, they either take a physical step backward or, if seated, drop their bifocals down the bridge of their noses to get a better look. Without a doubt, she is Smith's surefire storefront ringer for repeat patronage and definitely the gal I'd want to sit next to at bingo, slots, and every dinner party. She couldn't have been more ecstatic to get me registered, explain the benefits, and share the tips and tricks to corral additional savings—things I'm sure she tells everyone, but made me feel as if I was on the receiving end of some pretty privileged employee know-how.

The stores are clean, the produce is fresh, the organics are plentiful, and the associates race around like mad to open lanes for anyone in wait. No staff members ever question why you might be there shopping and they don't look at your eco-friendly bags as if they were bleeding. There aren't nomadic carts careening off automobiles or children locked up in cars with the windows up. The employees don't extend their breaks smoking on the patio furniture for sale outside and the only group to solicit me for something has been a Girl Scout troop. The parking lot isn't life-threatening, either.

I don't really care if Smith's marks everything up just to mark everything back down at checkout. When you look at your receipt, you feel so young and rich and beautiful. And thin.

Because powdered donuts are a choice, not a lifestyle.

GIMME BUFFET

I had only been to one, once.

And it was on land, at the port of the Pair-A-Dice gambling boat in East Peoria. (Still the coolest eightieth birthday party I've ever been to.) On that occasion, we went for brunch the morning after a collective seasick nickel-slot hangover and I doused my plate with all participating beige and yellow food groups.

Though for this missive, we will be referring to dinner—something I've always assumed hails from the word *dine*. And you will probably need to be familiar with my main restaurant requirements, most of which people are quick to deem finicky.

First of all, I believe the restaurant should actually *be* a restaurant. Which, in my storyline, is defined foremost by table service. A place where people in smart black bottoms kindly help by bringing you things to eat. I don't particularly care to order at a counter, pay a cashier, or teeter a tray back to my sticky Formica table, to later march the tip back up to a counter or leave it under the syrup shaker. At least, not before 2 a.m. Nor, as an alternative to carrying my own food on a coaster, I don't wish to be excused from a place-order-here line, curling a tented table topper that labels both me and my meal a number. Don't let the word *line* go unnoticed, either. I can impatiently stand at the bar on a waiting list, but I don't want to creep through a queue to be fed. That's grocery shopping.

Two: I like ambiance. And usually, much more than the average recommended amount per person. I prefer all applicable lighting to be on

13

dimmer switches so I don't flail for tweezers or SPF. I also won't hesitate to ask for a booth, which is hereditary, and a checklist item to be considered a proper *dining* establishment. I don't care to sit too closely to the next party where everyone has to stand up and push their squeaky chairs over echosome tile when I need to powder my nose or launch a complaint about something irrelevant, like not being in a booth.

And lastly, I wish to enjoy my meals with either a glass of wine or a Cosmopolitan, sometimes both, and need the option to close with Grand Marnier. In a snifter, not a shot glass. So, a full bar with wedding registry-level glassware is also a stipulation if I'm hoping to be fed and watered outside of the home.

See, only three very basic needs.

When we first visited our local Buffet (a word I honor with a capital B), I noticed it spilled right into the gaming floor—no doors or walls. It was like a human feeding show or life-size sixth grade science fair food diorama that included its actively-pursuant inhabitants. I began to groan, loudly, voicing my objections over the slot machine trills. The eating space was the size of three hotel ballrooms with the accordion doors pushed back. There were an infinite number of naked tables with lots of chairs and at least thirteen islands of assorted provisions buried under sneeze guards. A few staff members circulated, carrying only sodas and ice water. I watched paper chefs' hats and wide meat cleavers wax through their stations under only one fixed bright UV setting for the overhead lamps.

With ample pause, I asked Driver if we could check out the steakhouse or Mexican joint. Both were closed; I was trapped. Just like that time I didn't plan to eat taquitos and Corn Nuts from Quick Trip. *Inside* Quick Trip.

After winding through a superfluous squiggle of velvet ropes, we approached the lively hostess team chatting at the podium and asked if they had booze inside the food museum. From that angle, the booths lining the perimeter started jumping up and down as the duo pointed to the main bar in the gaming area. "Bring over whatever you want," they recited in stereo. I turned to Driver with a *well, well, well* can-do attitude and we wobbled over without further hesitation. Driver got a beer; I received enough red wine to drown.

The entire expo can be overwhelming for a beginner and is a potential playground for indigestion if you were to mix everything together. I revolved around each trough carefully, and with caution. There were hardly any identical food stalls and lots of Easter-colored Jell-O mounds available at the main dessert headquarters. I observed the other Buffet people, engrossing myself with recommendations and instruction made by the body language and self-serving etiquette of my fellow piglets.

Everyone kinda looked the same to me. At least, from the waist up. I learned there are a lot of professional Buffet eaters, many of whom strictly prefer tables. (I figure this is so they can get up often and not disturb the other eaters in their party!) It's a very hungry society slipped plainly inside the satiated common population. This regulated format for binging is not unlike having thirty seconds to grab as much blowing cash in an airtight acrylic box as you can. Only there is no timer, just human heads hurtling to make sure they haven't missed anything, as if forgetting you can go back up until you impair a few feet of your large intestine.

I have to say, I wasn't looking to be wowed. I wasn't even looking for a Buffet. But because they are always associated with casinos, and since I never knew anything about those, it was time for some personal enrichment. I had no expectations. Though there's something to these Buffets, with all their crazy coupons, comps, and vouchers. And how many mouths they can feed in one day and how much traffic they can withstand in a single meal session. Determining just how many people will wait in line and how many will (also) request a booth is quite a mind-bending brain game. Both searching for a group that doesn't know the drill and admiring the parties that do, beats any average day at Walmart.

If it wasn't one of the best eclectic meals I've ever dumped onto my own three plates and one bowl, then my new gambling name ain't Buffy Lucky 7 Caesar Salad Barbie Dollars.

Bright lights, big servings, new pants size. *Two-for-One and Prime Rib for all!*

TWENTY MINUTES

When I began calling real estate agents about properties before we moved, there was nothing more agonizing than trying to get a feel for a location in Greater Las Vegas and hearing, "Oh, it's about twenty minutes." I was convinced everyone in Las Vegas was lazy as hell or couldn't count very high. How could absolutely *everything* be accessible in twenty minutes? I was reduced to thinking Utah was twenty minutes away, not that I knew where Utah was anyway. I couldn't even get out of my driveway in Atlanta for twenty minutes because of all the pedestrians, beer bottles, pedestrians breaking beer bottles, pedestrians distracted by the contents of their Mrs. Winners Styrofoam boxes, and pedestrians shoving their Mrs. Winners boxes and plastic bags in my bushes. (It was a very busy alley.)

Then the twenty-minute people on the phone would mention specific names of roads; "Well, it's right off ____ and ____." Oh yes, because "I've never been there before, *ever*, but you're right, the satellites for Google Earth do dwell in the third eye right next to the hole in the back of my head." So yeah, I knew exactly what and where they were referring to, in every instance. Then they'd say, "Well, I can show it to you this afternoon, but I can't promise it will still be available tomorrow." Clearly, my overly-informative opening monologue shot straight up and all the way around their *it's-a-dry-heat* dehydrated brains.

So I decided to revamp my questionnaire after I realized I was fighting a crippling collapse in communication. "How far is the house from the airport and how far is it from the Strip?" Little did I know, but pilots can simply reference the reflectors on Las Vegas Boulevard when landing just a few blocks over at McCarran Airport. A truth evidenced by the closing scene of Hollywood's 1997 *Con Air* starring Vegas sweetheart Nicolas Cage. The hallucinatory finale will leave you stumped that three hundred tourists weren't deleted during such dewy-palmed, white-knuckled suspense. But don't take my word for it, rent it today. And fly in at night.

Now that we live here, the twenty-minute tenet has been tested repeatedly and religiously. Since I'm much better at keeping up with the log than logging any time behind the wheel, Driver has shouldered most of the actual labor. And sure enough, by interstate, surface road, back street, carriage path, sidewalk, and camel trail—there is nowhere you cannot arrive safely within this timetable. Your twenty can also include getting lost, getting sidetracked, and getting left behind. Thus, a powerfully-Pulitzer set of stanzas.

> ### Twenty: I Ode You So
> *You can add it, subtract it; slice it or dice it*
> *You can carry the two and stop for a brew*
> *You can rush it, you can slow it*
> *You can roll it, or just tow it*
> *If you try it, you should buy it*
> *If you can hike it, you can bike it*
> *It's twenty; it's veinte*
> *The big vingt, the true zwanzig*
> *So in Bahasa Malaysia*
> *(For you, I have to do some math)*
> *Lapan + dua belas*
> *But no matter what, it's still twenty, fellas*

THE WINDCAST

Sometimes, I fall asleep prepared to wake up in Kansas.

I've altogether given up trying to diagnose the schizophrenic winds that regularly whip through Las Vegas. In my previous slushy and stagnant Atlanta climate, there was no motivation to ponder the atmospheric conditions of a city two thousand miles to my left, so I was altogether unaware of Mother Nature's effects on a major host town for the World Series of Poker. And trust me, I had never heard of WSOP, either. I thought this place was just a free-standing theme park where Wayne Newton lived. A temporary, over-the-top bubble of captivity where the weather was controlled by a da Vinci instrument and swamp cooler.

"Are the winds always like this?" I queried, pulling the hair out of my mouth and plucking a displaced yellow Wendy's napkin from around my thigh.

The answer was, "We get winds, but they don't usually last long."

Since then, I've come to realize the wind here is just like rain, pollen, more rain, and humidity in Georgia. It's part of the area's complexion and blends subtly into the backdrop, unless deemed "severe."

Here, local weather anchors only get to milk their glossary of meteorology terms during the spring and early summer months—when Vegas is enjoying gale, storm, and hurricane force winds, squalls, shears, blowing dusts, gusts, and whatever else you can measure on a Fujita Scale. Winds so burly they lift sheds onto tile rooftops, blow nail polish off the manicured, and send shallow-rooted palm trees down like inflatable

Bozo Clown Bop Bags. A definite contrast from the typical pithy report describing Vegas as, "Sunny and hot for the next 108 days." (I'm not sure if these people have ever seen a rainbow.)

If it's any indication just how breezy it gets here, not only does dog pee fling sideways and foliage specimens bow in half toward the ground, but pigeons look like they're trying to fly the wrong way into a jet engine. I've had full drinks in actual glassware blow over in the driveway and I've almost been decapitated by wayward cardboard scraps trying to pick up my ice cubes. Several nights a week, as the wind whistles sharply through the screens, Elphaba's silhouette can be seen as she pedals by on her 3-speed in front of the moon.

Though I will say, it's exhilarating to sleep with the windows peeled wide open, free of any disturbing urban noises—both of which took some getting used to. It had been over a decade since I'd lived in a home where the double-hung Craftsman windows weren't repeatedly lead-painted shut and inoperable over the course of their ninety years. And leaving either the front or back door open for fresh air just wasn't an option, at any time of day. Not only would people come in, it was like leaving the hood up—a universal sign of distress. Then the cops would show up with guns drawn, needlessly distracted from the truly active crime sprees that were advancing around the corner.

But now in Vegas, drifting into peaceful slumber amidst interior curtains pelting both the sheetrock and glass issues a different sense of comfort compared to DeKalb County's sirens and gunshots, loud music and car alarms. Instead of waking up to the dog's excitement over the scurry of attic rats, it's now just the chatter from the Seven Dwarfs who have been ejected from the Forest of Hesse and deposited into my serene boudoir. Which reminds me how different property management is here. Fortunately, we were already in the good habit of bolting things down, but not because they were going to blow away.

Many mornings, I walk outside in my jammies to survey the exterior land and can barely believe my eyes. The spectacle mirrors the aftermath of our going-away party, minus the blue eye shadow, pink flamingos, and faux beauty marks. I find the largest terra cotta pot on its side, the outdoor rug bear-hugging the chairs, cushions realigned against the concrete wall, the grill cover twisted up like one of my grammy's late-70s turbans, and the dog poop needs recovery from places unusual. I'm usually afraid the patio fan blades are going to spin off and harpoon a hard-working landscaper blowing the decorative rocks back into their beds; no one needs that on their conscience. I would never want to be a wind chime, new flag, or even a bean stalk in this town—too risky.

Oddly enough, prior to this prevailing wind cannon, I used to worry I'd never be able to wear my steampunk goggles outside of Dragon*Con or any other alternative Victorian history convention. So it goes without saying that I was downright tickled to learn there is no better defense from the thick sand dunes that splash through the habitat than those. Still, when trying to maturely converse with a complete stranger in a parking lot and your shirt blows up over your brassiere and gives you a bank robber-pantyhose face, it's impossible to make proper eye contact.

And *that* is so rude.

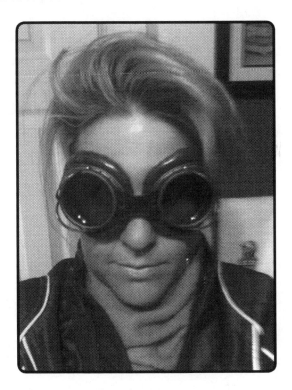

GLORY DAZE

Dearest Megan—

I pen this missive because you crept into my mind today when I was looking at bananas. Actually, I thought about your mom first. Remember the Real Thang Fruit Swang? She *loved* it.

I imagine you've been pretty busy since high school. Have you popped out any kids? Let me guess; they're doctors, too. I have a bunch. None of whom are doctors, or ever will be. They were all adopted, so no stretch marks or saggy boobs for *moi*. That's probably why I was recently called a "MILF." (Who am I kidding? I get that all the time!) Mine either poop in a box, eat the poop in a box, or are behind bars. I also have a Driver. And a blog.

You'll never guess where I live? Time's up. Vegas. As in *Las Vegas*. It really reminds me of home—only with strippers, casinos, and if you can believe, a lot more tourists. I left corporate a while back and got a little artsy, so I can basically go anywhere. It's not really a long story how we got here, but I don't think I've actually told many people.

Until now. Thanks to the bananas.

So, it was exactly however long ago that Driver was asked to dinner to discuss a new position with another company. I was also invited, which was insane. I even did a final triple-check to make sure that was the best idea. You know, that I should attend.

We met the Big Cheese at the bar for a drink before our reservation was called and just as we extinguished the first round, our table was ready. We shuffled to the other side of the restaurant and Boss Man asked if I'd like "another one of those pink things." Clearly, it would have been indecorous to decline. As you know, it's fine for a lady to drink, just as long as she never has a photo taken with a drink in her hand. Especially if ever considering a presidential candidacy. Which I sometimes do.

Basking in Atlanta Fish Market's finest, we discussed the job description and brainstormed incentives, while more pink things kept ending up stamped to the cocktail napkin just beneath my right hand. (I can drink with both hands, by the way.) All other patrons had soon evaporated and it was only the three of us left to reverberate below the vaulted ceiling. By the time Driver finally had to use the restroom, the future deal was nearly hermetic. But I felt a little uneasy in a few of my leading organs.

Once I made sure Driver had turned the corner, I leaned into Big Daddy. "This sounds great. And in case I didn't tell you earlier, I'm truly flattered you invited me. Means more than you know."

He smiled and said, "Well, this affects you, too. And I know that."

I previewed the restroom vestibule once more and leaned in again, this time closer, bravely preparing to spew what could possibly be a very divisive and risky request. "Really, it sounds great. But you got anything out West? We're not married to Atlanta and this position sounds like we'd be stuck here. *Forever.*"

The Big Kahuna pushed himself back in the chair and crossed his arms, kinda like my dad does when he has a toothpick in his mouth. I was clutching a rabbit's foot in my head that he would return with something positive, even if it meant Driver would have to climb poles and hang power lines somewhere. Then a euphoric grin beamed, "Are you being serious?" I was most particularly serious. That was my serious tone, saved for negotiating other people's jobs, specifically when they're unaware I'm doing so.

"Like where out there?" He sought with wonder.

"I don't know. How about Phoenix?"

His grin morphed into an entire cartoon and he was all, "Do you like Sedona?"

And I go, "I love Sedona. I have a dog named Sedona. Any other questions?"

Then he was like, "I have an even better offer out there."

Just as I hoisted my empty martini glass into the air to conjoin with Big Daddy's highball, Driver returned to the table. "What are you guys so excited about?"

The mister nonchalantly noted, "Your new job."

In that instant, I electrocuted myself with six hundred volts of teeth, eyes as wide as wagon wheels, nodding my head up and down, declaring, "In *AR - I - ZO - NA!*" I was an entire cheering section of myself.

Driver's neck snapped in half while an unrecognizable face looked at the two of us like we were scheming to become unicorns, begging for explanation as to what the hell just happened. "He's got an ever better gig in the Phoenix-Sedona area. So that's where we're going. Totally different job, but that's fine." It was a relay that ricocheted with a ringing mental squeeze of *Aren't you glad I came?* and *You're welcome*.

"Your territory would probably be Arizona and Vegas. We're still creating the position," the

Big Wig added as a supplement to my two-sentence synopsis.

Delicately encouraged by the staff to close out, Driver's head was still swiveling like a Kewpie doll on the dashboard of an elephant as we flagged down the sleepy valet. A completely sober e-mail the next day asked for confirmation if we were serious about moving. I dove on top of Driver's keyboard to reply. I couldn't be any more serious about being serious. Especially in my serious tone.

From then on, every fifteen minutes, I would ask Driver to check in with the brass. Foot-tapping, motor-running, time tick-tocking—I needed to know when we could leave. But plans slowed and flapped in the wind while all of the arrangements were being fleshed out. Then a few months later, Driver came home with an update.

"Looks like it's going to be Vegas," a statement I wasn't expecting.

"For what?" I played dumb, but continued. "We cannot move to Vegas. People don't live in Las Vegas. How am I supposed to tell my parents we're moving *to Vegas? Las* Vegas."

Driver carefully responded, but only after decorating my fist with a drink. "That's where the market needs the most attention."

I sip erratically, suffocated in thought. "Well, then I need a convertible. A Mercedes, probably a 1960-something. You think he'd throw in one of those? You know, sweeten the pot. People don't just *move* to Vegas."

I actually forgot about the whole collectible car thing (until now) the more I started to shrink-wrap my gigantic brain around the motion of this ridiculous notion. "V E G A S." I started saying it out loud. In a very *loud*, whispery, drawn-out, Kathleen Turner-Molly Shannon hissing pitch. To other people. To myself. To my other selves. Some were shocked I had never been. Others (most people I know) chuckled that Vegas seemed perfect for me, with lots of embellished emphasis around the *perfect* part. The rest of them (Barb and Denise) raved about how beautiful it was there. (Here.)

So, I just started owning it. All out, had it designed, tailored, and delivered to the doorstep by the sequin fairy, signature required. Just for me. And sometimes Driver.

Basically, that's how it all happened, my dear Megs. And I know there are thousands of conferences and conventions in Vegas every year, which means, I expect to see you. I can take you everywhere in town with the best martinis. And you can buy. Because doctors are rich.

Please give your parents my love and the biggest banana you can get your hands on. I look forward to hanging out in our prom dresses again. Mine still fits. I wear it as a tube top now.

Proof that I can also drink with my left hand.

THE STRIP:
LAS VEGAS BOULEVARD

LUCK BE A LADY

It was my very first day on the Strip, my forty-eighth day living in Las Vegas. (Clearly, I didn't rush right down.)

We had been roaming Las Vegas Boulevard for nearly seven hours, taking in the sights, the eyesores, the blender drinks, and the sensational sensationalism when we arrived at the conclusion we needed to get off (or take off) our blistering feet. Driver was prepared for a fancy dinner; I wasn't exactly hungry. But I was starved for entertainment. And something *Vegas-y*.

You currently can't sweep along the Strip and not notice the vast silk-screened Donny & Marie rendering from every direction. It nearly tackles you. It's a great shot; they look like kittens.

"*That's* what I want to do!" I darted an unwavering index finger midway up the Flamingo, confident my proposition was unrivaled. *Carpe diem!* Driver would have rather gargled thumbtacks with fountain water, but I was somehow able to lure us into the clutches of the pink casino, while still snapping photos of tipsy tourists. It was no breezy feat, any of it.

I danced through the game room to Michael Jackson's "Thriller" (one of my best routines) and Driver deliberately bobbled about six feet behind me, looking to get stopped by anyone who needed directions or a photographer. We glided around a corner near the concierge and got in line. I was so elated, glitter misted from my elbows. The line was cluttered and unkempt, like it wasn't really a line at all. More like a deli in gridlock, out of French Onion soup. We saw heaps of merchandise and a lot more pink and knew we were in the right place. I made a bunch of noise and everyone parted like pig tails, giving us a clear view of all the wingding and worry.

Then my sparkle balls deflated and Driver's smile widened like a worn-out elastic waistband. They had cancelled. *Whatever were we going to do now? Who says they can just cancel a show on the very night I was trashed enough to go?* It was an abomination of my spontaneity and *savoir faire*.

"Fine, let's go see Celine. It's last minute; they'll probably have $20 tickets. I don't care where we sit, she's probably pretty loud." We walked over to Caesars and Driver had reached the desk by the time I returned from the restroom downstairs. I passed by the door guy to ask if it had started. He said we had five minutes, and he was very nice about it. Driver turned to me from the front of the queue and slowly mouthed, "Two hundred and fifty dollars." I shrugged, which meant, "Per ticket?" That inspired a whitewashed nod and Driver ducked back under the dividers to join me doing nothing in front of the embankment of Colosseum doors.

"Well, *now* what?" I offered, empty.

"Can we please eat?" Driver inquired.

"I still have too much of that sour mix in my stomach. Here, see what's going on tonight." I flung Driver the *Vegas2Go* book, alleviating at least six ounces from my overloaded handbag of helpful resources.

We were now sitting on a portion of the raised floor just outside the former Bradley Ogden restaurant. There, I took off my shoes like total white trash and waited for gladness and charisma to present itself. We read through the events for the night as our options waned, given the time. Driver noticed my dire pedi peril and suggested we take a cab over to Planet Hollywood. We stood in the ever-present taxi line at Caesars for seventeen minutes and were finally whooshed right around the corner. I was deposited at a stool in the center of the game floor while Speedy Gonzales went searching for Band-Aids. It took days. We had less than fourteen minutes before the show started and had no idea where Saxe Theatre was located inside the Miracle Mile shops.

I had read about *Vegas! The Show* and was eager to see it. The upbeat, historical timeline brings quintessential Las Vegas to life through a musical anthology featuring the icons that have overwhelmed and stimulated our visions, memories, and wits of Sin City. It's a carnival of choreography, a festival of fantastic. A vivacious platform for the glamorous, the gaudy, the gifted, and the grand—performed by an energetic, vividly-voiced, and able-bodied cast, visibly in love with what they share with audiences on a nightly basis. It's nothing short of the get-you-off-yer-ass kind of exciting.

This talented troupe nails the authentic likes of Sonny, Cher, Tina, Wayne, Sammy, Lena, Ella, Elton, Tom, and Dean with unstoppable song and dance fervor. All your favorites, under one roof. The versatility of the players in this ensemble excites, leaving local and long-distance witnesses breathtaken, blissful, and beguiled. It's a must-see if looking for a little bit of everything—including showgirls, now a dying Vegas breed left only in the hands of the long-standing *Jubilee* production at Bally's. Just pepper in some Can-Can feathers, a Liberace marionette, a dazzling tap dance duo, and a magician with more white doves than Elvis had rhinestones, and you've got yourself a one-stop memorabilia shop.

How can I, how can I tell them
This is not a puppy love

BOTERO AT ENCORE

I don't like to write about restaurants because we all have different agendas, different expectations, and different tastes. And restaurant reviews aren't what they pay me the big bucks for anyway. Besides, as you now know, I'm most concerned about ambiance. Which is strictly a matter of opinion.

But there are times I'm ruled by my exceptions.

So I will tell you, the entire Encore experience is worth a repeat. The namesake fits. And the gastronomy to be trifled through at Botero is an irresistible come-hither reminder of that well-spent notion.

I love this restaurant so much I could marry it and flourish handsomely for the rest of my ravenous tomorrows. Not only is it easy on the eyes, showcasing heaps of attentive design and artwork, it makes waiting to be seated—and waiting for a drink while waiting to be seated—a saturnalia of sensations. I ogled over all the semi-caricature pieces of pleasantly plump people on the walls and beamed below the wildly colorful vessels that rainbow across the ceiling over the bar. Fernando Botero, as you may or may not know, is a Colombian artist and responsible for these fabulous fat figures—presumably why his portraits get such prominent positioning in a joint with his name on the shingle. There's something very comforting about his work—if only just a jovial overture to eat, drink, and then eat some more.

Smart. *And* subliminal.

There was no room for a true appetizer after the velvety sourdough bread, and my salad fell nothing short of formidable Egyptian architecture.

To peruse this aerial edifice of thatched crops, I could more easily fathom how pyramids were forged *sans* machines and steel-toed sandals than how a creature other than a hare could do that with (and to) lettuce. I wanted to stand beneath it for an updated Facebook profile picture, send for my belongings, and live inside for just three days and two nights. I wanted to dip it in gold and wear it around my neck to a pawn shop, a nice one. And leave abruptly. I was in no way equipped to raze it with flatware or prepared for its heartless deconstruction. I took great pause to weigh my options and exorcise my qualms before tipping it over as if it was a Jenga game of groceries.

Driver and Tim ordered a savory cattle creation while I sanctioned the Dungeness Crab Agnolotti, an expensive word for ravioli that makes it taste better. My penchant was nearly deadlocked between that and the Seafood Tower, but knew I would end up backed into the same corner as my spar with the salad—eating it strictly with my mind for the first few minutes, then searching for the right size cuticle clippers in which to prune its layers and carry it gently toward the toothy break between my cheeks. Dungeness Crab also sounded like a good name for a betting horse, which is how I decide on what to eat when I'm two martinis in.

Driver can always squeeze in dessert, so we usually end up ordering one. And in this case, two: the Bananas Foster Crème Brulee and the Frozen Chocolate Candy Bar with Godiva mousse. I doled out my ratifying, "I'll have just a bite, won't even need a spoon," and fell face first into each wistful, creamy, who-needs-sex-anyway chimera of confections and sweetmeats. My thighs weren't far behind. Both corrupt calorie clusters stretched the world's natural boundaries for joy just a little further and refused every means in which to disappoint.

That was, until the next morning. When I noticed there was an original Botero where my full-length mirror used to be.

*Critic's Note: Seeing as most professionals rate with their opposable thumbs, diamonds, Michelin, or some kind of star, I will not be so trite... I give Botero a full '5' out of '5 pounds!'

THE BELLAGIO

You might not believe me.

But I'm known all over the orb for my heavy betting, high-rolling, and stringent poker face. I've grown rather accustomed to choppering into garish casinos via helipad and being nodded through to the haughty, deep-pocketed VIP districts where I'm impervious to laypeople and polysynthetics. Velvet ropes snap before me like brittle rubber bands and I'm whooshed to the comforts of my embroidered, diamond-studded twirling roost. A nameless someone delivers an expensive, imported white pelican to my left shoulder and nestles a Cosmopolitan between my unaltered bosoms. Time after time, and comp after comp, the tables orbit around me on mechanical pulleys while I estimate my chips and pat the chimpanzees that amass at my feet being pumiced by a convivial chap called Dottie.

Rare, pale-winged flamingos meringue over my dice so no transmittable airborne diseases infest my immediate space as blowing on them has been unilaterally abolished. My earnings are silently wired to my offshore bank account, managed now by Punjab, who many believe went underground after little orphan Annie left the Warbucks mansion. (According to rumor, she left for a better life bussing tables and rattling around a fifth floor walk-up in Brooklyn.) Dot, you should know, is also responsible for baling broad sprays of metallic glitter into the atmosphere, a routine that announces my arrival and charts the way back to my private suite. Every few hours, I must rest. The finger-pointing and exotic bird-stroking I endure while gambling is grueling. My arms have been known to quiver and even spasm. In these instances, my masseuse, Helga, is called immediately.

That being said, I was naively unaware that even at the grandest of gaming houses in Las Vegas, they offer *free* self-parking. And there is so much of it, it's like they knew people would congregate in a single Nevada setting to both flush money down the toilet and win enough to buy scores of commodes. They also knew that if you didn't go there to spend any money, you would be bored as hell. And if you failed to show up without as much as a flip cam, a flask, or a Siegfried and Roy, you would soon enough vanish and your one of six trillion parking spots would avail itself for the next American tourist or foreign traveler to occupy. *At no charge.*

It's lushly documented that the Bellagio accounts for a great majority of awards and top ratings cited for true superiority in Vegas. And for reasons quite justified. The Bellagio is like an enormous five-star ocean liner, outfitted with inescapable shopping, dining, entertainment, and art. Guests collectively smell of fragrances by Tom Ford and unfurl into a European Willy Wonka world adorned by Bernini in a prized pasture of tulips somewhere between the Trevi Fountain and Piazza Navona. And it should, seeing as Bellagio (outside of LV) is an Italian municipality long-renowned as "The Pearl of Lake Como." Which, if you've ever been to that particular luxury chunk overlooking the Alps, you would agree it's perfectly tolerable.

That is, if you *like* geographical coordinates that postcards, George Clooney, and romantic fantasies are made of. Just soil in a dapper bellhop, some Chihuly glass installations, Cirque du Soleil's *O*, five majestic swimming holes lined with infinite cabanas, and you've got a palatable place to holiday in the lower 48.

Some could argue the Bellagio is an opulent resort with a 22 million-gallon water feature in front of it. Others might tell you it's exactly the reverse; that the more than ten thousand annual fountain shows give life and meaning to the massive hotel. The sophisticated fountains have the versatility to dance to any song, and all productions last between two and five minutes. White lights, a fog system, and endless speakers support this renowned attraction, one that dramatically sends streams of water as high as 460 feet into the air. The 8.5-acre lake is positioned on the grounds of the former Dunes golf course, utilizing the pre-existing private well beneath the property as its water source. No water is drawn from the already-strained Colorado River and shows are cancelled when the winds exceed 25 mph to limit further evaporation. Given its desert coordinates, the cleansing and baptismal effects of water often create a subconscious emotional experience for many unsuspecting admirers. Some have even been dumb enough to jump into it.

Another one of my opinions includes the fact that people-watching is at a premium in front of these fountains. Central on the Strip, this must-see-at-least-once spectacle is a pleasure to peruse, whether standing still or walking by, and plenty gather along the wider sidewalk. Street performers of every dimension assemble and pose for photographs while recreational magicians take to their folding tables for shell swaps, card tricks, and other convenient sub-Copperfield illusions that leave the attending crowds holding yard-sized plastic beverage bongs dazzled. (As with anywhere or any service in Vegas, please be sure to extend your appreciation by tipping these hard-working folks.)

There's also a collection of small trees that contour the water's edge, so tired and weary vacationers can stop to rest and take shade during the warmer summer months. You might see some wheezing faces growing various shades of rouge, and sometimes they're fighting over the last splash of bottled water bought from the guy with the illegally-poised rolling cooler. Strollers, too, cluster up in this area, and occasionally, parents opt to dangle their children over the heavy concrete banister for fun like Michael Jackson once did with Blanket. You can also spot moms sitting atop strollers while their little ones climb on dads' shoulders. Their little arms surge out of the sockets pointing at things, usually the people who are spray-painted silver or look like one of their toys. What I'm really saying, the tourists can often be more colorful than the people they are watching if you're free to stop and stare for a few.

Within the Bellagio, the Conservatory is another splendid tour de force. Its five revolving seasonal displays consisting of live plants, flowers, trees, and topiaries are tended to by over one hundred horticulturalists. Gazebos, bridges, ponds, fixtures, and characters are raised and alternated for the Chinese New Year, spring, summer, fall, and the winter holidays. It's *Alice in Wonderland* meets the *Wizard of Oz*, and time of day drastically changes the demeanor of the florally-perfumed open-air space.

But personal sacrifices to such indulgence and beauty aside, I learned in one easy afternoon that it's much more fun to slum it with the general public in the common areas of the Bellagio than in my usual over-birded private spaces. We saddled up to the Baccarat Bar in the utmost axis of the gaming floor—populace-watching at its pinnacle, vodka-pouring at its most overpriced. (I just order the clear kind.) I knew nothing about baccarat, but we played for an hour anyway. Without Dot and my devoted rabble of water fowl, disaster can strike at any given lemon wedge. I should have quit when I was ahead, at four dollars. A fleeting moment that had me rocketing into the abstract embrace of the Italian Riviera like a third-string understudy from the cast of *Fame*.

…I'm gonna live forever. Baby, remember my name.

Thanks to Punjab and some creative financing, who *can't* live forever on four dollars? I belted out the entire song start to finish because the nice guy on the baby grand had the sheet music tucked into his paisley vest. He said every full moon he gets the same request. He wasn't the commissioned pianist, but a very fun drunk.

The Bellagio undoubtedly delights. And truth be known, it's essentially a self-contained, petite replica of every redeeming quality that subsists on planet earth—intoxicating aromas, breathtaking architecture, interesting inhabitants, plenty to drink, clean lavatories, and it's composed of mainly water.

The clear kind.

Fountain Schedule
Monday-Friday: Every 30 minutes from 3-7 p.m. and every 15 minutes from 7 p.m.-midnight
Weekends & Holidays: Same as weekdays, begins at noon

GAY PAREE

Henry Mancini is the kind of guy who makes me want to be a famous musical composer myself.

He was the one responsible for giving *Victor Victoria* the film score that later went to Broadway. You know, the story of a penniless female soprano in Paris pretending to be a man pretending to be a woman. It's a spotless plot and one that bears the song "Gay Paree."

> *When people speak of Gay Paree*
> *They think that when they say*
> *Paree is gay, they mean that Gay*
> *Paree is gay; it is!*

The term *Gay Paree* actually materialized as the Belle Époque reached its apex around 1880, when the new liberal government introduced a host of reforms. This was about the time July 14 became a national holiday (Bastille Day), freedom of the press was propagated by the abolition of crimes of opinion, and Parisian cafés multiplied and prospered. And in Vegas, designers for the desert's Paris resort did a more than acceptable job recreating "The City of Light" and a French lifestyle conveniently in a place that's been dubbed "the brightest city seen from space."

Atop the 460-foot, 50-story, half-size version of the true Eiffel Tower is an observation deck that any paying anyone can enjoy from morning past nightfall. It flaunts a significant city view from the very center of the Strip's excitement and is worth the wait and the cost. But you can also just scale two-thirds of that steel lattice and rest comfortably at the sophisticated Eiffel Tower Restaurant, consuming Crème de Cassis and a great angle for the Bellagio fountain show directly across the street. As you exit the elevator at restaurant level, a stimulating vision of the bleach-white kitchen and its shiny silver things unfolds before your Francophile eyes. It's a heavenly dandle for germaphobes and small appliance bon vivants alike. (p.s.—there's an attendant in le toilette, so plan accordingly.)

Don't worry, I had the same question.
What's with the hot air balloon in the driveway?

Conveniently enough, Driver and I had just spent an entire day recovering with a few scholarly documentaries at Carpet Kingdom (our house). These detoxing intervals often consist of me drifting off into gangling thoughts, needing to repeatedly ask what the television is talking about. But on this particular Sofa Saturday, I had the wherewithal to notice (without any help) that the same guy from *Sideways* was playing the role of John Adams in some really long movie where they all spoke with weird

American accents. It was a dynamic contrast coming from the wrath of grapes in California's wine country, so it was a little hard for me to follow. (That John Adams can sure act good.)

But there it was, in the protracted and educational mini-series—the same exact hot air balloon as the one you see on Las Vegas Boulevard—bearing all signs of the zodiac, the fleur-de-lis, lion heads, and happy-faced sunshines slapped on a satiny blue bulbous sail. World history suggests the original mini-blimp took flight before the Palace of Versailles, French royalty, and 130,000 onlookers in September of 1783. So this eye-catching inflatable was indeed much more than a spare-time craft for Sin City, but an intrepid replica of the first hot air balloon to surge for two miles in eight minutes carrying a sheep, a duck, and a rooster. Invented by the Montgolfier Brothers, I know they wouldn't be prouder knowing its metallic southern Nevada clone has even clutched a large woven basket with a Barry Manilow screensaver on all four sides.

My favorite division of Paris Las Vegas, aside from Napoleon's dueling piano bar, is Mon Ami Gabi. The always-bustling brasserie buoyed brilliantly on the boulevard flaunts a robust outdoor patio, dishing out authentic *moules-frites* and a unique Metropolitan martini—morning, noon, and night. The service itself liberates you to any Place de ___ en France and with such a handle on the seating chart, associates even ask if you'd like to dine under an umbrella or tan directly under the soleil. Frankly, I'll sit anywhere on the veranda as long as the champagne's cold. And I'm there all the time.

So *bonne chance*, Victor. And Victoria. Come to *Fabulous Las Vegas*. Where, oddly enough, you can do everything but get gay married.

Must not be a sin after all.

NINE DINING

Driver said the look on my face was unlike any other. And granted, I do make a lot of faces, but that meant it was quite serious in nature. Though one probably not *found* in nature.

I don't know what I was expecting, but I know I wasn't expecting *that*. Maybe I just wasn't expecting to be the one signing the check, even though I usually do. I just never pay. Apparently, I have better vision and more discretion. Just a lot less income.

The dinner zoomed right past me, like I wasn't even there. Only sucking up perfectly good oxygen and a few drops of Ketel One in the center of a rectangular table beside several people I had never met. From start to finish, the six of us only kept the seats warm for an hour and a half, which should speak for how hurried we were. And not by scurry to be elsewhere, just a meal accelerated by the people bringing food in a very busy eatery. Lots of people appreciate this, but I do not. I'm not keen on being asked what I would like as an appetizer, a side, and an entrée the moment my derriere crashes into the furniture, no matter how starving. If I'm that hungry, I'll order from the hostess, a bus boy, or whomever passes first. Sometimes, another patron.

Also, I'm not really a carnivore, so I require a little extra time when faced with a house built for steak. But, I need even longer than that when I'm at an authentic pub, like say, Nine Fine Irishmen at New York-New York Hotel & Casino. I've never gravitated toward bangers and mash, corned beef, or shepherd's pie. Though I do like tartan plaids, bag pipes,

---

and Lucky Charms—probably in that exact order. There, we had a gift certificate from Tammy, who received it from someone in Reno, who got it from someone who no longer worked at the restaurant, and we were ready to use it. It was on official letterhead, and after some phone calls, scanning, e-mails, and finessing, management approved.

Nine Fine is also the kind of place you can get lost in a folksy musical set list played during Kate and Leo's third class taboo dance-off in *Titanic*. Such Celtic beats loosely mask the sounds of the reverberating Coney Island roller coaster that outlines the building's exterior perimeter. You can also enjoy six different ways to prepare mashed potatoes. I don't know if that's leaving a few other traditional ways out, I'm not an Irishman.

But back to our party of six, at N9NE, inside the Palms—a resort often associated with Hugh Heffner, located on Flamingo Road. I felt a tad overdressed in my black-on-black-on-black dry-clean-only outfit. I had also never seen a valet line so long and wide, anywhere. It was like returning a rental car somewhere on Florida's I-75 North during a procrastinated, yet mandatory hurricane evacuation. Only younger and a lot less clothed—as evidenced by all the bathing suits and beach towels shaking off like golden retrievers, clutching plastic cups in every paw. The Palms is either always having a pool party or it was an isolated affair, but it was definitely shades of spring break. Just fewer parents incurring the expense.

It goes without saying, the evening at N9NE was a business dinner. Why Driver invites me to these things, I just might devote four minutes to wondering. All I know is that I usually do all the talking. And sometimes I have to siphon out extra energy to not croak from the slowness of woe. With my help, we don't talk about business or the supporting climate of anything. I'm usually on hand to lecture about Vegas, current events, and my inner ear imbalance. Or, how bad or good my last martini was. But I never speak of how often the latter happens, sounds like I'm bragging. And you know, business dinners are *sooooo* modest.

It was an incredible meal as far as the parts I remember, the ones that didn't whoosh by at breakneck speed woven through some pretty mind-altering martinis. And make note, when you spend a residential mortgage at N9NE, they give you a few passes for the upstairs Ghostbar. It's a sexy, celebrity-courting venue at the top of the Palms, some five hundred stories up in the sky. Sleek sofas, dark as hell, and the music is so loud, the pounding in your chest can give you a black eye. That's why it's so hot. And cool. From the balcony, you can see all the way to Sarah Palin's house. *And* all the way to China through a glass cavity in the floor. It also delivers one of the best views in Vegas.

By night's end, I was friends with a nice young hipster pair in from France smoking long, slender cigarettes, wondering what all the fuss was about. We saw nary a Hilton or even a Carrot Top. I didn't see any ghosts, either. So I started signing autographs as Wayne Newton and posing for millions of pictures.

Because drunk people will believe anything.

Drunk person.

AIN'T IT GRAND

I have no designs to break the news to the Alpha Delta Pi sorority. *Not one iota.*

What they didn't know, or already knew, wouldn't hurt or would only sting. And then chapter houses all over the nation would spiral into a deep, dark, bow-and-pearl-melting chasm of hopelessness upon learning their mascot is one shared by others: the lion. A universal and honorary symbol heavily appointed, mentioned, bronzed, displayed, gilded, promoted, and worshipped at one of the largest resorts in Las Vegas, and the world.

But who knows, I may have just initiated the next destination for a cheery, under-age-drinking, week-long, Facebook-damning Panhellenic convention that would render parents both hyper-proud and tremendously broke from their scholarly sacrifices for higher education and meaningful collegiate sisterhood.

You don't know how grand the MGM Grand is until you've had to cover its diameter in less than thirty minutes. It's enormous. There are at least six different zip codes inside those four emerald greenish-teal towers and it's a potential breeding ground for blisters, a proud endorsement for shin splints. In walking from Diego restaurant to the parking garage, we were reduced to searching for vagabonds just so we could unload our gourmet leftovers instead of making the complete round-trip back to the Garden Arena. But we didn't pass anyone who seemed indigent. Only inebriated. And busy.

The afternoon was a result of the morning that stumbled with tiresome miscommunication and minimal agreement. All because of the Lion Habitat. Really, all because of Driver, who told me "they" keep the lions off-site. And I assumed that meant *we* would be boarding a bus, a tram, a trolley, or joining a caravan to see them. Pain in the ass.

En route to MGM at 1 p.m. for the power-packed itinerary Driver had planned for us…

Driver: "What do you want to do first? CSI: The Experience or the Lion Habitat? We have dinner reservations at 5 p.m. and the concert starts at 8 p.m."

Me: "Let's do the lions so I have good sun for photos."

Driver: "It's indoors."

Me: "They keep them in a building?"

Driver: "Yeah."

Me: "Well when do the buses leave? Every hour? Half hour? Do we need a ticket? Did you *get* tickets?"

Driver: "What buses?"

Me: "The buses that drive the people to where they keep the lions."

Driver: "They're at the MGM."

Me: "But *where* in the MGM?"

Driver: "They are *at* the MGM. The lions."

Me: "You said they were *off-site*?"

Driver: "Yeah, they keep the lions off-site."

Me: [banging my face into my hands to catch my frustration before manually deploying an airbag] "Okay. Then what are we doing?"

Driver: "Or, we could do the CSI thing first."

Me: "What time does that start?"

Driver: "It's whenever."

Me: "So they're both *whenever*? I still want to see the lions first, but I don't understand. This is why I have to plan everything, you know. Not because I *want* to."

Driver: "The lions are at the MGM. [huff] They have about sixteen or eighteen of them off-site and they rotate them every few hours. [huff]"

Me: "Oh. So *they* ride a bus."

Driver: "Huh?"

Me: "We have *got* to work on that."

Driver: "What?"

Me: "Being on the same bus."

Driver: "Why a bus?"

Me: "They have a tendency to break down."

Believe it or not, we found the Lion Habitat. All by ourselves, and without any of my golden tresses being thrust to the tile in thick, matted clumps. It was very easy to find, but it wasn't what I expected. Naturally, I dressed for an African safari and thought we'd be on a guided tour (bus), so the only other people who looked like lion handlers *were* the lion handlers. The Habitat has closed since this outing, but it was once a multi-million dollar indoor environment in which two lions could be observed—snoozing, frolicking, or simply staring back. It was definitely not a petting zoo. Everyone would just circulate around the massive terrarium that was accessible for observation, twenty-four hours a day.

Because lions always make me thirsty, we paused for a few drinks before embarking on the CSI Experience—an interactive, hands-on exhibit that features three crime scenes that are chosen for you or your group. To demonstrate a(nother) way Driver and I maneuver differently through the world, I will share our notes. And as discreetly as possible, so not to spoil the pursuit for anyone interested.

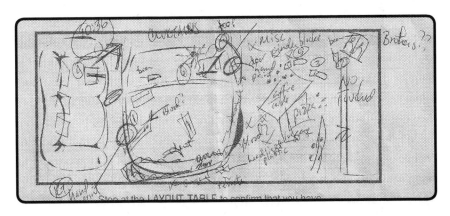

Please tell me you knew the above sketch was not *my* hideous interpretation of the full-scale setting. I've seen doodle pads decorated during conference calls that are more legible than this ball point pen portrait. If I was Driver's field partner and had to decipher this in broad daylight without an intern, I would say the victim was a chili dog-eating seagull and pooped to death in a beach parking lot.

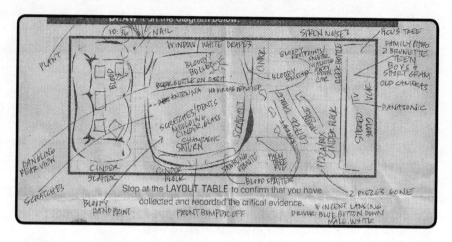

This one is mine. You'll notice the level of detail and the use of real words. It's perfect. The only thing I could have added was Braille and a link to Google Earth. Even upon first blush, anyone would know that the lions were positioned on the grounds, mapped by exact location, and there was no bus required. Period, problem solved, case closed. Tell it to Nancy Grace.

Thereafter, we settled into a snuggly seat at Diego and feasted on a trio of salsas and hand-tossed sangria. We discussed things serious and irrelevant and how full we were before ordering the main course. Suddenly, the two gals at the next table asked if we were going to the concert. They said they assumed we were going, which I thought was weird. So we assumed they were gay, which they thought was weird.

Samantha and Laurie, escaping from their respective broods of husbands and sons for the evening, were just as euphoric as we were about the show. They had really good seats and we had only gotten our full price, last-available tickets two days prior. We exchanged numbers just before scampering to the parking garage (and back) to drop off our leftovers. They thought it was disgusting that we were going to keep our food, warning of all the possible contractible diseases, confirming my suspicion that straight lesbian mommies are *such* alarmists.

The concert was essentially what led to our day-long agenda at the MGM...

Driver: "Sade is gonna be at the MGM this weekend."

Me: "Oh yeah, wanna go?"

Driver: "Sure. I'll see what kind of tickets are still available."

Me: "Let's not spend too much. I think she just stands there in a white flowy gown with a few oscillating fans. I'm fine wherever, just maybe on an end somewhere."

We got tickets alright. And seats at the end of a row. The very last row. At the very tippy top right side of the arena. Nothing behind us but the dark, textured acoustical wall, across the aisle from some other spirited fans who liked to dance with lighters just as much as moi. It was hardly a bad seat, even up there. And Sade did *not* just stand around in a white gown, either. She was incredible.

By the time we left the MGM, our rations were much warmer than when we consigned them to the trunk. I had two enchiladas when we got home and they were just as grand.

And I did not die, new friends.

SIT & SPIN

The evening included three "firsts."

As you know, that means a number of circumstances that had never happened to, near, or around me, ever before, almost four different times. My experiences were completely unfamiliar, unsolicited, and uncontested in regards to the situation in which they unfurled. And I had no expectations that would include, or exceed, a metal detector. I knew better. I also knew we weren't going to dinner in an airport terminal or a courthouse because I picked the restaurant.

Yes, the very restaurant plopped at the pinnacle of the Stratosphere Casino, Hotel & Tower, established in 1996 that punctuates the northernmost end of the Strip like a bright beacon on a blinding bay. The tripod-ish spire waves exaggeratedly to all of Las Vegas and afar like a new Miss America, hailing landmark recognition like Lady Liberty. Owing to its north-of-Sahara Avenue coordinates, officials actually consider it part of Downtown, not the Strip. Known as "Stupak's Stump" to insiders, this iconic lawn jockey favors Seattle's Space Needle, but at 1,149 feet, it soars almost twice as high. A marvel in modern architecture, it's the town's tallest structure and the country's highest observation tower—one that single-handedly directs all glazed-over eyes from any widespread perspective to the axis of Sin City's hustling bustle. A long red-lighted dowel shoots from its saucer-shaped head, warding off airplanes and lightning bolts, while two radio stations have on-channel FM boosters positioned from an antenna on top.

The tower features four amusement rides and my DNA will never be traced back to any of them. I don't understand how these metallic death porters can be deemed *attractions*; nothing about white knuckles and temporary face paralysis is attractive. At conception of the Stratosphere, one of the original rides was going to incorporate a gigantic ape that would tote tourists up and down one of the columns. I guess like King Kong, but probably not as believable. Though when engineers decided to shrink the height by almost 700 feet because of interference with McCarran Airport flight paths, the primate idea was nixed with what I'm sure was tearful disappointment. But still, the Big Shot remains the highest thrill ride in the world, something which has been compared to taking off in a space shuttle. A level of exhilaration that has never once crossed my mind, or any other practical body part.

The well-named Insanity is the second highest thriller and looks like a big mechanical tarantula that dangles endless out-of-towners over the edge at 900 feet and then spins them around in circles at 40 mph. I would rather eat all of my t-shirts. The SkyJump is a controlled descent free-fall because it is bungee-like, though the fixed wire makes it less bouncy and bungee-*y*. I can barely hear a difference. But it allows flight-suited dare devils to plunge to the concrete from a platform affixed at 855 feet.

And finally, there's X-Scream, the third highest thrill ride in the world, topping out at a still-disastrous 866 feet. If you ask me, this one puts the rush right back into Russian roulette. It's a cross between that swinging pirate ship pendulum set-up and a steep flume ride. Only there is no water. You're just suspended off the side, very high in the air, over unforgiving pavement. You slide up and down in a back and forth pattern, wondering how a steel see-saw frame will combat the gravity of the cart *and* fare against any unforeseen weather conditions and the fatsos in the back—all while preventing those aboard from an accidental splat straight down to the sidewalk. But who am I to critique what other people do some eighty-seven stories in the sky. Not my beeswax.

Top of the Strato, by day. I took this from I-15. On the left, Insanity. On the right, X-Scream. You can vaguely see the SkyJump wire also on the right, and the Big Shot travels the top column.

So, back to my first "first."

Given the tower's soaring dimensions and extreme visibility, proprietors don't pull any punches when it comes to public safety. Nope, none. As with many high-traffic and prestigious architectural prodigies in the United States, security is of chief concern upon entry. And this is for everyone, not just me. Stepping through the aforementioned metal detector is required to ascend hundreds of feet above the clean and quiet casino. Someone mans its controls and noses through handbags, bookbags, and quite fairly, saddlebags. Along with anything else that appears askew or not part of your intended, standard human model.

Had I known our scanner guy was going to be such a grump that day, I would have loaded my purse with maxi pads. The ones that are the size of mattresses. Along with some clingy unwound thread. Then I would have taken the sanitary feminine napkins out of their plastic wrappings and removed the adhesive strips so they would have exploded like Navy lifeboats and stuck to both of his hands like the Crazy Glue cap. Not to be mean, just to see if he was alive. He gave all indication that he would have been happier putting binder clips on his tongue than peek inside one more stranger's container. Even Driver noticed, if that tells you anything.

Second "first." I had never been to a dining establishment that made a point to wield the disclaimer for a fifty dollar minimum spend, per patron. It washed over me like seaweed in a swimming pool, something I just wasn't used to seeing. Normally, when approaching a restaurant that doesn't give away bumper stickers or plastic playthings, it's easy to expect a check well over one hundred clams, especially if those are on the menu and you drink like we do. Besides, I didn't pick this place because it was cheap. I selected Top of the World restaurant because it has the only 360-degree, rotating panoramic view of Vegas. And when you spend at least fifty bucks a head on consumables, the starry sights and flashy lights are complimentary.

Personally, I don't believe expensive always means better, for many things in life. But I think if anyone has the balls to advertise their billing requirements, I presume they have the confidence to deliver. Especially in a town teeming with chefs whose household names alone generate a waiting list. I actually thought about this prerequisite from a truly practical and professional perspective, one that's somewhat difficult to verbalize without being offensive. But when you're a revolving restaurant known for the most exquisite surveillance of the city, you've probably seen your unreasonable share of ungrateful tire-kickers, trick-or-treaters, and dipshits. All who assume just a few minutes weaving in between authentic patrons like third-graders, flashing cameras, and pressing their greasy foreheads into the glass won't bother anyone.

That's why I've been thinking of some alternative slogans instead of broadcasting what is essentially a camouflaged cover charge. My brilliance includes: *No Spring Breakers, January through December. No shoelaces for women, anywhere. No visible boxer shorts or other undergarments that may cause accident, injury, or loss of appetite. It's only an all-you-can-eat, if you can afford every course. This is a sneeze guard-and-linoleum-free setting.* Then my list starts to get real specific.

The large round dining room makes a complete rotation every 117 minutes. At 833 feet, you're eating where helicopters fly and are a potential witness to anyone jumping off the building on a wire from twenty feet above. Level 107 Lounge is situated like an overhead loft above the restaurant and live music fills the ambiance from 6 p.m. on, Wednesdays through Sundays. You can enjoy your crab cakes and lobster bisque next to the window, in the center tier, or on the slightly raised echelon in a cozy booth near the stationary core. We raised our glasses and filled our bellies alongside a full fiery orange moon that I could have just plucked from the night's sky and taken home with me. Like mints, or monogrammed appetizer plates.

First-timers and photogs should definitely request a window seat. You won't get dizzy looking out and it won't flip your skirt up or anything, but it moves faster than you'd think. And if you have to tinkle but forget what the people sitting near you look like, the staff is skilled in reminding all guests where they came from. Also, be careful where you leave your purse when sitting closest to the window. If you set it on the floor, make sure it's on the side of the track that moves with you. Otherwise, you may lose it. And let's face it, that handbag is usually worth more than what's in it. Protect your investment, girls.

After four easy-to-swallow Blue-Tinis, I forgot to ask if the dining room spins twenty-four hours a day or just during hours of operation. Like my head the next morning. I do know the kitchen is motionless because I wound up there a few times trying to find my seat. (Such a fun-loving staff, that bunch!) And since I already knew the scientific definition for stratosphere is the atmospheric layer lying between the troposphere and the mesosphere, I didn't need to waste any time asking.

I would certainly recommend the food and the venue. As well as Brian, our perfectly conversational, baby-faced server who has been there since Top of The World opened its doors. But justifying the $300 we spent, as two people, would be a little hasty on a routine basis. That's why we went upstairs to Level 107, to break the bank into tiny little pieces. We came in on the tail end of a music session and I walked up to the small stage to watch the last of what I could. I'm not sure why, but I sometimes need to get within spitting distance of people performing. As I nodded them goodnight, making my way back to the tall table Driver had picked for us, I was obstructed by a pair of men. One who was older than Driver, the other closer to my age.

The less old one stopped me like I was a stewardess on a busy plane and told me I looked familiar, which impelled my third "first." I smiled and told him politely I had definitely never seen him before, that I must have one of those faces. *I don't have one of those faces.* He paused and caressed his hair, lending a small eye squint and lip scrunch. "No, really," he pleaded, "are you a ventriloquist?"

I have never wanted to kick my own two shins with metal cleats, ram my head into a thick plate of white porcelain, and disappear. Of any job, any profession, any role—he manages to muster up the *one* career, the *one* character I have never played, portrayed, or studied. Ever. My repertoire was inadequate, my rebuttal vacuous, and my discourse doomed. *Damn it!* I broke, too. Totally smiled. A very defeated grin that left only enough for, "No. As much as I'd love to tell you I was, I can't. I don't like to talk with my mouth closed. Unless I'm eating."

"I swear you look like the ventriloquist we saw earlier. How 'bout I buy you a drink?" He *insists.*

"Sure, but you'll have to buy two. You can send them to that table over there," I motion toward my puppet with a Bud Light attachment.

Turns out he could read lips just fine.

KNIGHTED MARES

It was almost exactly what my mind's eye would have predicted had I thought about it on the walk down from Paris. Only it didn't smell like manure and I must have counted at least four hundred brunettes sitting in Spain from where we were seated, somewhere along the Austria-Hungary border.

The attendees with darker hair were easier to count because the tiered and boxy stadium in the 925-seat amphitheatre is evenly-distributed, not unlike a House of Representatives chamber with beaming red judges paneling as a contrast. There was a bounty of children seated in every country, all decorated from top to bottom with the toys their parents brought, bought, or bribed them with during the course of their running Vegas junket. And *they* were almost as excited as I was when I learned our joyous serf had access to vodka. Therefore, a close-enough version of the Cosmopolitan was delivered, not a lighthearted request when it comes to the Middle Ages.

Soon enough, a wise-looking, white-bearded, glittery-hatted, sparkly-caped master of ceremonies descended to the Wrigley-raked infield from his stained glass DJ booth. The entire potpourri of people in the stands started banging their fists on the table and stomping their feet on the floor like it was a pep rally for camera-clad tourists at a 4-H Club. And we all had instinctive license to act like weak-kneed teenagers, launching our team spirit across the yard and rattling our tonsils with shouts of

"HAZZAH!" every time Merlin instructed us to respond. Sometimes with his sorcerer staff, sometimes with his midget jester.

I hadn't devoured a meal with my bare hands since I stood braless over the sink flicking pepperoni off leftover pizza the previous morning. And it had been even longer since I palmed fork-usually-required food in public, surrounded by other patrons who were doing it as well. It was Moroccan at Imperial Fez in Buckhead, fall of 2008. My party was barefoot and nested on silk pillows, rapt with beige couscous and olive-skinned belly dancers—an overall experience that rarely includes disproportionate intimacy with intact animal skeletons. There, you're usually only exposed to the collective germ force of the immediate bodies in your reservation, an outing in which I never believe "more" hands are ever merrier.

Though when our costumed wench slid a heavy pewter plate and Cornish game hen onto my utensil-free place setting, I was a natural. It was effortless, just like sticking your hand in a bag of M&Ms and washing them down with champagne. I tapped into that universal drunk hunger formula when the only thing those people you just met have lying around on their coffee table is a half-eaten rotisserie chicken and a warm two-liter of Diet Dr. Pepper. And maybe a roll of paper towels and some Sudafed.

Growing up, my mom always took me to the Medieval Fair so I embrace this particular time period with seasoned jubilation. One year, I wore the tunic we were asked to make out of a pillowcase for school. I was the only one in my class with a knee-length king-size satin baby blue number, purportedly the only set of sheets Mom was willing to part with. Mine looked more like one of Miss Hannigan's negligees than a walking history project. I didn't care, though; it was extremely comfortable. Wore it until it was threadbare and faded of its magic markered-on Heraldry. I also went waving the sword and shield we made as part of the same assignment. Fortunately, our next door neighbor's son, Dan, liked to do professional carpentry in their garage after midnight. Not only would his electric saws send my father over in his pajama shorts to complain, I obviously nabbed the highest grade for Dan's craftsmanship. That, plus some gold spray paint and hot-glued jewels—killed it. Everyone else used white poster board or Styrofoam. Had there been an advanced crafts program at McIntosh Middle, I would have been beating off the recruiters. With my own weapons. *HAZZAH!*

That's just to say I don't think they had real jousting at our festivals, or at least that I can recall. I don't remember past the speared meat, elephant ears, and tie-dye booth—all of which may have happened at an elementary school carnival anyway. Point remains, I never knew the object to jousting was to unhorse the adversary. I just assumed they were trying to impale one another, which would loosen most from their pony, eventually.

There are two things you have to consider. First, this is Vegas. And second, this is Vegas. The Tournament of Kings at Excalibur could really go either way—spectacular spoof of Renaissance horse ballet, or dramatic recreation of martial sport. I was up for either, if not a woven and inspired macramé of both. Anything to fluently accompany my dragons, fire-burning sconces, and jingly chainmail while yelling a consolidated "Hooray/Hell Yeah/Amen/Cheers" in 15th century slang and counting the brown-haired clergymen over in Spain. All while managing to dissect my dinner without letting any imported hooch slide through my greasy phalanges.

Named after King Arthur's mythical sword, Excalibur is recognized as the gloriously overstated castle on the corner of Las Vegas Boulevard and Tropicana Avenue. It's beefier and wider than Disney's Magic Kingdom, more believable than Gargamel's cartoony fortress, and has four thousand more rooms for families than the cliffside Chateau Eza along the Côte d'Azur. A fief that swallows seventy acres of southern Strip real estate, this property is the epitome of the "themed resort" that was popularized in the early 1990s. Fortified by bold red and blue turrets, parapets, and crenellations, this structural dandy also includes an interior arcade, appropriately named the Fun Dungeon. Just don't get any creepy ideas; kids play there, too.

Back to my Canterbury tale...

Pyrotechnics rocketed over the ring and a large round table was lowered from the ceiling. I don't think the muscular men representing each country (and thus, our seating sections) actually ate, but the rest of us sure did. The knights huddled together for dinner to celebrate Babylon, but they kept yammering over pretty-boy Prince Christopher. That's why I'm not sure of anything. You really have to pay attention because there's no commentator.

Then, *POOF!* The big table and its burly chairs vanished clear into the solar system and the dashing, long-haired romance novel men leaped in their leggings to corresponding horses, grabbed their lances, and started running around in organized, emotional, and choreographed sequences. Charging at one another and lunging longways and sideways like macho polo players in bright and shiny flowing dress, all donning robe-gowns bearing a strong resemblance to my sultry preteen pillowcase. Always the brains behind the vision, I should've known Mom would have referenced our burgundy set of *World Book Encyclopedias* before she sprang for the linen closet. That woman's a genius.

Complete with a frenzy of fireworks and stunt smoke, a halftime marching band and minstrels, colorful troubadours and bards swiveled around in what looked like dark Hawaiian beach sand. The audience roared with equal parts impatient anticipation, eager participation, and unopposed bursts of supple mirth. Trained horses dodged regaled competitors and marched like disciplined soldiers to the concise musical fusions in the atmosphere. These stallions—unfettered by the loud, crisp clinking of metal swords connecting with visible sparks—were the loyal vehicles that generated the velocity such cavaliers used to hike javelins in which to impress the beautiful ladies of noble birth. *HAZZAH!* Their long sticks snapping like Louisville Sluggers as well-orchestrated equestrians tumbled like dice when faced with their ruggedly handsome opponents from the oncoming direction.

Constantly shifting positions throughout the underground arena, the monsieurs showcased their hand-to-hand skills of mortal combat, doling out immeasurable superhuman feats and chivalrous live action. These heroes are not only employees of Las Vegas, this 32-member cast is among the finest amalgamation of athletes, actors, and acrobats in our current century. The near two-hour production is worthy of an extended spot between halves at the Super Bowl. A feudal feast for the eyes, a fattening treat for the thighs.

And to all, a good knight.

PLAYS WELL WITH BUNNIES

Had I known the night would end up like *that*, I would have worn different shoes.

Something a little less vintage and a lot more user-friendly. A pair with actual ambulatory abilities, not just conversational ones. A set of three-inch heels that don't even look sexy sitting beside me on any surface because of their age. So old, I've just repeatedly plied whatever-color-available Dr. Scholl's cushion or gel inserts onto the disintegrating insoles. What's worse, I bought them with birthday money twenty-some years ago a half size too big anyway. I had to have them, even if they flopped off like bedroom slippers when my sodium was low or it wasn't humid enough for my feet to inflate. And now, glaring into them is like to peering down the throat of someone with a bunch of discordant tongues that have been dragging the floors of Circle K stores since Clinton announced his candidacy.

Just days before my designer shoe kerflooey, we watched a special featuring the glitziest Vegas accommodations on and around the Strip. As usual, the semi-informative Sofa Saturday of sloth involved all quadrupedal domestic animals, an IV drip of aspartame, Orville Redenbacher, and an impressive exhibit inspired by Hershey wrappers. With nominal energy, we guffawed at the exaggerated extravagance of Sin City's endowments, wondering why anyone or any company would pay anywhere from ten to forty thousand dollars per night. That's basically a Lexus.

That's also why I'm glad it wasn't our money.

Thanks to Driver's largest annual business (geek) convention, we got up to one of the illustrious Sky Villas in the Fantasy Tower at the Palms. Six thousand seductive square feet enclosed in solid glass with a can't-avoid view of the omni-twinkling town, it was everything that show host promised it would be. A heated pool dangled over the side of the building like a balcony, balancing on cantilevers and shamrocks. It was an overgrown hot tub that could house thirty not-too-fat people like civilized sardines. Of the multiple suites within, one chamber even included a round, rotating bunk that I spun around on with Driver's biggest client. No one even noticed.

On the way up to the Villa in the elevator, my passel decided that if anyone asked, I was "in Marketing." *Got it.* They punted me through the double doors and I landed smack dab in the middle of someone's high school reunion with the mathematics team. Or maybe the people who write crossword puzzles. It was a tiny baby microcosm where everyone was so excited about Red Bull, may have well been the cast of Victoria's Secret. Things only escalated when some new guy finally arrived with vodka. I'm sure the same guy from Accounting they never talk to, but knew he'd be more than happy to pay good money for liquor and the chance to meet all of three ladies in the Villa. Or, given his indifference to my questions, he could have been another butler. Didn't matter. I heard cherubs howling and bells clanking when he dished out a very holy grail of Grey Goose. I could now narrow the wide discrepancy between tee-totaling me and a pageant of flushed engineers.

All I could imagine in my peculiar future were curly-haired and balding, bespectacled men slipping into Red Bull comas and I would have to make copious calls to wives on phones I didn't know how to use as the lone vodka leader with an able tolerance. *From Marketing.* The only survivor who elected not to mix perfectly good alcohol with a hyped-up heart attack in a can. Well, besides Driver and Tim. They were guzzling beer and laughing at me and my masculine audience from behind their slender brown bottles.

I swear, it felt like a Camaro in there. Or a Trans Am.

Something with red, waterproof furniture and lots of easy-wipe leatherette. And definitely a T-Top. A cocky sports car I should have been washing slowly with real soapy water in faded cut-off jean shorts and a studded biker jacket while Alannah Myles' "Black Velvet" fed the acoustics. I'd ignore everything beyond my wash-n-wax, only flopping over a hand wide enough for someone to set an icy drink and I would sip without it even touching my mouth. Those same persons would collect my beverage until I needed it again, as signaled by me swinging my hair around, also in slow motion, and tossing it out of my face with the upper part of my forearm. All the while, I'd never get wet and it would be the sexiest thing, *ever.*

But as an alternative, I was bookended by two very large men, sitting with my black slacks rolled up over my unshaven kneecaps while my pale white calves splashed against the surging jets of the big pendulant sink populated by a haphazard caboodle of delegates from the field of mobile technology. It could have been any prearranged visit to a swingers lounge with your all-male book club, but no bother with trapezes or reading material. And there I was, holding my own in discussions I never knew I could, seated next to my black-and-white spectator pumps carefully stacked on a perilous tiled surface. I'd smile when I couldn't understand a foreign accent or hear over people plunging into the bubbling bath, altogether incapable of concentrating on more than the courteous chap who kept surfing the slick surface with his forehead while getting in and out of the warm basin for reasons that somehow pertained to me and my vital marketing impedimenta.

The Palms Casino Resort salutes the Strip from its high-class hutch on Flamingo Road, courting a wide range of concerts, conferences, and confessions. The Fantasy Tower was once recognized by its legendary Playboy bunny ears situated for illumination halfway up its midriff, but the establishment's image overhaul recently sent the iconic trademark into the sunset. The two main towers favor shiny, reflective PEZ dispensers minus any characters, which means they look like enormous cigarette lighters poking holes into the desert sky. Though if you ask me (and my Four Ps), these high-rises should be topped with humongous Hugh Hefner heads to demonstrate real Vegas chutzpah and a consistent branding regime. Just a minor upgrade to the existing façade that would exude the apt promotion for a hedonistic holy land where dilapidated high heels are optional and smoking jackets should be required.

Long live the perfect destination for thirsty marketing liaisons and traveling tribes of all kinds, where the accommodations wouldn't be complete without cascading rapids of Red Bull, mechanical beds, and some Armor All.

And Black Velvet, if you please.

A MOB SCENE

I've always been fascinated with organized crime.

Which is an overstatement, or flat-out lie, because I didn't even know what "organized crime" was for the better part of my first decade. Organizing crimes had nothing to do with my Cabbage Patches or Care Bears, my white plastic Porsche phone or any of my Judy Blumes. Of the few times I'd even heard the term, I figured it was a positive undertaking, seeing as it must have been so orderly and efficient. Besides, my parents always praised organization, and boy did I have a knack for it. I should actually be a professional organizer by now, a rich one. To think of all the money they could have saved in tuition had we just known so many people wouldn't know how to sort their own shit.

By my early teens, I supposed organized crime was just a sarcastic expression or category for white collar pranks that flopped. You know, ponzi schemes and identity theft stuff. Not like I knew what those were in middle school, either. Organized crime was just never on my take-home list of words to look up in the dictionary and define with a sharp lead object, in cursive. Back when we watched film strips, had overhead projectors in classrooms, and walked all the way over to the media center to search for things on microfiche.

But I had definitely heard of the Mafia, though I don't remember where or who from. And sometime in the early 90s, I stumbled over Michelle Pfeiffer's 1988 movie and learned the word *mob* was its synonym.

And then there were those enticing family fables that fed my imagination. Stuff about bulletproof cars, side panels, and a circus.

I still haven't seen *The Godfather*, but I've seen *Dick Tracy* and most of *Bugsy*. I have a small crush on Warren Beatty. And even if he's not who Carly Simon is referring to in "You're So Vain," I still pretend she is. *Your hat strategically dipped below one eye, your scarf it was apricot.* I used to sing it under my breath every time Todd, a debonair gent I worked with, would promenade past my office. He never knew that; guess he should buy this book.

I don't remember much about either movie, other than having the entire Dick Tracy soundtrack committed to memory since my senior year of high school. I even played the role of an adapted Breathless Mahoney for a college homecoming skit at the Leon County Civic Center and reenacted parts on the float. We were playing Georgia Tech and since Dick wore a yellow jacket, Amy hatched a brilliant plan and the rest is history. I couldn't attend rehearsals the day the speaking lines were recorded, I'm sure it had something to do with my unpaid internship. Or Bacardi. That meant I had to lip-synch in a 12,500-seat arena to Marcey's voice, a good number of octaves higher than my husky Brenda Vaccaro version. If not for the skintight strapless bra beneath my gold sequined gown, I would have never been able to pull it off.

West Jefferson Street, Tallahassee. Go Noles!

So anyway, I suggested to Driver while lunching at Pink's Hot Dogs that we walk down to the Tropicana so I could poke my head in on the Mob Attraction. Times like these, we always seem to notice Driver has the wrong shoes for movement. Antiquated leather flip-flops do not make for a good half mile's hike in the heat, on a very hard surface, some stairs included. And not too many moments later, I have to yank Driver—who is asking about Band-Aids—from some storefront to remind that I keep a minimum of fifty adhesive bandages in the secret zipped section of my purse, right next to the tampons and fabric swatches. It's always been this way, how forgetful "we" can be.

I love the Tropicana so much I could wear it every day as a leotard made of shea butter and coconut lime verbena. A backdrop for many feature films and sitcoms like *Designing Women* and *Charlie's Angels*, this comfortably-sized (~1,650 rooms) beachy resort reminds me of Florida. It's a cross between a self-contained luxury condo on Longboat Key and the city of Miami before it was canonized in rap songs—all with just a relaxed sprinkle of the Caribbean. There's a weightless aroma of Banana Boat suntan oil that socks you in the kisser the moment you slither into the Sports Book when crossing over from the MGM Grand. Ballrooms named after barrier islands and Cuban cigars, the dining establishments have sprung from layouts in an upscale design catalog. It's a paradise of palm fronds with a pineapple mojito chaser, trust me.

Opening in 1957, early suspicions surrounding the involvement of Phil Kastel and Frank Costello confirmed links to organized crime by 1959. The Trop saw steep competition with Caesars Palace and the Las Vegas Hilton (now the Las Vegas Hotel & Casino) in the 1960s before a skimming operation was discovered in 1979. It's had a resilient timeline of changes and evolutions in success, suffering, and supervision. But still, for more than five decades, the Trop has continued to grow, holding up its rightful post on the corner of one of the busiest intersections in the state. Therefore, it's easily an appropriate site dedicated to notorious mob memorabilia.

Honestly, I was expecting the Mob Attraction to favor a costume party prop shop with some science fair tri-fold boards plopped on top of an enclosed glass case with semi-authentic trinkets inside. Not because I expected the arrangement to be down-letting, but because the lifestyle was led in such confidence. I figured anyone who gave up any information, whether fact or fiction, would end up drooped over a meat hook. I just wasn't sure how anyone was supposed to donate or contribute artifacts and information without getting whacked. But what do I know about being a museum curator. Or made man.

As you know, these wise guys' strategy for assigning nicknames is uncanny. Many of which include *Big* or *Little*, their dominant shooting hand, or the best adjective that describes their faces. Take Charlie "Lucky" Luciano, for instance. He should have died in his early thirties after being beaten and stabbed and dumped on a beach in the New York Bay, but he didn't. He was lucky.

We entered the Mob Attraction with extreme caution and a non-committal disposition about going inside. I wanted to see it, but wasn't sure if I was in the mood to do it *that day*, especially after we discovered there was an interactive part. I'm usually into that kind of thing, but after the hot dogs, French fries, and taxing walk over, I still felt like a Hydroxycut "Before" picture. Lethargic and lacking flair, I watched staff members shuffle around in striped slacks with suspenders and white long-sleeve button-downs, topped off with tweed driving caps and fedoras. I turned to Driver and landed a shrug that said, "Fine."

We got two tickets and boarded the impressive set that starts at Ellis Island. Pretty soon, we were into it. From the high-tech holograms to the light spurts of participation, visitors are able to experience the various phases, processes, and archetypal settings of mobster evolution as they pass through dark alleyways and surveillance rooms, money counting tables and period wood-paneled offices. The actors were my favorite, so fun.

Guests are then directed into a chic and airy self-guided gallery area. Complete with genuine articles and modern art from each decade, every space has been crafted to keep the information concise and easy to understand. There's a lot of reading involved, but it's enlightening—even I could do it. They strive for solid character-building that highlights the most prominent of men, versus every charismatic anti-hero who swore to a code of both omertà (silence) and no facial hair.

***

Across town, the Mob Museum, former mayor Oscar Goodman's baby, opened in 2012 and makes for a friendly turf war with the Mob Attraction. Located just two blocks north of Fremont Street, the city of Las Vegas purchased this particular downtown property from the federal government for one dollar in 2000. The three floors of the 1933 Post Office and Courthouse are devoted to the various hues of American mob life and their well-known grapple with law enforcement, from here to Havana. Since the building is on the National Register of Historic Places, the only two stipulations in this thrifty turn-of-the-century transaction were the mandatory restoration of its original appearance (upwards of $25 million) and the structure being used for something cultural.

Oscar and me.

The heirloom piece of the Mob Museum is the second floor courtroom, where one of the fourteen national Kefauver Committee hearings to expose organized crime was held in 1950-51. The Museum, which opened on February 14, was also able to acquire a portion of the bloodied brick wall where seven mobsters were slain in Chicago on Valentine's Day, exactly eighty-three years prior to Vegas' ribbon-cutting for the controversial "cultural" addition. Some veteran Las Vegans, those who've been around since Benjamin Siegel gave us The Flamingo Hotel & Casino, might tell you they preferred when there was a heavy mob presence in town. Now with the Mob Attraction and the Mob Museum, those days aren't completely outmoded.

It was at the Museum I learned Mayme Stocker is known as "The First Lady of Gambling," recipient of the first license for the Northern Club in 1931, now home to Coin Castle. It was also where I read Clara Bow and Rex Bell were both largely responsible for encouraging the Hollywood set to rendezvous in the desert. And much to my surprise, Vegas was where Ria Langham filed for a quickie divorce from Clark Gable, just before his 1939 release of *Gone with the Wind*.

That actually reminds me of a gal who could have achieved a little fortune and fame for creating the first real tagline for Las Vegas. What could have easily been the most timeless and telling phrase, penned well before 2002 when Jeff Candido and Jason Hoff birthed the familiar-to-all and all-too-familiar "What happens in Vegas, stays in Vegas" slogan. But instead, Margaret Mitchell just put it in a book and called it a day.

For every action within the Las Vegas city limits, there is a reaction—cerebral, physical, or verbal. And whether it's murmured silently to one's self, shouted over a roulette wheel, or whispered to a new best friend—it's what *here* makes happen. A singular and sacred place where the hearts, bodies, and minds of men and women all profess the same declaration with repeated conviction.

Frankly, my dear, I don't give a damn.

PET NAMES & OTHER REASONS WHY

I never thought I'd stagger over a few roots from my own family tree while researching the Flamingo. But I did.

At first, it was all pretty innocent. I was really only hoping that maybe, just maybe, he was there around the same time—once I learned when that *time* really was. I remained optimistic that he, or they, had been in town on a night when all the big names had descended on Vegas sand—whether performing, playing, philandering, or philosophizing. And that he may have nodded to any of them or passed one through a cloudy fog of cigar smoke on the sidewalk.

Maybe I was just hopeful there was a better story, which simply meant, actually having a story. And I'd finally be able to press all the fragment sentences into the skimpy unsupported captions, forming semi-cognitive paragraphs and explanations regarding the things I'd heard or had been told. Something that would either explain or formally liberate the harebrained memory of being bounced over a tall concrete wall and let into a drug store in the middle of the night for orange sherbet. With *him*. A story that would, at thirty-something, finally procure the needle in which to weave all of the lively dead-end threads together and finish with a poufy bow so elaborate you'd have to unwrap it with a blackhead remover tool.

She told me to "Be careful," more than once. But I won't tell you who she is. Or he is, obviously. But we're all related. She was serious, too, as if it was a fair, yet non-threatening warning. More like, she knew all the things I didn't and it was still evident, after all these years, no one was going to make this scavenger hunt easy. I decided to just ask her everything in one fly-by, five-hour cross-country phone conversation. I was dying for the answers, at least some of them. I was dogged to make those answers become more than slippery images, all conveniently cloaked in wobbly controversy, cool conversation changes, and quieted hush-hushedness. Hazy events from my youth that stirred wonder ever since I watched that long dark limousine sail away when I was five.

I never knew the story behind the Flamingo, but I knew it would be one of my favorites. It was the third casino built on the Strip, the first "carpet joint" in Vegas, and remains the last standing mob-built model on Las Vegas Boulevard. That's plenty of intrigue already.

This whole reconnaissance mission started at the Tropicana Mob Attraction when I kept seeing blurbs about Meyer Lansky. And it was like some unclear cosmic riding crop kept winging me toward his artifacts and other exhibited particulars. I sensed he was smart and self-made. Probably because he was Jewish, and you know how smart Jewish people are. He also reminded me of *him*. Staring deliberately into that display case, I imagined them meeting regularly at Pumpernik's Deli several decades ago to kvetch about business after an hour of shuffleboard. Though I don't think he even played shuffleboard. But I pictured them, together, drawing their handkerchiefs from their pockets, blowing their noses, and wiping their brow, in unison. There was cream cheese everywhere.

I adored him. I had memorized the silhouette of his thick wavy hair, knew that he would beat me at Atari games, and could put my Rubik's Cubes back together just moments before I would give up and move the stickers around. He loved German cars and antique watches. Once older, I learned he liked women with skinny legs and big boobs. And Vegas.

I knew he was the main reason there were Caesars Palace ashtrays and other flashy swag at my tea party table. I just never knew who Vegas was, or why her name was on so many of my things. There always seemed to be a well-nourished collection of casino memorabilia for me to play with around the house—everything from match books to swizzle sticks—all of which became significant aids in the architectural programming of my more complicated Tinker Toy elevations.

In the 1940s, Lansky knew there was enough potential in Vegas to whap anyone in the face. He just didn't want to be the one to take any heat should the idea implode. That's why he sent his dapper young ambitious friend Benjamin Siegelbaum instead, who wasn't too thrilled about leaving his schmoozy hopeful acting career in Tinseltown. He was also known as Ben Siegel, but you probably best know him as "Bugsy," a name he earned from being so paranoid and jumpy. A name no one ever called him to his front side and not just because he didn't like it, but because he had a temper. And this playboy wasn't going to flee for Vegas without maximum coaxing, if he could help it.

Siegel was born in 1905, the same year Las Vegas became a city. Once he finally realized this was going to be his opportunity for greater personal legitimacy, he discovered and cultivated a whole new world of illicit exhilaration in the desert, setting the new-fangled standard that swept Vegas into a magnetizing and glamorous frontier. Bugsy sought out and convinced the drained founder Billy Wilkerson, owner of the *Hollywood Reporter*, to allow a few of Siegel's associates to invest and help complete the vision he had already started on thirty-three acres he purchased from Margaret Folsom in 1945. Wilkerson wanted something more elegant and European, cushier than the going-rate "sawdust joints" a few miles away on Fremont. It was an undertaking that landed him about $400 thousand shy of its successful execution. After taking the reins, Siegel would soon name the resort after his ladyfriend, Virginia Hill, a redhead with the nickname "Flamingo."

At the time, Mr. Siegel's machinations for extreme luxury outrank even the extravagances birthed from Steve Wynn's empire of world-class wonder. He spared no expense, slating lavish riding stables and individual sewer systems for each bathroom in the then 105-room hotel. He often paid twice for building materials because his workers would unload them in the morning to be pilfered come nightfall. Poor decisions and an oversized ego also contributed to overtime costs and change orders as he wrestled to get footing as a good-looking rookie in the construction industry. Though his method may make him sound like a pompous asshat, those who worked for him always spoke of his generosity and kindness. Which I'm sure would make Mama Siegelbaum very happy to hear.

Siegel also created a fortress-like private apartment on the top floor for himself. As evidenced by the trap doors, gun portals, dummy hallways, and escape hatches that led to his getaway car, there just might be some merit to those infamous paranoia charges. Left completely intact, his personal quarters are now referred to as the Presidential Suite, a site that rumor implies is haunted. And why wouldn't it be? If I started this whole razzle-dazzle depot of debauchery and never got to enjoy it in the flesh, I'd be back to drink for free and jiggle a few light switches, too.

Bugsy had big designs for The Flamingo Hotel & Casino's Grand Opening on December 26, 1946—an event that was originally billed for March 1, 1947 by Wilkerson. Though not yet complete, he was hoping to raise some money from his Joan Crawford-Lana Turner-kind-of-famous friends who would be coming to see headlining Jimmy Durante the wintery evening he assumed would be a promising christening. Alas, inclement weather prevented travel and the lack of rooms sent gamblers elsewhere. Siegel was staring the $6 million dollar mark in the face, a good $5 million more than planned.

The next six months of Siegel's life went something like this: First week The Flamingo lost money, closed in two. Completed construction, reopened in March as The Fabulous Flamingo. Reported profits by May, but not enough to save him from the suspicions that he was skimming, planning to skip, and was sending his redheaded sex bomb to deposit monies overseas. Then on June 20, 1947, while reading the *Los Angeles Times* in the Beverly Hills bungalow he shared with Virginia, several leaded rounds found his head through the window. No one was ever officially convicted for his murder, but the incident put Las Vegas back in the spotlight.

Since then, the Flamingo has seen slight name variations, different management groups, renovations and demolitions, Donny and Marie Osmond, Jimmy Buffet's Margaritaville, and even its rowdy share of references in popular literature. It's where Hunter S. Thompson stayed while attending a seminar at the Sands when he wrote about some of his experiences in the 1972 facty-fictional tome, *Fear and Loathing in Las Vegas: A Savage Journey to the Heart of the American Dream.*

Today, the Flamingo is about as pink as you can get before you lose your entire straight male clientele altogether. So pink, it may as well be jumping up and down with a sonogram and a skirt-shaped balloon shouting, "IT'S A GIRL!" So pink, it's the comprehensive palette for a late-80s Bat Mitzvah held at Stardust Skate Center, buoying neon Lilly

Pulitzer fruit punch tutus and big bright fuchsia fondue pots of Pepto-Bismol on its roseate cheeks. The interior is stuffed to the gills with every hue of pink on an updated Benjamin Moore paint color fan deck—from pomegranate to powder puff. It's art deco meets Miami Sound Machine and radiates from deep behind its vermilion tonsils. Each guest is greeted by several bougainvillea-colored showgirls standing outside the southern entrance, glistening in full regalia and posing for photos with tourists of all shapes and clashing shades.

It's a little bit kitschy, a little bit rock-n-roll. It's like being onstage with Jem and the Holograms, alter egos and rival cartoon bands welcome, and then whizzing off into a double rainbow on the hood of a bubble gum Barbie Corvette. The Flamingo is a sense of humor that would rather be ignored if not taken for being blissfully flamboyant.

The Flamingo is everything you believe about Vegas, everything you've heard. And everything you never want Vegas to change. So you can imagine how I felt when she told me. *Everything.* When she told me he and Meyer actually *were* friends. And they *would* meet at Pumpernik's. And the Flamingo. And that he also knew Virginia Hill.

Who must have had skinny legs and big boobs.

TITANIC MEZZO-SOPRANO

For nearly twenty years, I was distracted by the whole arrangement.

I was preoccupied exclusively by the chest-pounding, the arms flailing, the rapid cheer moves, and the thunderous howls that would rocket into the rafters of the infinite cosmos and never again return to terra firma. Then, after the ribbons of ricochet and resonance had shattered the sound barrier and were drawn into the eternal vacuum of outer space, I realized the physics of it all was much too great. I'm just a periodic table kind of gal.

For so long, I could hardly decide where to pledge the allegiance of my concentration. And when. Or how. It was like watching a phantogram on a fake location with fake clothes, fake hair, and fake vocals—faking it. Some figment of a woman blaring songs into the present and the periphery that may as well have been fake, too. Powerful, chart-topping numbers that ended up on nearly every motion picture soundtrack in the late 90s, serving as the venerated anthem for this box office smash, or the acclaimed ballad for that blockbuster hit. I call fake.

But then, everything changed.

All of my opinions and impressions, instincts and interpretations, began to suspend and liquefy the evening I watched a special on Oprah's OWN Network. (I had this thing with OWN for a while, still can't explain it.) I heard about the presentation, *Celine: 3 Boys and a New Show,* and scheduled to be home.

And that was the very night I fell in mad, incurable love with Celine Dion. Pronounced *Sa'leen Dee-YON!* Real fast, real hard. I went from skeptical and curious to smitten and convinced. Maybe even a little bit lesbian, *maybe*.

As her season series drew to a close, I got tickets to the 4,300-seat Colosseum at Caesars Palace. Red and velvety, regal and rotund—there isn't a bad place to sit from the main floor to the second mezzanine. It's a fancy and expensive womb for strangers to cavort and extol entertainment made from famous people we usually refer to on a first-name basis. For perspective, the farthest point from the half-acre stage is only about 120 feet. That's seven feet less than the distance between second base and home plate on a baseball diamond. The Colosseum in Rome, obviously the inspiration for the Vegas rendition, once sat 50,000 spectators. (I didn't even know that many people were alive in 80 AD, let alone kibitzing in one place.)

When it comes to musical experiences, hers is an affair, not just a concert. It's like a reception sponsored by Harry Winston, not the tailgate for a corn hole competition in the parking lot. It makes the Cadillac of recitals look like a hitchhike. It's an occasion, not merely an event. It's the wedding part of the engagement, the Eucharist of the holy stampede. The production combines documentary and cinematography with videography and art, all French-braided through music and evening gowns, roused by the strength of one woman's influence, a handful of background singers, what looks like a 30-piece band, and endless ever-changing interactive LED screens.

The consummation involves lifting and shifting along mechanical stages with illuminated risers that descend below, retract left and right, fan open, and reunite through a commanding chorus. For whoever has the job, it must be like orchestrating a puppet show from behind a lemonade stand the size of Antarctica. One that's inspired by timeless classics and sentimental meanings, embossing a modernized signature on musical history and the majority of our five senses. It's a big damn deal. The two-hour assembly hurls audience members into recollections and appreciations of our accrued sweethearts, heartaches, and heartbreaks. It rattles unconsciously through an entire lifetime of things we've gathered and become along the way, seasoned with a few milestone cantatas introduced to the world by other premier artists.

I know every vocalist relies heavily on their instrument, but Celine's is an entire ensemble inside her esophagus. When, just standing behind a microphone breeds crackerjack magic and the words spring from the pages of her mouth like winged elves on dandelion florets, forcing nature to sit up and take note of the man-made beauty springing from her Canadian parlance. It's ridiculous. The whole thing is an unblemished enchantment that drives standing ovations and encores, courting tearful beginnings and affecting endings. I sat there, swaddled by a multitude of superior moments that made me feel as vulnerable and emotional as if watching a Lifetime original movie marathon interrupted tenuously by Sarah McLachlan animal commercials on the second day of lady menstruation.

Celine is the set of pipes you don't mind bursting and every song you'd never lock horns with during karaoke. She's like watching a space shuttle launch from Cape Canaveral or Fourth of July fireworks over the Hudson River. A supernova or gamma ray burst, a blast of such high energy radiation that it can outshine an entire remote galaxy. She's spontaneous symmetry of the fundamental forces, something electromagnetic and even harder to pronounce. She's something so seemingly fictitious that every detail is worthy of intrepid over-exaggeration and flashy imagery no better presented in less than a thousand words. Which, I know, can be so *distracting*.

She's really just something you need to see to believe, especially the fake parts.

ALL SHOOK UP

Driver has this weird-to-believe story about driving to Graceland.

One that I will translate on my own, as it was loosely confessed to me. Mine is an important interpretation, drawn straight from personal opinion, judgment, and healthy suspicion. But first, we should embark on this anecdote with a trickle of accuracy, at least in the first paragraph. That's why *riding* to Memphis would be more appropriate. And not because Driver wasn't driving, but because they were on a bus. I don't know if it was a school bus, a public transportation bus, a tour bus, or a Greyhound bus. But it was, in fact, a bus. A bus that departed from a legitimate bus depot, somewhere in or around Southern Pines, North Carolina.

The junket was designed by a travel troupe as a vacation package to experience the life of Elvis Aaron Presley. An enterprising itinerary that generates searing images of everyone's arrangement on board, thirty years ago, when Presley's private home was opened to the public. Circa 1982, when I was still towheaded and peddling Tagalongs for Brownie Troop 181. My subsequent daydream of the bus contents reveal boxy shoulder pads and pleated pant sets, thick blue eye shadow, and crunchy crowns of White Rain hairspray. Maybe even some twister beads and other accents erupting with the color teal, while wafts of salty snacks and eager conversations bubble over seatbacks with schoolgirl infatuation.

I spot a few round souvenir buttons impaled into printed polyester blouses and that one lady even brought a rolled-up poster in hopes of getting an autograph. By 10 a.m., everyone's seen it, kissed it, and there's pink lipstick all over it. I spy busy Polaroid cameras developing maimed photos of whirring landscapes and picture the tour guide smacking grape bubble gum well after it's lost its flavor. She's Southern, obviously, and has geese crafts in her country kitchen. And there's Cheerwine on board. Lots of Cheerwine. And some canned spray cheese.

To my knowledge, no bus (of any faction) has ever been confused with the Concorde, so there were likely a few stops along the 700-plus mile route. And this probably meant staying overnight in several convenient, low-slung interstate motels. Included was a scheduled performance by Engelbert Humperdinck somewhere in the throes of this matchless adventure, and of course, a rendezvous in Tupelo. *Did you hear that?* Engelbert. Humperdinck. Had I ever been exposed to Engelbert Humperdinck, all of my complete sentences would begin with, "When I saw Engelbert Humperdinck..." I would work that into any discussion between me, myself, and everyone else. To this day.

Driver doesn't elaborate on the Graceland experience itself, but I assume the bus people arrived safely enough to devour every felicitation the Tennessee property professes. I, on the other hand, remember my visit to Graceland with bold affection and crystal clarity. So does Security. And though I was keenly aware of Elvis by a young age, I only knew "Graceland" to be a Paul Simon song and title track to his 1986 record. I was told that was "where Elvis lived," but the familiar hymn makes no specific mention of The King himself. So I snubbed these pointers and sought only the truth in Simon referencing the land as a holy place, where *poor boys and pilgrims with families* went. Ladies, can you say *GIRLS WEEKEND?!*

You're probably dying to know how the rest of Driver's trip played out. I know I was. Seems that sometime after Graceland, but before re-entering the city limits of Southern Pines, there was a guard rail. A guard rail that separated the bus and other vehicles from a fatal drop along the side of a mountain. And for the sake of this narrative, it was either a Smoky Mountain or an Appalachian Mountain. But don't quote me on that; mountain ranges were never a top priority in Florida classrooms.

So, all of a sudden, and out of nowhere, a tractor trailer plowed right into the rear of the bus, forcing it into and nearly over the railing. *BAM!* The bus lay flopped on its side, half its wheels spinning in mid-air, sparks blazing and parts smoking, while tacky mementos ran the course of the aisle and handbags lay slung in every direction. All disoriented passengers were separated from their kin and forced to escape through slim childproof windows. Driver, the baby on the bus, crawled out first, thanks to being so tiny. The very youngest passenger just dismounting blindly from any obtainable opening, splatting to the coarse gravel like a water balloon. I'm sure it was also raining. And lightning'*ing*.

It's reported that everyone made it out intact because Driver caught the largest and strongest man who was able to help amass everyone else bounding out of the disaster wagon. There were wolves, snakes, and hungry people scattering everywhere without any room on the slippery shoulder to stand. And wait. For a back-up bus and driver so they could leave their original bus on the side of the road, on the side of a mountain. Then, the new bus took the tour group to a courthouse, where they all spent the night. Clearly it was a courthouse historically esteemed for its prompt procurement of cots and sanitized linens for those exact, just-in-case situations when large sects of Elvis groupies fall on hard times.

I know it wasn't a satire at the time, but look at me, "laughing at it one day." I don't know if that's the end of the story, but it is now, I promise.

Elvis passed away at Graceland on August 16, 1977, the year after he finished his Vegas stint. He was forty-two. Presley's seven years in Sin City may as well have been fifty given all of the images, likenesses, impersonations, conventions, paraphernalia, and wedding ministries that adorn the streets and souvenir shops of the Las Vegas interior. Elvis is everywhere. In every size. On many corners. In several shows. He's part of the fabric, community, and history—enough to make all of metropolitan Memphis envious.

For me, the Viva ELVIS Cirque du Soleil show was the most sentimental way to acknowledge the thirty-fifth anniversary of the legend's passing. A detail I'm not sure the kid on his Gameboy next to me knew much about. And I took being front row center at Aria's Elvis Theater to be an omen of my unswerving good luck. Driver appreciated it, too, you know, considering the rolling doom cruiser ordeal.

I wouldn't have wanted to sit anywhere else. The blue-shoed performers jumped and danced and swung from the very ledge where I originally set my fourteen ounce clear plastic cup of pinot noir. The 75-artist, ninety minute production briskly ticked through each period of Presley's life and we were mere inches, feet, and yards away from those who shimmied and sprung from the stage like bursting kernels of kettle corn. We were in petting distance of the bright, tights-wearing, leotarded set of super heroes flinging from one tilted trampoline to another like helium-filled cannonballs in a forest full of face masks and ab muscles. Either Elvis had a thing for comic book adventures or I completely misunderstood the syllabus.

Impressive was the throbbing in our chests from the legion of acrobats camouflaged in military fatigues rocketing from the floor to the parallel bars as if they were part chimpanzee-part racquetball. A band and a banquine stacked four persons high brought Elvis and his music alive with genius and praiseful church-like swaying. There was a spectrum of rhinestoned Elvis onesies, complemented by tall feathery headdresses and gifted gymnastics, all just as flamboyant and as inspired as Graceland itself.

At the end of the vivacious performance, the attractive cast saturated the entire congregation with signature red satin scarves featuring the Viva ELVIS graphics. I received one, but they skipped Driver. And I'd tell you to go see it, but you can't. The curtain was lowered for its final bow August 31, 2012, so you missed the bus.

Still beats tipping over in one.

AMATEUR NIGHT

How was I supposed to know what was required of residents on the last night of the year in Las Vegas? I was still trying to find a farmers market.

Sin City provides options that can be as overwhelming as a disoriented gaze across a Waffle House menu. Here, *all* three hundred and sixty-five days are set aside to form a glutinous stage for domestic and foreign swashbucklers to celebrate like it's New Year's Eve. But the events for one night in particular are arranged and choreographed to outsmart even the most extraordinary of dates in The Entertainment Capital of the World.

I hadn't made an arrogant effort to ring in anything since 1999, the time with Prince. When he cashed in on the best song-writing decision of his life and I left a dent on Hoedown's dance floor. A horizontal partition of parquet that, in turn, left a dent on my pelvis. That was probably the last laidback and relaxing year before everyone thought the world was going to twist inside-out and disintegrate if we didn't organize enough rations and battery-powered backups for what was billed Y2K. In my opinion, New Year's Eve is overrated. We shouldn't need an excuse or occasion to drink champagne and kiss people at midnight. We just need the right supplies.

Notably, Las Vegas swells of the most hotel rooms in the United States, maybe even the world. And when NYE promises full capacity in Vegas, you'd better be splitting a friendship charm with Fergie or part-owner of a pack mule if you think you're getting direct access to the Strip by automobile. Practice stagnating in the Disney parking lot during a commemorative anniversary year when the trams are grounded and the monorails are down. That will help with stamina. It's like being able to see Cinderella's Castle, but you won't be wearing an ear hat any time soon.

I suggested to Driver that we venture down early in the day and stick to the north end so we'd avoid getting trapped somewhere in the middle. And since Las Vegas Boulevard was already going to be full of clowns, I chose Circus Circus. Somewhere I knew there would be at least three rings and I'm never opposed to jewelry jewelry. It's also at the very top end of the Strip's chaos; my strategy was perfect.

The whole casino looks and acts like a carnival for good reason. But namely, a circus. I'm convinced the gaming level—as in balloon darts, not Craps—foots the electric bill for the entire property. There's no way the slots and tables could hustle half as much dough from the traveling gambler like those impossible optical illusions. Vertigo lights, a sundry of noises, and a palette of hovering fluorescent prizes all react to things with balls, guns, rings, bowling pins, mirrors, and milk bottles. Things with all sorts of things, yet free of any outdoor dirt. Therefore, no black snot by day's end. *A revolution!*

Circus Circus was a lot to take in, especially on New Year's Eve. After thirty bucks, my hands were clogged with the fuzzy dice I'd won and greased with the remaining dollar bills I'd lob haphazardly at the mischievous attendants manning each Midway amusement. Chummy staff members clamored to sway passers-by that they could knock over three stacked blocks with a bellybutton lint beanbag and people stepped right up like it was actually doable. Once again, Driver insisted on squawking back, "She used to be a pitcher!" A tactic that, as you know, proves very intimidating to an inanimate opponent. Like wood.

If 315,000 people descended upon Las Vegas to celebrate New Year's Eve, then 314,000 of them rubbed up against me and the drink I held high over my head as we shuffled through. I don't know what it is about Vegas. There's something about this city that not only makes some visitors act like complete morons, but detains the pervasive majority in a state of elevated euphoria. It's a frame of mind that magically maximizes civility toward other organisms of their own kind. Or, close enough to their own kind.

I believe that's because it's a fairly neutral territory, sans any rivals or school colors, despite most people thinking everyone who works in Vegas is an apparition and gets bussed in from Milwaukee. *I sure did.* Vegas doesn't discriminate, either. It's a temporary fire escape from the lackluster inferno of everyday, low-voltage life and folks deserve that every once in a while. Travelers hail from anywhere with only one concrete blueprint for Vegas, just one. And though the layers within that master plan vary per lifestyle, the overall objective for hedonism is kindred.

There isn't much you can't achieve in Las Vegas. You can purchase ladies and gentlemen for the evening, peruse exotic animals from land and sea, be married by Elvis and divorced by dawn, acquire liquor at your whimsy, and melt into a historical fabric that is purely Americana. But those are just the obvious and admired examples.

Now I can't remember if I was supposed to be talking about New Year's Eve or Circus Circus. *Oh well, plot twist!*

You can certainly find plenty under the big top at Circus Circus, that's for sure. It's even cozied next to the KOA Kampground, thoughtfully conjoined by a pedestrian bridge. Yes, there is a KOA on Las Vegas Boulevard. So you can also come by Winnie, Airstream, or fifth wheel, and sleep under the signs. Vegas has thought of everything.

That humongous pink canopy clinging to the rear of Circus Circus, it's appropriately named the Adventuredome. This hippodrome alone consists of five overactive, climate-controlled acres of everywhere you don't want to be if you don't like children, especially your own. Just a few of the banner activities your heirs can enjoy include roller coasters, a flume ride, a free-fall, a bungee bouncer, bumper cars, airbrush booths, strong man mallets, a carousel, even the swinging pirate ship. But that's not to minimize or compete with the tight ropes and trapezes or acrobats and gymnasts that soar from scaffolds every fifteen minutes in the Midway. Circus Circus is the leading response to the argument that Sin City is not family-friendly. It's also the largest permanent circus in the world—which means it's pretty big, every day of the year.

And that's *fair grounds* for naming it twice.

DOWNTOWN:
THE FREMONT EXPERIENCE

THE FREE MONTY

If there's anything I've learned about living in Las Vegas, it's the indispensable need to manually override, if not delete, whichever one of our anatomical senses, sensitivities, or synapses it is that stimulates and hosts the emotions of shock and surprise when it comes to individuals and events.

Sure, I noticed the guy zip-lining over the car as we necked around for Hennessey's Tavern and legal parking, but I didn't think much of it. I was much more provoked by all of the classic neon signage and older, crustier charm of the original Downtown casino corridor known to true aficionados as "Glitter Gulch." The famed Fremont Street dates back to the founding of Las Vegas in 1905 and became the city's first paved thoroughfare in 1925. This area is also close to Cashman Field, home of the 51s, Triple-A affiliate for the New York Mets—our ultimate destination for the eve of Independence Day.

On the eastern end of this lane, adventurers can enjoy what is officially coined the "Fremont Street Experience." I had never heard of it, so it wasn't on my bucket list.

As we whet our whistles at Hennessey's, the weather took a bizarre and dramatic turn. I stepped outside to indulge what felt like the quintessential backdrop for a Florida hurricane party. I chatted up a few patio servers, other non-descript patrons, and two officers peeling a guy off the ground who had passed out. The bicycling, helmeted, bright yellow-shirted officials were rife with smiles and kindness, genuinely concerned about the gent's welfare and wherewithal, but I was confused. When Rip Van Winkle came to, he not only apologized to the authorities, but also to me when he saw that I was near-drool gawking from over the railing.

Where the hell was I? A dormant and potentially homeless man, simply misplaced and untimely, awakes graciously and not roaring undecipherables or blaming everyone in the vicinity for his status, while the police are humanely making sure he can stand up securely and make it safely elsewhere. Clearly, I'm not in Atlanta anymore. Because that affair would have included handcuffs, backup uniforms, a bevy of four-letter words, sirens, more four-letter words, and a lot of Arsenio Hall fist-pumping from the divided audience. It would have also been witnessed by Baton Bob, Blondie from the Clermont Lounge, and the guy who walks up and down Briarcliff with what may as well be a pork tenderloin rammed into his white spandex shorts. And then we could have watched it all over again on the evening news because a not-so-innocent bystander triggered a water main break with a black plastic bag and a stolen MARTA Breeze pass.

But on Fremont, the fronds of the surrounding palms curtsied like sugarplum nymphs in the winds as a dense grey stratum built thick, heavy shelves in the southern Nevada sky. No one seemed phased—after all, summer *is* monsoon season. Which means the ceiling could fall out with a flash flood, washing you and your car away in a matter of minutes. *No bigs.* But, we wondered if they would call the game or not. I felt inclined to ask the distinguished couple standing under the awning outside how they felt about the ominous storm. For the sake of privacy, and because we didn't exchange names, I will refer to them as Moondrizzle and Sassafras.

"Just moved here from Atlanta. Think it's really gonna rain?" I probed.

"Never know," Moon drizzled.

"We've got tickets to the 51s game, not sure if they're gonna play tonight," hoping for further repartee.

"*Whooooa*, we haven't been to a Stars game in a long time. It's gotta be cancelled," Sassy said.

"The Stars?" Huh?

"Oh. That's who they used to be. Guess they're the 51s now," Sassy smiled, slowly.

"This area's pretty cool, never been down here," again, hoping to continue.

"Yeah, we like to come over and get a room for the week so we don't have to worry about drinking and driving," Moon replied.

"That's a good idea [glimpsing at his beverage]. Even though you're drinking water [from a one-gallon jug]?" I grew interested.

"Ha-*haaaa* [he doled out in a long, delayed chortle]. We are *sooooo* stoned. Grow our own. Have a whole mess of it," Moon beamed.

"Well, that is so interesting." I grinned, nodded them a good night, and shot back to my assembly. (Who knew reefer grew in the desert?)

Despite our valiant efforts to check on the game, I can't say I was feeling ambitious enough to conduct electricity with my underwire from a stack of metal bleachers. So as dusk sat down, Paige waved us over the crosswalk from the tavern and into the clutches of the Experience. Greeted immediately by one of several persons we'd see dressed as a chain-smoking Spider-Man, he asked if we'd like to have our picture made with him. This was going to be rich.

Known as "Viva Vision," a 1,500-foot overhead barrel vault canopy is the canvas for a 12.5 million LED lamp extravaganza, one that made me want to glide barefoot through the outdoor pedestrian mall in a voile tie-dye mudmee long bell dress with a grapevine wreath of baby's breath in my unkempt hair, tossing long-stemmed daisies at strangers from an oversized picking basket, swaying to the vibrant and acoustically-perfect music in such strawberry fields forever as if I was Jodie Foster in *Nell*.

Every half hour come nightfall, all casinos and merchants dim their fizzy exterior shingles and exterminate their luminous bulbs as not to compete with the ten-minute production. The Golden Nugget, Four Queens, Binion's, El Cortez, the D, California, and the Fremont Hotel are all casino headliners in this unmatched five block radius where you can buy Mardi Gras beads the size of playground balls and find psychics and tarot card readers atop stage coaches.

Just down from the canopy, powerful industry voices impromptu their talents at Don't Tell Mama piano bar, while live music and karaoke scatters from the center stage in the main galley. Inspired costumes debut year-round as Asian contortionists, jugglers, the fully-regaled KISS crew, and SpongeBob SquarePants dot the corners and breezeways everywhere between Heart Attack Grill and Oscar's Beef Booze Broads restaurant. It's like being on Barcelona's La Rambla alongside Lucy in the sky with diamonds, dodging street performers and tourists, shoulder-to-shoulder with kiosks of snacks and crap at every twirl, but less the mention of pickpockets and pirates.

Although the baseball game was cancelled because the stadium lost power in the storm, we arrived just in time for the 51s fireworks. A supple presentation indeed, but a dramatic pale in comparison to the unforgettable hippie trip three miles down the road. When visiting Vegas, be sure to skip the schlep of the Strip one night and head to Fremont Street. Just ask for Spider-Man. He, too, will be drinking copious amounts of water, but will point you to me and Bobby McGee.

I'll be the girl with kaleidoscope eyes.

My mom made me do this.

SOLID GOLDEN

I had never heard of it.

When Singer said it was going to be her costume for our casino-themed going-away party, my irrefutable realization of knowing nothing about Vegas was in full swing. I liked the name, but had no idea if it was a person, an impersonator, a place, or a thing. Or, some of each. But common instinct told me it was probably famous, or infamous, if she was going to commemorate it as an outfit. I imagined endless bolts of shiny metallic fabric, nine pieces of processed chicken, America's cholesterol level, and a mascot for the San Francisco 49ers—all rolled into one. Kinda gaudy-kinda gross-kinda fantastic.

Coincidentally, just before we moved to Vegas, I had a conversation with Miss Shelby. I don't think she's actually from the South, but refers to herself like that, and in the third person, as "Miss Shelby." It isn't even her real name, I've always admired that. She told me, "Girl, I can totally see you as Sharon Stone in *Casino,* when she throws all those chips into the air, like 'fuck it.' Miss Shelby can totally see you in Vegas. Yes, Miss Shelby thinks Vegas is perfect for you."

It wasn't until we had been to Fremont Street a second time before I cobbled it all together into one coherent understanding. And then I was sadly disappointed in Singer, who portrayed the gracious hostess role as "Lady Luck," and not the Golden Nugget. Yes, to answer your question, Singer is her name—her real one, not her profession, nor does she sew. She's one of my sorority sisters, so we both have embarrassingly high tolerances

101

and are very good at pranks. And pomping. Which pertains to parade floats, and little else.

With all of the action and distraction swelling around the Fremont Experience, the visual saturnalia can give you a hangover before you can even focus on one concrete example of crazy. You really need to extract teeny tiny sections of the activity, slowly, so you can feed it to your conscious intuition with miniature forceps as to receive the moving parts rationally. But retrospect is always 20/20.

The Nugget is legendary, but I didn't know.

I didn't even know it had a pool. The same one directors used in a 2012 *CSI* episode featuring sharks gliding through spotless swim-up tanks and boasting of a three-story tube slide that winds suited swimmers through the massive 200 thousand-gallon aquarium. I assumed, since the property is Downtown in "Old Vegas," it was made of all old people. Old décor. Old smells. Old fixtures. Old hairdos. Old bar maids. Old oxygen tanks. Old mothballs.

But I was wrong.

The Nugget's majestic pool can be admired from the hotel's three-sided, all-glass, wrap-around interior corridor. Fish dancing, sharks circling, lights gleaming, fires burning, lifeguards perching, mixed parties relaxing. The palatable and open-air arrangement nestled in the middle of the not-too-tall towers may as well be a sound stage. Unassuming, yet dramatic. To look up is like peering through a skylight that has been permanently rolled back to reveal a cloudless planetarium. Abundant sofa settings, secluded hot tubs, live palm trees, running waterfalls, even seating built ergonomically into the water at just the right level so you don't sink.

The Nugget was constructed around 1950, emerging as Downtown's most stylish gambling hall, a staple for poker playing and poker champions, to this day. And under the vision of a guy called Steve Wynn, it was revamped in the mid-80s. I'm not very good at pie charts and stuff, but I think this was when Mr. Wynn cut his teeth on casinos, just moments before completely laying a hefty claim on the Las Vegas Strip. In 2004, old Goldie got a two-year, $30 million dollar facelift and now looks nothing like her age. So if that's what they call Old Vegas, I'll gladly start saving for my own renovation now. The Golden Nugget is a classic landmark for good reason, and I hope *it* never has a going-away party.

But if that were ever the case, I would definitely go as Singer.

PUTTIN' ON THE FITZ

We found it.

We finally found the murder mystery dinner theatre I had been searching for so impatiently. And *Marriage Can Be Murder* runs, without exhaustion, seven nights a week.

Until the fall of 2012, the Fitzgerald remained one of the delightfully wilted anchors on Fremont Street. If you were to delete all the commercial glitz, Hollywood glam, and Strip sparkle from your imagination and reference roll—the Fitz would be the archetypal casino to play the lead in every gritty, realistic motion picture portrayed sometime after the Rat Pack, but prior to Steve Wynn. Renovation schmenovation, it was perfectly fine the way it was. In fact, they should have just renamed it The Fitz-Carlton.

However, a set of brothers, Derek and Greg Stevens, have transformed this great institution into the D, for Downtown, though I've also heard it has an affection for Detroit and Derek's one-lettered nickname. But for the purpose of this explanation, let's forget present tense and actual meaning altogether.

On our search for the showroom, a twangy and befitting "The Weight (Take a Load Off, Annie)" piped through the lightweight blanket of cigarillo smoke as we passed every species required to match the ultimate gambling stereotype. Specifically, the one about multicolored and catatonic people who unapologetically live and die for Vegas. The slot machines on the second level dole out authentic American coins (even post-regeneration) that you can field with small faded buckets. The stacked plastic cups dwell at every cluster of games, like bone-colored plates on a buffet trough. In its heyday, the Fitz felt like a well-oiled living room, catering to your entire extended and unrelated family on Thanksgiving Day. The Sports Book seated no more than twenty wide-eyed men in low red velveteen chairs, with about eight residential-sized televisions on the wall. It was a true man cave fit for a bluegrass garage band. Affable attendants, generous bartenders, and patrons assorted. There was no better place to wear a velour warm-up suit and every piece of jewelry you own. Especially rings, lots of rings. On every finger.

Now, back to the mystery.

For me, nothing is more rewarding than participating in or facilitating murder mystery dinner parties, even full-blown destination weekends. And I'm horrible at them. I'm apathetic to the plot and stirred by the performance. *My own, that is.* I can't follow along with any of the reasons why because I'm too engrossed in the whodunit. Or, if *I* should be doing it. Or *can* do it. That's if I don't get too tangled up in trying to make everyone think I'm guilty—whether I'm in the script, have penned the script, or have even read the script.

That night, we were first in line and the first to be escorted inside. A few minutes into our opening salads, all guests at our long, narrow table had been formally seated. Driver was unnaturally more talkative than usual, chatting up visitors on the left end from Missouri, while I introduced myself to the mismatched married couple across from my silverware. I didn't find them suspicious, but the things we had in common were suspect. How on earth could they possibly live in one of the same neighborhoods I grew up in, forty-some states away, *and not want to talk to me?*

Our playful server misheard my drink order and returned with a full plastic cup of Absolut and a side of soda. As in, Diet Coke. As well as a bottle of red wine. Some may snub their noses at this combination, but it's a helpful conversation piece for others who are generally shy. Or judgmental.

Sometime during or after the main course…

Driver: "How did you get involved in this?"

Me: "What do you mean? I think *you're* involved. You did something when I went to the ladies room. You told those people what to say to me."

Driver: "Paranoid? You need to be quiet. One of the rules is keep talking to a minimum."

Me: "I can't help it."

Driver: "Well, you're going to ruin it."

Me: "We're *supposed* to interact. You're in on this, aren't you? You know, I'm always the one who gets killed in these things."

Driver: "Shocking."

That's when, all of a sudden, the ███████████████ in front of me launches ███████████, ███████████ the room, and █████ cheap ██████. And dies. The gal playing the ███ followed ██████ ████████ death march and the victim's ████████████████████ just kept ████████████████. ████ I stood up to discuss what I had seen, without being asked, and I tried like hell to implicate ██████████ ████████. Total fail. And the incriminating evidence in my head was much better than what sprang from my mouth.

I couldn't keep up with the next few victims, but I was elated to be lumped into the elite pool of diners nominated for the Best Supporting Actor/Actress in a Non-Supporting Role. I don't think I would have received such a prestigious honor had I not added my name to the sleuth sheet as the last one to be slain "for having a big mouth." Sadly, I didn't take home any trophies, at least with figurines on top. Only an anonymous bruise and a cute new friend, Nikki. She was the female half of the odd couple. It also marked the first time I've ever lost anything to anyone named Cupcake. Including my keys and virginity.

Obviously, portions of the aforementioned pursuit were redacted to preserve the sanctity of the surreptitious sequence and original experience. *Marriage Can Be Murder* alternates the cast and conspiracies frequently, so I will go often. With the intent of just ordering vodka. Or wine. But not both, at least in unison. And rest assured that although the building changed names and took on some fancy upgrades, the mystery theatre is still there. The cast is quick-witted, insanely clever, and downright endearing. You also don't have to be married or even engaged to participate in the show, so you can lie about everything else.

But trust me, being hammered does not count as a murder weapon. *Or* cause of death.

LIVE AND IMPERSONATOR

I don't make it a habit, but I did ask Reba McEntire how it felt to be Reba McEntire.

Meanwhile, sans any prearranged agreement, Driver slipped away from me to pace around under thousands of golden light bulbs fifteen meters to the fore, pretending we were in no way associated. Driver wasn't even mindlessly toying with a cell phone or fidgeting with a shirt collar to occupy distraction, just combing the enclosed sidewalk, solemnly tracing the lines and wearing a visible divot in the worn cement. This continued well after my conversation was complete, which couldn't have lasted more than six minutes. Serendipitously, I had caught Reba only seconds before curtain and Reba was very busy visiting with fans and cutting up with a few other famous faces.

It looked like a red carpet affair, one that we snuck into without tickets, a valid invite, or opera glasses. The paparazzi were everyone, and anyone with a camera. Fortunately, the standard attire in Vegas is casual so it didn't matter that we were dressed for doing laundry. Folks here can come and go as they are, were, or want to be. Even wannabe. Vegas is what you make it, if not whom you make it.

And you see what I've been making with mine.

I wanted to go to *An Evening at La Cage* at Four Queens. I needed to be entertained and serenaded, within a desperately urgent time frame. After all, I promised Reba we would be there three times. But Driver was, as evidenced by the extreme detachment and vacuous expression, not interested in my proposal. Something grouchy about having already seen the performance twice, so I was given the option to "do anything else." And going to the *Country Superstars Tribute* next door at the Golden Nugget starring the *other* Reba McEntire did not count as an alternative, either. I was left to my own devices, dissatisfied by Driver's dreadfully funless rejoinder stating we had already seen that show, too.

I know for a fact Reba wasn't expecting a few of the questions that were collated into my oral examination. I didn't even know I had them in me. Though I will admit, sketching out celebrity connectivity and the multi-dimensional degrees of separation with Reba as the fulcrum has monopolized more than one of my rainy days. I'm obviously pretty private about that part, but I'm very open about my love for Reba McEntire.

I'm certain Reba thought I'd ask something about hair and makeup, gowns or nail polish, lyrics or clothing lines. Possibly how long it takes to get ready or if, secretly, there *was* more than one chance for Fancy after all. Maybe I'd even ask where Reba puts his manhood when pouring into wardrobe, but not ever the query, "Is imitation *really* the sincerest form of flattery?" Life, art, and Madonna seem to think so, did Reba?

The first time we went to see *La Cage*, I snapped one hundred and twenty-two pictures with my phone. It's the only show in Vegas that encourages photography. And throughout the course of the two-hour concert, mathematics suggests that's an average of one photo per minute. The next day I had to delete all but six because they came out like wobbly color studies. Purely indistinct images that yielded a dynamic cross between electrocution and the microscopic enhancement of an amoeba.

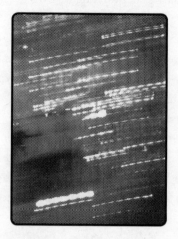

That's because I believe bartenders on Fremont are required to make the strongest drinks in the whole wide world. Or they use firewater, gasoline, and lemon-flavored non-poisonous poison. Two large plastic cupfuls and I'm inserting myself into the performances and telling people they need these beads.

The second time we ended up at *La Cage*, I had won enough money at Pharaoh's Fortune in the Fremont Hotel to pay for our tickets. That was part of the deal. We would go only if my winnings covered the cost. And you know Driver was thrilled I actually came through. Like Oprah was right there yelling, "We're going to *AUS-TRAL-IA!*" That kind of thrilled.

And because I had only seen *La Cage* through the screen on my phone, I was dying to see it when I wasn't so preoccupied. I was also curious to confirm if the person playing Michael Jackson was really a man playing a man. Or a woman playing a man. Or a man playing a woman playing a man. Because the first time around, I could barely tell any of the women weren't women at all. Until Bette Midler and I had a quick exchange after the show, parting ways at the restrooms.

What's fascinating to me about female impersonators in particular is that not only are these men impersonating women, they are impersonating *famous* women. They aren't just a bunch of transvestites running around in slinky plus-size, surplus stripper fashions. Nope, they are real-life avatars with obscured Adam's apples and flawless electrolysis who have to match someone we all know. And they're everywhere, of every design.

Vegas is also one of the few places you can catch a demonstration from almost any pop culture icon in history. Usually American, but that's not a hard, fast rule. Pretty soon I need to decide who I would be if I was an impersonator. And maybe by the end of my life, someone will want to impersonate me. Or maybe one day someone will just help me put my hair in Bo Derrick braids like Kim Kardashian did. She is definitely one of my favorite celebrity impersonators, and probably the most successful one, too.

Chances are, I'll end up Suzanne Sugarbaker from *Designing Women*. I haven't seen him-her or her-him-her here yet, so that could be a promising niche. I would work strictly under the canopy at the pedestrian mall of the Fremont Experience, on my very own stage, at the top of every hour. I would be "Suzanne: The Pageant Years," who repeatedly *sweeps every category except Congeniality*, slinging syrupy Southern sayings around with bewitching abandon. And I would be the *only* Miss America contestant to have ever spun her baton into a transformer, triggering the impetus for a 550 thousand-watt Viva Vision light show. A spectacle so arresting, that when they first plugged in those millions of synchronized LED modules, the charismatic surge of electrifying rapture was felt all the way across the country, two thousand miles to the east.

And that, Marjorie. Is the night. The lights. Went out. In GEORGIA.

AROUND TOWN: VEGAS LOVES LOCALS

A PENNY FOR YOUR SLOTS

I can only imagine the mottled cornucopia of reasons, excuses, and alibis many casino patrons are moderately suited to brandish when they are politely asked to leave a gaming establishment. I'm sure they are all quite textbook and trite scenarios involving disorderly conduct (or clothing), exposed private parts, a crinoline-laden tiara, ripped fishnets, some kind of heist, a blow-up doll, an ill-fitting weapon, or someone's mother.

That's why it was certainly news to me that there are *other* painfully sedate motives available for staff to indulge when they wish for someone to leave the premises. And swiftly at that. Who knew that in a boisterous building with blinkety lights and profuse drunk people, one could be as quiet as a mouse, not making a peep or lifting a finger, just slightly leaning over, and garner the meandering request to be relocated? I didn't, but my learning curve is pretty special.

I wasn't snoring. But even if I was, it's not like anyone could have heard me over the ding-dongs and ding-a-lings anyway. I couldn't have been napping for very long; I was only resting my eyes. The whole dance-off with Chuck Rawlings the night before took a lot out of me—trying to keep my shirt buttoned while doing the splits was grueling enough. So it had to be such that my peaceful slumber was aborted when Driver tapped me on the shoulder and said it was time to go. Sounds like the nice drink-bringer lady at Treasure Island advised my responsible tribe that I should be awakened and impounded to a real bunk before I was confiscated by the security department.

That's just a little tip in case you ever want to wind your party down, pronto.

But after a full night's sleep in a real bed and a day of disturbing television shows on the sofa, we were back up and at 'em by 9 p.m., sharp. It was decided, if I could function, that we would take Singer to one of our favorite neighborhood casinos, the Cannery.

The Cannery is fairly new, the décor is pin-up girl chic, the restaurants have all proven to be edible, and the people-watching is marvelous. That night, I was better suited for non-bra activities, but I rallied. It would have only subtracted more energy to boycott. Upon entry, the three of us circled around the large Wheel of Fortune command module like city slickers at a campfire and I lost $7.50 before I even had two self-respecting swigs of my four dollar wine. There were no vowels or consonants, anywhere. My slot was obviously broken. And I sure as hell didn't recognize what the policy was, but I was determined to find a game I liked. One that would become "my game"—the one that would transform me into the complete Vegas cliché, just like you read about. Or at least see on shows starring Dan and Roseanne Conner.

I ditched the Wheel like a burning bag of poop and assessed my exploitable options. There were forty-nine alternatives in reaching distance to choose from, but Super Sally's Shrimp Mania slot was calling my name. It was loud, and it was clear. Comic strip sketches of shrimp, crabs, oysters, pelicans, snails, and other unidentifiable shellfish garnished the screen in numerous rows like a patchwork quilt with a bunch of squiggles that kept surfacing like dot-connecting televised football replay diagrams everywhere. And if that description didn't make any sense, then I made my point. I injected my remaining $12.50 and began pushing all the buttons that were farthest from my wine. Driver sat down beside me to play It's a Blast, some harrowing mutiny featuring a lamb with a stick of dynamite in its mouth. "Danger" barrels sliding to and fro with hideous fight music and TNT rockets racing next to small atomic bombs. It was pandemonium. And so dumb.

Every time I spun, Super Sally transmitted an encouraging hymn that told me to "Bait it up," "Land them shrimp," or "Work those reels." But I'm not a fisherman. Or a hillbilly. My high-rolling twenty bucks evaporated in just one drink. Granted, it was a heavy-handed pour, but I wound up with *another* broken machine. One that didn't know how to win. "This is so stupid. All I'm doing is throwing money away," I murmured. "That's why they call it gambling," Driver, the leader of perpetual positive thinking, reminded.

I slid further over to what I hung even higher hopes on, the Dam Beaver-something game. Red-and-black lumberjack button-downs, furry hats, climbing boots, scary axes, and chubby-cheeked woodchucks all spun around without matching, even when I ante-upped and doubled down. Whatever that means, I wasn't even doing that. So, I smooched another papery Andrew Jackson portrait goodbye and pouted. Not only was my glass empty, but I was losing and Driver wasn't silencing the lambs. Meanwhile, Singer was off taking pictures of other guests and trying to get us registered for bingo.

This, it shall be documented, was when and where I began my reunion tour with the Bangles.

I only put three dollars in Pharaoh's Fortune so I could get a free cabernet before we sauntered over to the bingo hall. Unsure if they had full service within, there was no sense taking *any* chances. To note, I've always been fascinated with Egypt. In fact, I wanted to be an archaeologist in sixth grade, but it was against the law. So I was drawn to this flickery gold box like a moth to a closet and immediately made friends with the nice gentleman beside me. He wasn't playing, just chain-smoking generic menthols and hitting on the girl to his right.

I don't even think I touched anything, but my credits were adding up like travel calories, by the penny. Then it froze. Completely *frozen.* Driver and I were still sitting in the same block of machines, without a drink-bringer in sight. But now I needed an attendant, too—one with a skeleton key, a monkey wrench, or a corkscrew. I kept jumping up over Pharaoh's like a neurotic Jack Russell, trying to flag anyone down, sending a repeated and pathetic SOS into the smoky ceiling tiles that my game, the one holding my entire fortune, was deceased. I was convinced no one would ever be able to find me.

"Hit the 'Attendant' button," Driver shouted, as if I were a stranger.

"I don't have one," I volleyed back.

"Do you have a 'Change' button?" Driver, still policing lambs.

Turns out, the "Change" button also makes the sirens on top light up and a nice woman arrived immediately. Almost like she had been standing there the whole time. She reviewed the situation, looked at me funny, and then drove her fist down on it, nearly compromising my warm cabernet. I was back in business. And in what felt like sixty seconds under water, I had 9,600 credits on the screen. It would continue to occasionally freeze up and I would just pound the shit out of it myself, like I worked there. I alternated between soft presses, strong pummels, and deep pours, dancing in my vinyl high-backed seat like Nefertiti. I was as "WINNING" as Charlie Sheen.

Singer: [laughing like a hyena through the skinny straw speared through her rocky vodka soda] "Have you even gotten up to pee?"

Me: "No. This machine is way too hot. You shoulda seen the crowd around me. And when I tipped the gal that five dollars, she definitely didn't forget about me. I bet I've had a box of wine."

Singer: "Is it like Memory; how d'you play?"

Me: "Dunno. But I keep getting the King Tut Bonus and it plays 'Walk Like an Egyptian' every time you spin. Then I get to pick my stones like I do tarot cards [waving my hands over the screen like a blind magician to demonstrate] and the whole machine kinda rumbles."

Singer: *"Ohmygod."*

Me: "You need to leave, you're bad luck. Shoo, shoo. Go."

Singer: "Okay, I'm gonna do another lap and I'll be at blackjack with Driver."

Another hour later…

Singer: "Have you peed yet?"

Me: "No. But I can totally see how people get addicted to this. I'm down a little, but I told myself I wouldn't go below 7,000."

[Starting Credits: 300, Credits Remaining: 7,001]

Singer: [slurping sound spun through a snicker, her right index finger jabbed the "Cash Out" button] "Okay, looks like you're done."

Me: "But—"

Singer: *"Seriously?"*

Me: "Did we miss bingo?"

Singer: "Um. Yeah, Jackpot Judy. We did."

FREDERICK

ACT 1, SCENE 1:
North Las Vegas' acclaimed steakhouse, in search of treasures from both land and sea. With the semi-restrained request for a booth, we are escorted to the center slot as if dripless, untouchable, wait-in-line-to-see, standing-room-only ice sculptures displayed on a flashy cruise ship's all-you-can-eat smorgasbord. Opening dialogue performed with the velocity of a competitive Chinese ping-pong duel, internationally televised, and translated into English on most networks.

Frederick: "How *are you* this evening?

Me: "We are *wonderful*, thank you."

Frederick: "Well, you *look* wonderful."

Me: "*Oh*, stop it some more."

Frederick: "If I had a nickel…"

Me: "I'd owe the bank."

Moments later…

Frederick: "I went ahead and brought two glasses for the wine. And here's your Cosmo, Blanche."

Me: [grin] "Now, do you mean *Golden Girls* Blanche or *Streetcar Named Desire* Blanche?"

Frederick: [gently gift-wrapping himself around the scooped shoulder of the sofa-style dining throne] "Or there's Joan Crawford, *What Ever Happened to Baby Jane?* But I'm thinking Devereaux."

Me: "Frederick. This is going to be a fun night."

Driver: *"OH.GOOD.GOD."*

Driver, again: "Well, who would—?"

Me: "Dorothy."

Frederick is easily two parts Andrew Lloyd Weber, one part William Shakespeare. If not the reverse. Animated, theatrical, and worth every encore. So much so that guests call in advance to request his station and/or wait feverishly for even a tulip to open up in his territory. (Kind of like Kelly O, our favorite restaurant goddess back in Atlanta.) How we were magically dropped into Frederick's orchestra, we can only blame big bright pinwheels of destiny coupled with escargot and she-crab soup. All of which filled us up entirely, that by the time our entrees arrived, we only had room left for a little more wine, a corpulent chocolate wedge, some Irish coffee, and two boxes.

Over the course(s) of the production, I doled out my entire playbill of questions to Frederick—business, personal, and all things Las Vegas. By the end of the evening, we had exchanged cards and were convinced Fred probably had more personalities than everyone who had ever appeared on *The Love Boat.* (Just like Gilda Sue Rosenstern, same person as Kelly O.) Whether he liked it or not, we had just placed ourselves into his everyday life.

Driving home from dinner…

Me: "I *really* like Frederick. Wonder if he's a total freak."

Driver: "Anyone who hits if off with *YOU* [annoying overemphasis] like that, yeah, probably."

Me: "Drivers are supposed to be silent. We should probably get you a hat."

Me, again: "And a Lincoln."

So, of course, we said yes when he invited us over for dinner three nights later.

ACT 2, SCENE 1:

Frederick moved here about ten years ago from Manhattan and still has lukewarm feelings about Vegas. It's hard to compare the two, really. However, after spending six hours with the Atlanta cast of *Ignorance is Bliss*, there's no way he couldn't have a renewed sense of city merriment. He has four fancy "tuxedo" cats, which I had never heard of before. None of them liked me very much, but Driver reminded that when I grab at felines like a four-year-old, they have a tendency to scamper and retreat. At least Frederick didn't seem to mind when I did the same to him.

Naturally, the three of us began planning family holidays and trips to wine country together. We have long-term goals to swap recipes and sew matching ironing board covers, take our cats for long walks, and learn how to turn balloons into poodles. We'll lobby to be background dancers for Celine and go bike riding after school with James during our summer vacations. And by the time we've seen each and every show on the Strip, they'll be calling us *The Golden Girls*.

Dorothy: *"OH.GOOD.GOD."*

HALF BREED

Trying to decide was a real barnburner.

The Pure Aloha Festival and the Celtic Festival were in town the same weekend; you can imagine the conflict. Both sounded intriguing, but it all came down to who would have the better souvenir tents. I was pretty sure I could find a pair of coconuts if I sat under the right tree long enough, so the decision really made itself. And then the seersucker suit I would wear was a no-brainer from there.

In honor of the occasion, not only did I miss Passover, but I learned my Jewish side's family name has a Scottish origin. *Huh?* Obviously, when you're a quarter Jewish and round up to a half, you don't have to be accurate with your "holidates." You just need to know which ones apply to your people, considering the postal service and banks never close to remind you, unless they happen to fall on a Sunday. You also don't ever expect to discover anything about your religious roots at an event where people are plastered in plaid. And by plastered, I mean Guinness and single malt whiskey.

I thought it would be a scream to run my mother's maiden name through the computer system at the ancestry booth. I was certain it would send the machine into catastrophe, like the time I asked to have it traced at the Genealogy Center in Salt Lake City—a very liberated kind of place. There, the bitchy attending librarian returned my paperwork as if handing me a demerit and whispered, "Yiddish." She never revisited the station I was tarnishing for others, so I obnoxiously tested all sixteen ring tones on my cell phone to retaliate. Repeatedly.

This particular Celtic jigfest was held inside Floyd Lamb Park at Tule Springs, a natural setting fifteen miles north of Downtown. With views of the Sheep and Spring Mountain ranges, it surges with abundant vegetation, lakes, and engaging peacocks. *I love peacocks.* There were bands playing, hammers throwing, cabers tossing, foods greasing, and Highlanders dancing. And I believed with everything in my bosom that the crest or coat of arms for my clan was going to be twinkling with menorahs, Maccabees, and matzo balls. But I was wrong. Instead, it was consumed with stately silver knight heads balanced by big regal lions. And there were stars alright, but none of which had anything to do with David.

Driver found these results to be the most amusing news in years. Thus, I was treated to a complete kilt kit—a do-it-yourselfer that includes everything from the flashes to the sporran. (Driver has this quirky thing for kits.) I was so dismayed by this identity crisis, my mom essentially had to talk me down. With things like, "I think the name was shortened by my grandparents" and "I assume it previously ended in –berg, –stein, or –man." I was somewhat receptive, hearing the name was abbreviated and I can still half-lie about my heritage. I was also relieved to know I can now add Scottish holidays *and a kilt* to my repertoire, when necessary.

That was also the very day we received our first invite to a BBQ. The picnic genre has always been a challenging theme for me to work with, but nevertheless, it's a consistent one—a function involving a grill and things that begin and end with salad sides and Saran Wrap. Remarkably, in Vegas, you can diagram an outdoor event without executing the labor-intensive, seventy-eight step precipitation contingency plan—any time of the year. The locals really dig the rain because it means something about the climate is actually different than always. If even just a quickie monsoon or good-humored haboob.

Little do these folks know that I not only brought my Apple Bottom jeans all the way from Atlanta, but also my raindance boots with the fur. And my customary scissor kicks court only sunshine and moon beams.

Sometimes, just moonshine.

TOWN SQUARE

If I were the "old me," cynical and plunging animal crackers into my misery soup amidst a tiny township known as Atlanta, I would have never let myself be detained by two smooth-talking, good-smelling Israelis peddling products from the Dead Sea at an outdoor hut.

Had I been at Lenox Mall and passed this same roofed retail coop with the same cabana boys, I would have extended a very piercing, red-eyed, snake-haired Medusa glare, effortlessly turning them both to stone between forced blinks. They would have slumped to the ground with a reverberating thud and I would have continued on to the next belt or jewelry stand, unleashing the same salutation to him, her, or them manning little gimmicky tents. All accessorizing and self-improving merchandise islands in my sweeping path would have been demolished, their shopkeepers left smoke-signaling for assistance from FEMA with a ruddy wand of patchouli incense.

Likewise, any and all arms reaching out at me with sample packets or spritzy things would have been twisted off with fast-acting jiu-jitsu and flung all the way across Peachtree Street giving Phipps Plaza a black eye. *BOOM!* But at Town Square, an outdoor galleria, there aren't any slow-going herds of consumers billowing around people who hate their jobs, hate serving you, and now hate the smell of The Cookie Company. Town Square is situated a few miles south of the Strip just off Las Vegas Boulevard—a sprawling complex with an intimate feel, originally designed for travelers who wanted a break from their bender. But moreover, it has turned into a sublime atmosphere for locals.

And we are locals now. Of course, we accidentally happened upon this sanctuary of subdued opulence because we were hungry. Considering the suggested number of meals per day, this happens often. I can break out into starvation just about anywhere, at any time. Locals probably don't even share this gem with other locals, it's so precious. Town Square hosts a range of upscale and specialty shops, fine dining, a few nightclubs, even a family area and movie theater in the rear. It's like a trophy wife in the world of one-night stands.

I didn't recognize Kosher Salty's accent at first. I thought he was from the South of France. His intonation was indulgent enough to be its own Ben & Jerry's flavor, one that would no doubt entail Toblerone. He caught me escaping Banana Republic to feed the parking meter, leaving Driver to make unilateral decisions about trouser cuts—a duty that should have redelivered me to the dressing rooms in approximately four minutes or less. But three quarters and a nickel later, I was still perched atop a swivel chair, reflecting in the mirror while Kosher massaged away the dark circles under my eyes and his sidekick Yarmulke exfoliated my forearms.

"Crap, I gotta get back in there. My Driver might buy something awful, but I'll come back. And I promise to buy whatever that was." I fled back inside; Driver was checking out.

Driver: "What you been doing out there?"

Me: "I told them you'd buy something. We have to pass them on the way out."

Driver: "Who?"

Me: "The Jews. They rubbed their sea salt all over me. See [showing the comparison in my forearms]. It's dry here. Dead skin, Dead Sea. *Voila.*"

Driver: "Who *are* you? You hate when people try to sell you stuff."

Me: "I know. But he told me he'd give me a gift. Come on, let's just buy it and get to the Bellagio. I'm thirsty."

Soon enough, Driver was also being awkwardly caressed by Yarmulke while I rotated around the hut scratching and sniffing things that pledged eternal youth. Never has the sentence, "But for you... [insert reduced price here]" ever moved me further than a curtly offensive cackle that gets me shushed and gleans dirty looks. But this time, I swooned. "We'll take it. All of it. How much? *Who cares!*"

As the credit card slid through the machine, Yarmulke heaved other gratis items into our already-strained aqua blue Beauty Effects bag. This made me think we (or Driver) had completely overpaid and they felt guilty. But the "new me" didn't care; I wanted all of it. I wanted them to put everything they had in my big embarrassing bag. And they did.

Now alive with inventory, I plan to thatch palm fronds together to erect my very own stand-alone sea salt lean-to in which to vend all surplus beautifying agents in the 'burbs. It will be the sister shack to the one run by my fresh-faced fellow Jews. Though at my casbah, there will be a cover, two drink minimum, and a disco ball.

Naturally, the slogan will be, "Beauty: It's the thing you *rock!*"

IN-N-OUT

It had been about three weeks since Ralph, the appliance repair guy, professed his true love to me with a refrigerator magnet shaped like a service van. For some reason, three of the four burners on the range started popping and clicking. *Clickety clickety effing clickety.* And then the last click ended like a crochet needle pricking a helium balloon inside a Toyota Corolla idling inside a squash court.

Ralph looks like a total Ralph. And a total appliance repair guy, too. He left his glasses somewhere the first time he came out, so in his Bostonian accent he asked if I could squat down under the stove and read him the serial number with his mini flashlight. The same flashlight he left for collateral, I'm sure, so he could come back and show me his butt crack again when he and his glasses could crouch down to see things himself.

Meanwhile, Driver was out of town and I was still waiting on "the part." Via Ralph. I don't think I had eaten in hours.

There was a small window before meeting my new reflexologist-Reiki master-glass artist-electrologist-cat healer friend, Judy, so I swung through Target in hopes they would have a wok. Something I had never used or owned before because I'm not Chinese. I just knew I didn't want some cheap, ugly one that looked like a hand-me-down or came from a yard sale. I scoured each designated culinary aisle, asked a few associates, and wound up void of triumph. I made some revisions to my basic needs, and still wound up starving. I took a moment to pick up several Father's Day cards, including an imaginary one for Ralph, while I continued to rack my gigantic brain for a substitute cooking apparatus. Something I could plug in, as well as stow away. Something that cooked food in between me turning it on and turning it back off. I only wanted to stir the contents like twice.

I had heard about electric skillets (once) when Linda told me that's how her mother used to make Drunken Liver Chickens—outfitted in heavy eye shadow, skinny jeans, high heels, listening to Jackson Browne. But I had no confidence these widgets were still manufactured so many years later, nor did I picture more than a waffle iron without the little indented squares. And I certainly didn't know what the hell a drunken liver was. Well, that you eat. However, to my astonishment, a small display flagged me down and I bought the skillet with a picture on the box of what I had planned to burn in my wok anyway. It was a long shot, but I took it as a reassuring sign.

The trip to Target has little to do with anything. It was only the unintentional vehicle to an overdue hot lunch. Not cold Boar's Head in a blanket, not a handful of pretzels, not a bouquet of stale Twizzlers. I needed something dramatically above room temperature and nothing replete with radioactive bias.

So, as I was leaving the all-red supercenter, a hypnotic aroma streamed over and above the commonness of skating rink provisions prepared fresh in the Target grill area. I smelled onions and unfamiliar blobs of warm, tender loveliness from somewhere near. There was an unbeknownst and unmistaken pull toward its sovereignty like I was the pointer thing on an old wooden Ouija board. I scampered across the parking lot to follow the likes of that scent, tracking like a floppy-eared bloodhound and sliding into the joint on foot—completely unannounced and empty-handed. That smell, I swear, had the wings of Icarus.

It should be noted that before we moved, Tammy was all, "Blah blah blah, In-N-Out Burger" and I was all, "When have you ever seen me eat a hamburger?" But apparently, a west coast thing and so good, she raved. It hardly matters, but I'm not a vegetarian. I just hadn't had a hankering for an all-beef patty in the last twenty-four years.

I passed outdoor tables and umbrellas on a spacious patio, but there wasn't a single jungle gym, netted ball jail, or precocious child in sight. This since-1948 burger studio begs not for a birthday party or creepy cartoon character, but for non-dieting, discriminating adults to boost their cholesterol levels, as fast as possible. I tucked the aerosol kid repellent back into my purse and continued inside. All associates don croquet whites in a clean environment, while polished faces smile beneath wedged caps the gals have to batten down with bobby pins the size of crossbows. You have four choices: a burger, a cheeseburger, a double burger, or a double cheeseburger. As well as fries. And milkshakes. They also have a merchandise catalog.

My most favorite part is what I assume to be their mascot, the palm tree. My second favorite part is that I bought a medium frozen yogurt the day before and it was ten cents more than my burger, fries, and lemonade. Which proves that interest rates on mortgages may be at an all-time low, but this country can still rake us over the coals for rainbow sprinkles. All hail the mighty ramifications of our ongoing obesity problem in modern America. *Think Thin - Act Fat!*

It's not the typical burger operation where you can milk your own ketchup and mustard at a desk next to the trash can. In fact, you only get those condiments if you request them prior to preparation. Their burgers are smothered in a more calorific and drippy Thousand Island-colored "spread," but those thunder thighs are worth every bite. Their spread is substantially lower in sodium than the usual toppers and there are no trans fats, anywhere on the In-N-Out menu—something fast foodies always take into great consideration.

In-N-Out's burgers are stamped out with beef that's never once been frozen and the buns are made without preservatives from *real* sponge dough. Which is a relief, because I've had artificial sponge dough and it gave me TMJ for three days. I'm also thankful they "hand-leaf" their lettuce. Feet-leafing is still pretty gross if you ask me, even by today's standards. No one ever needs to explain to their primary care physician (or dentist) how they got athlete's foot in their mouth.

Shall Ralph's affection or my wok-substitute ever wane, you and Jenny Craig will know where to find me: laid out under a palm tree, face down in a sponge dough bath of top-secret spread, with a milkshake in my left and a side of fried Kennebec potatoes in my right.

At any one of six greater Las Vegas locations.

POSTCARDS FROM THE CANNERY

Dearest Maureen—

Remember when we took that Caribbean cruise twenty-some years ago and we thought we were so cool because your parents let us do whatever we wanted so they could drink Red Stripe beer? And one night we sneaked into the comedy club and I screamed out the punch line, "Holy Shit!" I don't remember the joke, but it was pretty predictable. We had those horrible high bangs, bad spiral perms, side ponies, and all of our outfits were by Ultra Pink from Burdines. Remember?

On the ship we met that tall, hyper Angie girl and those two older boys. I know we called one of them Ducky because he walked like one. Didn't you kiss him? If you did, that would have made you a cheater on Martin, your boyfriend at the time. You were such a hussy back then! I'm still surprised the word we invented didn't catch on: B-GONG. Perhaps it was more like a sound, so no one understood how to use it. But we sure did. I think at the time I was hanging with Steven, who had a retainer. What a weirdo.

Do you remember the number one song on the Billboard charts that year? Sure you do, you must. It was the only song I didn't make us do a routine for in an effort to get us on Star Search. It was way too slow, especially for the ribbons. And no, it was not "Spring Love" by Stevie B, our first concert at Robarts Arena when I wore those olive green MC Hammer pants, a black leather bolo tie, and a purple rayon vest with flowers. Matching scrunchee, of course. I don't remember what you had on but I'm sure it was just as stupid, only ten times worse.

So, you'll never believe what we did last night…

We went to the Cannery, this time for a live musical performance at The Club. It's a neat venue because it opens up into an outdoor amphitheatre and spills into the courtyard in front of a section of the guest rooms. (Those people got to see the show for *free*!) It's not too big, not too small. We'll go when you come. We can just throw your kids in a crate, I have all different sizes. And you don't have to stand like we did at Robarts. Do you have any allergies?

Anyway, I didn't even know the group was still together, nor could I remember any of their other songs. But I did know there were three of them and they harmonized exceptionally well together. They also had a brief role in the movie *Bridesmaids*, which almost made me pee my pants. I'm still really good at holding it, by the way. The best part about it was they gave everyone band buttons upon entry. I didn't put mine on, though, because I was wearing a new gauze-weight blouse and had a funny feeling it would have ripped my top in half and exposed my bra, or a ta-ta. And that might have made others uncomfortable. But who knows, Vegas is pretty loose. I'll send you Driver's button and will let you know when I've got mine on, so you can wear yours. Just like old times.

We had a blast at the show. Well, I did. They even covered a few ABBA songs. Driver wouldn't let me get up to dance because the crowd was rather sedate. But when I went up to the bar, I met Michelle and Debbie. They were from Southern California and are huge Wilson Phillips fans. I asked the girls if they would dance with me and they were ecstatic to oblige, like they had been waiting for me the whole time.

We tried to rush the stage (twice!), but the little security guy wouldn't let us pass. We could have taken him, especially because the girls were wearing their buttons and I had a few credit cards in my back pocket. We even picked up two dudes who looked nothing like WP fans whatsoever—more of a slender Gerard Depardieu and a less-Italian Big Ragu—and approached the front from another angle. The guys, who were there separately and solo, were more into the music than Shelly and Deb. They were like *crying*. The five of us were only inches away from Carnie, Wendy, and Chynna. We were just in time for an encore the audience would not have been able to "Hold On" for one more day without.

In a word, *B-GONG*. Don't let Steven see this!

LORDS AND SOME LADY

Picture it: 1996. *The First Wives Club.* Goldie Hawn's lips.
Now hold that thought.

Without even disclosing my routine inventory of seating requests and conditions, we were escorted by the bartender who was pressing fresh grapefruit juice to what was easily the best table in the house. On the outer banks of the restaurant, pure waterfront dining on Lake Jacqueline in Summerlin.

Lake, lagoon. Tomato, tomahto.

Beneath a faintly windswept wrought iron cabana, neutral canvas draperies coasted in the euphoric breezes. Blissful summer swimsuits were spinning the pond in leg-powered paddle boats and plush, thoughtful landscaping enveloped a patron's palate for perfection. A destination bistro and utopian setting for consumption, reflection, and peace. The nautical theme sprawled into each and every rank of what felt like Thurston Howell's private yacht, docked at the pier of a resort in the Lesser Antilles.

The stately composition of this serene maritime milieu had me hankering for a long-stemmed crystal glass of crisp pinot grigio. Jacqueline's bogus blue water rippled with Canadian geese that snaked about its insides with poised webbed strokes, rejuvenating the spirits of landlocked onlookers in every direction. The restaurant was picturesque and pacifying, and if planted somewhere in the South, patrons would enlist floppy pastel hats, argyle cardigans, and polka-dotted bowties.

If it's not yet obvious, I'm a huge proponent of people transporting their overactive and bored offspring to fine dining establishments. Especially before the server has even taken my drink order. More especially when a mismatched trio has been seated at the very next table and is brought waters with straws right away and I've only been extended a reticent index finger while the person at the end of it whispers, "Someone will be right with you." We watched the youngest member of the trifecta flip erratically through folded up note papers and tap holes in her cell phone with neon pink nail extensions. Remember the lips I was referring to? Twinsies. Only Goldie is a brunette in this story.

We hung on Brownie's every life-altering word and tried to configure the connectivity of this eccentric threesome. Driver guessed daughter-in-law or realtor to the older couple. I predicted middle-aged exchange student here getting plastic surgery and dining with her hosts. The married pair (or very close siblings) seemed to be regulars. I will refer to them as Stan and Sylvia—a very lovely duet, much quieter than Brownie. Sylvia was probably a famous watercolor artist and Stan was likely a retired ophthalmologist or periodontist.

Stan must have thought it was Sunday and could order smoked salmon from the weekend brunch menu, his evident usual. When he was reminded it was Monday, he was also told they would bring his lox out right away. Mind you, it wasn't until *after* their food order was taken and we had learned about Brownie's entire jewelry collection and the gift card she was waiting for in the mail that we were asked if we'd like anything else to drink. Again, by the bartender, who was acting as the understudy for the server we had yet to meet.

By this time, Driver sensed I wasn't too crazy about the whole special treatment situation, as if my Chanel sunglasses weren't ten times bigger than Brownie's Prada knock-offs. But just breaths before a meltdown, all was renewed when a small carafe of white wine was submerged into a leaded glass, then into my fingertips, and safely down the hatch. We then ordered the grilled artichokes.

Brownie couldn't talk about herself while they were eating so we regained a few moments of solace for our sippery. But there was no verifiable reason we should enjoy the afternoon without a table of ten's two preschoolers descending upon our perimeter from their guardians twenty-five feet away. They laced in and out of the fencing that separated us from the lagoon, trying to reach their grubby little hands into the water as if they were feeding their skin to the bluegills. They did this for seven minutes until they chased one another around and around and around our chairs. They banged into our seatbacks and scattered like splinters of Gremlin-shaped broken glass. We noticed their parents didn't notice they were missing. I could have put them in my purse right there and then and traded them at a swap meet for Hello Kitty backpacks.

Once our appetizer arrived, they had scampered off. And with much relief, we ogled over the celestial artichokes and decided on entrees, wondering if we'd ever meet the elusive server we had only seen darting around the starboard side. Two bites in and enter the children. *Again.* Only this time, they were waving squirt guns like butterfly nets. All expression in my face sunk to the patio floor like an anchor the size of the Titanic. *Are you fucking kidding me?*

Immediately, I couldn't remember if I said that aloud or not. Driver began to giggle when the server hurried over to apologize for his absence and asked if we were ready to order. I scraped my gusto off the ground with a backhoe and requested the blackened mahi and another glass of pinot. Driver requisitioned a flatbread thing and a draught beer.

Ten excruciating minutes with the water gun guild and the party of ten abruptly sucked their ‘ ids up and evacuated. But that wasn't enough cacophony, for anyone. Another mother set her two somewhat-older boys free, a duo that also found our area the most desirable. And clearly, the reason they have a picture of this table on their website. At least these kids had *manners.*

"We need to be quiet. Okay? *THESE PEOPLE ARE EATING!!*" The chubbier one yelled at the top of his lungs as they raced by, working their way through both ours and Brownie's tables.

Back and forth, in and out, up and down, side to side. They were on the rocks behind us, the railing in front of us, and the turf below us. I was in the same place, only beside myself.

"We're coming throoooooough! *EXCUUUUUUUSE US!*" Chubbier, clearly the spokesman.

Our server set the entrees before us and asked if we needed anything else. I had no response; Driver had to thank him. We couldn't find anything at all disappointing about our meals. In fact, it's still one of the best we've had in Vegas and have returned more times than I can count.

Now I just take my Bazooka Super Soaker and make a reservation under the name Stan.

HOLD MY PURSE

I don't know why the grandstands are declared "cigarette-free" when the people sitting in them are already secondhand smoking the fumes of forty aluminum death mobiles revolving for hundreds of laps at an average speed of 188 miles per hour around a D-shaped oval. But it's a rule.

I can promise, some bubba with a bunch of sponsor patches on his starchy polyester jacket drawing long on a Doral 100 through his yellow mustache wouldn't offend me in the least. I'd probably want him to hotbox it directly inside my schnoz to curb the complimentary jet fuel emissions that would have sent me ablaze if someone walked by with a can of Aqua Net. The immediate toxic inhalation occupied me for only nine warm-up laps before I realized Driver couldn't hear me ask (several times) how long we had to stay. Finally, just short of me moaning, I was led back up the low incline stadium steps to one of the paraphernalia areas. The long permanent souvenir station boasted a generous palette of stiff garb for NASCAR fanatics requiring even more panache to further bedazzle their limbs, heads, or pre-existing accessories.

"Do you have earplugs?" I asked the lady at the counter. Privately, I hoped they wouldn't. I wanted to just wallow in my wretched vociferous misery for however long it takes to vehiculate four hundred 1.5-mile Ds in boxy, vibrating road crafts that roll so close to the ground, they may as well be vacuum cleaners from a bad dream. But apparently, my query was not a dumb (or novel) question. "You want the headset, this pair, or we got these?" She questioned, loosely robotic, all but calling me "sweetie" while reaching into a tall cardboard box. She yanked out a set of foamy orange Flintstone vitamin-sized capsules tethered to either end of a blue plastic cord and held it up like a white rabbit from inside a top hat. It looked like a strand of fuzzy rear-view mirror dice, a concept that would have probably fit my ears better.

I wasn't there to make any impulsive or everlasting investments, so we dropped six dollars for two pairs of the cheap leashed silencing corks. I couldn't even get the sponge to stay in my left ear. It just kept falling out, unmistakably the reason they had to put them on a string. That meant the painful sounds were somewhat muffled in my right ear, but spotty in my left. Great, asymmetrical tinnitus. Driver's plugs seemed to work just fine, unable to hear anything I was complaining about.

For big events at the Las Vegas Motor Speedway, an entire fiesta of food and trademarked tents is arranged around the perimeter to feed those gathered for the day and camped out for the entire race weekend. It's a nice facility, one with an infield that can accommodate the overcrowded populace of Winnebagos and their people, places, and things creatively stacked straight up to the sky. It's an elongated hallucination that melts deep and away into the punctuating mountainous horizon. Multiple layers of seating and spaces were designed for upwards of 250,000 ticketholders— roughly 245,000 more people than I was expecting to rub Wranglers with at a Saturday event that began abruptly with a big case of *what the hell am I supposed to wear?*

Mesh caps and American flag clothes peppered the perspective as the aroma of corn dogs, sunscreen, and gasoline boosted the level of ambiance well beyond any traveling circus or county fair I'd ever witnessed. The Dale Earnhardt Tower overlooks more than three thousand feet of the front stretch and was where I should have been positioned instead of at the very end of the bleachers. We were just past the third turn, twenty feet from the sizzling black track and close enough for my epidermis to thump from the uninterrupted blurring-whirring-trumpeting-trombone-elephant-screaming-airhorny-clatter projecting through a megaphone. It was a sound that shot all the way from my torso to the pending aneurism in my hair, forcing me to self-diagnose with phonophobia. No doubt the irreversible kind. A scenario so complete, the only upgrade would have been watching the drive-a-thon from a hot metal toolbox in the back of a pickup truck, sucking down a strawberry Yoo-Hoo and sharing an expired bag of pork rinds with a stranger named Deek.

Driver was engaged and elated, tuning into stats on the phone, leafing through the thick program, and swinging big cans of cold beer around like it was a ship's christening. I sulked, sunburned, read Facebook updates for the three days prior, and texted people—none of whom believed my whereabouts or were envious if they did.

I know NASCAR is a big deal to those thousands of Winnebago people; it's just not something I can emotionally embrace. I also take the parents of these thrill-seeking car jockeys into consideration. "My child has to wear a flame-retardant jumpsuit every day he or she goes to work." It's not even a *controlled* crash; it's an undeniable, ever-present provocation for a real one. Competitors repeat the same circle-ish pattern at speeds most cars can't even travel, dodging a litter of other huge gas tanks built inside rolling cages with sheet metal wrappers. An activity that contracts a contestant to put on a helmet the price of Rhode Island and is equipped with everything from an air tube to a neck brace. I don't even know how you get insurance for that job.

Driver believes I should be interested in the pit crews and their strategies. To date, I've only been able to falsify caring about what each flag means. At least now that Black Flag commercial for the in-home pest control makes a whole lot more sense. Driver also needs to watch every televised race. *Indoors!* This is a delightful habit given it's the longest sports season known to man, with over 1,500 races at more than one hundred tracks in thirty-nine United States, running February through November. That is 83 percent of the year. Eighty-three, out of only one hundred. I would rather share a thermometer with a hobo than hear these races in the comforts of my own abode. And after that, I'd spend one full business day sewing my toes together with yarn.

To balance out my opinions, I did some research. I learned stock car racing has ancestry in bootlegging during Prohibition, even after its repeal in 1933. These forbidden booze dispatchers would shrewdly engineer their compact, fast jalopies so they could elude authorities and twirl down coiled mountain roads—a budding set of challenge courses that began for profit in Wilkes County, North Carolina during the late 1940s, around the same time NASCAR was officially founded by Bill France, Sr. A tidbit that proves if you look hard enough, you're bound to spot something of tolerable awareness, in any situation. This information definitely helps me feign a little more interest as I'm certainly appreciative of a special agent helping his fellow man hoist a pint, during any era.

Though I don't ever plan on throwing my bare arms around NASCAR with a "you complete me" exhale, I do think Danica Patrick is on to something when it comes to fashionable prizes.

Because purses, boys, are for *girls*!

OYSTER BARF

I gain little pleasure shedding limelight on dining experiences I opine to be less than remarkable. But with that dull disclaimer, there will be the occasional incident that produces a gaping emptiness in my enthusiasm, sidelining my rightful enjoyment of the reasons we seek meals outside the home. And understand, the word *reason* can turn plural on the rock of a high heel and the slump of a linen napkin.

We were starving, nothing new. And somehow, we were hypnotized by the carousel horse-sized plastic catfish tethered to the ceiling joists over the hostess stand. I wasn't fooled that it was real. Or once alive, ever. But it's custom that oyster bars (and some Mexican restaurants in Atlanta) are known for their aquatic taxidermy squatting on the walls, but usually such stylish trimmings consist of tarpon and sailfish, species that emit a plethora of polychromatic distinctions and fluttery fin flair. Said establishments don't typically boast of white tablecloths and a wine list, either. Usually just a paper bib and two color choices of jug wine. So it beats me why any proprietor would pay good money to build or steal a *false* whiskered fish best caught with corn meal dough balls steeped in tuna juice, stained with red dye and barbed with bacon, only swallowable if fried.

Besides, we thought it was an Italian restaurant. *Errore numero due.*

Still, diners seemed congenial, nothing smelled weird, and they were serving close to 11 p.m., precisely when we snorted up. I won't say the name of the restaurant, but it rhymes with something.

Led to a two-top, our accommodations were larger than a thimble, but smaller than a pin cushion. We were tattooed against some kind of screen or divider wall and I was quickly too claustrophobic to complain. The underzealous and detached server came to see us one calendar day later and asked if we'd like anything. Not anything to drink or anything to eat, just "anything." Like most guests, I'm sure he assumed we, too, just wanted chairs to admire the Goodyear catfish piñata. But we pleaded for the mussels and some wine, if it wasn't too much trouble.

I could feel the well-dressed bachelor party of ten men behind me request separate checks, and the last of my original baby blonde neck hairs curled up, started throbbing, and died in the back of my shirt. The gooey lovebirds to my left were in full receipt of enviable attention from their server as our guy dropped a bowl of black shells to the table from shoulder-height. Again, he didn't ask if we would like anything else, just continued on as if to install a louver door on a needy closet.

To be diplomatic, I should have ordered a new gag reflex. The mussels were huge, bouncy like basketballs, and the estimated shade of a poorly-managed spray tan—characteristics that lack promise and make me fret over hormones and hydroponics, red tide and paralytic shellfish poisoning. (Don't ask what the hypochondriac in me thinks.) I like my mussels to be about the size of a fingertip, not a Matchbox car, with a deep terra cotta hue, baptizing in a broth that's either painstakingly simple or highly unusual. I'd also prefer to eat them on the Côte d'Azur avec frites and the house white, watching sidewalk artists peddle their portraits and gain serenade from men in berets with Jean-something names. But, at times, I know this can be an inconvenient order. They look at you real real funny when you ask for that at Long John Silvers.

Wow, the view from this soapbox is amazing!

Signore Server of Permanent Zest indeed returned, so we rushed to place our dinner order. He was noticeably startled by our demands and put our check back inside his long black apron. I asked for the linguine with clams (please hold the retaliatory spit or soap), Driver clinched the chicken parmesan. And we yelled for another glass of wine as he trailed off, back to the taciturn installation of his slatted door.

I'd say it's pretty hard to screw up parmesan chicken. Even *I* can cook that, blindfolded and drunk. That's why Driver's came out piping hot, palatable, and satisfactory. Nothing seemed alarming about it. On the contrary, my linguine was a few questionable degrees below room temperature and, like the mussels, met the table with an illustrious thud. It was negligent of taste, annulled of affection. Just snoozy noodles and the gritty aftermath of what had to be canned clams strutting around like digestible rations. A pile of tomfoolery brought to my personal space by a waiter who wanted to be alone. So I showed him, I didn't eat it. But of course, I took it home anyway and ate it for breakfast. Because I was, once again, famished.

Oddly enough, we were in and out in under an hour. This never happens. We never spend less time in a restaurant than it takes to relocate a dairy farm. We weren't even upsold on a dessert, which also never happens. We are the ultimate poster people for: "NEW TO VEGAS. Not goin' to Weight Watchers until they call *us*." But this Romeo was on a tear to empty our table faster than a lucky blue hair can shout "bingo" from the interior of her dentures.

The true testimonial of our dining experience happened a few days later …

Driver: "What doing?"

Me: "Writing about Oyster Barf."

Driver: "Oh, from when the girls were here?"

Me: "No, I'm behind. This was when we had the mussels and that non-server server."

Driver: "Yeah, the other night."

Me: "No, service was fine there. This was when you had the chicken parmesan and I had the cold linguine."

Driver: [just looking at me, head shaking]

Me: "Bad service. We were starving. Small table."

Driver: "What did I have again?"

Me: "Chicken parmesan."

Driver: "Did I like it?"

Me: "You ate it."

Driver: [crickets]

Me: "Remember, mine was cold? We never saw our guy. I didn't even want to tip. Anything?"

Driver: [crickets and their babies]

Me: "The catfish. The big-ass *catfish*."

Driver: "Ohhh, that place. With the catfish."

Driver, again: "Chicken parmesan. Are you *sure?*"

WHAT A DRAG

Ernie opened with what most adults would consider a normal conversation.

He ordered a double shot of Crown Royal from the bartender I affectionately referred to as "Jammies" (long for PJ), and sat down beside me. *Right* beside me. At a wide open bar, *in* a wide open bar. Where there were at least 416 other compartments for him to roost.

We arrived pretty early because we went to dinner at Firefly pretty early. We got to the club about two hours before the show and there were only three cars in the parking lot. I was one seat away from Driver when Ernie washed up. We were beating on the video poker machines as the other six people coating the three-sided bar were busy without our input. When gambling, your drinks feel like they are free. But they're usually the price of a suggested max bet.

The first machine I sat down to play wouldn't accept the twenty Driver handed me, so I slid over. This gave me a little more space to chat up Jammies while Driver zombied with a grave face at the football game on television.

Ernie was partially involved with the game because he bet on it. Once the game was over, he muttered something about fifty bucks. I didn't care. That's when he formally introduced himself and told me Las Vegas was "no longer Las Vegas." That he was a poker and a blackjack dealer for twenty-three years. At another point, it was twenty-seven. I didn't care. Then he told me he used to fly helicopters twice a day to the Grand Canyon, for tours. I don't know if he did both at the same time or lied about his age. I still didn't care. Then he told me Vegas could be anywhere I wanted it to be, but it was "not Las Vegas anymore." It was not the Las Vegas he came here for thirty years ago, from another country, "a communist one." And that I had missed it. *I had missed it all.* I had missed the real Las Vegas. Because *this* sure wasn't it.

He said he left town because he was burned out. I definitely didn't care. And now everything in Vegas is "corporate." Then he mentioned Las Vegas was "not Las Vegas anymore." *Again.* As if repackaging his statement would make me more interested. I still didn't care. He told me that by 8:30 p.m., "a place like this" would already be packed, everyone's drinks would be free, and no one would be on their phones. (Like he was, when I would turn my back to dialogue with Driver. About him.) And "everyone stayed up all night long." He pointed to each and every person bellied up to the bar, described their states of mind, personality, and overall demeanor, just before predicting their levels of boredom and degrees of misery. He'd be the first to tell you he was "good at reading people because [he] was a dealer for twenty-three years." Maybe twenty-seven. I didn't care. If he was reading me, then he's dyslexic.

He slithered up closer than an ingrown hair and told me I was playing blackjack too fast. And wrong. That I should bet more, let it ride, bet less, watch the dealer's hand, think like the machine, play "the Vegas way." And not only is Vegas no longer Vegas, "the Sopranos are gone." *Sopranos, WTF?* I thought they lived in Jersey. Driver couldn't hear anything Ernie was pontificating about but could overhear spotty snippets of my responses, reactions, and the reverberation of my eyeballs getting clotheslined by the back of my head. So, I did what I often do when it's time to change the subject with an exasperating stranger. I leaned in and grabbed his eyes with mine. "Are you gay?"

"What? Why do you ask?" My subject quivers.

"Just wondering. We're in a gay bar. And there's probably no one in here because the drag show doesn't start for another hour and a half."

"This bar has been around for twenty years. And I'm meeting a friend. *She's* gay. But there should be more people in here. The economy has hurt everything. Corporations have hurt everything. This is no longer Vegas. Go ahead, name somewhere you want this to be, but don't say Vegas. Because it's not. It's not Vegas."

"Why are you here?" I didn't even pretend to care.

"At this bar?" He answered, with a question.

"No. In non-Vegas Vegas," I sarcasted.

"I come back to visit," he swigged.

"But you don't like it. Why do you bother coming all the way across the country if you don't like it here anymore?"

"I come to visit friends and I'm a helicopter pilot so I get free airline tickets. Anywhere I want to go, even international." His plumage slowly regained its earlier posture.

"So where are your friends? And if you can fly *anywhere*, for *free*, why come here?" I asked, studying the hangnail on my pinky that took precedence.

"Because it's Vegas," he suggested with confidence.

"But it's *not* Vegas anymore," I remarked, and turned around to Driver.

Jammies presented another Cosmo and I pretended to keep playing blackjack. It started happening again.

"Why are you guys sitting so far apart? Are you in a fight?"

"We're sitting apart because that machine is broken," pointing to the defunct video screen between Driver and me.

"Are you sure? I know these things," he reminded.

"Yes, Ernie, I'm sure. I was sitting right there just before you came in," I issued with my newfound chronic aggravation.

"Well, why didn't you just say that? You could have told me that," he pleaded.

"What are you talking about? I don't need to tell you anything. Do you always talk to people like this?" I turned to tell Driver he thought we were having an argument, but his face kept making atrocious sounds.

"You play too fast. You want me to show you the right way? How to play?"

"No. No Ernie, I *don't* want you to show me how to play—your way *or* the Vegas way. I don't care about blackjack. I care more about the natural habitat of paper clips than I do blackjack. I didn't care about this game before you got here, I'm not gonna care when I leave. I'm killing time before the show. And *this* Vegas [physically pointing down to my location on the floor] is all I know. And it's the only Vegas available. So if you don't like it, zip it."

"Why are you getting so upset? You need to calm down. Don't be upset. We don't have to talk about blackjack," he flapped, like I got all crazy ex-girlfriend on him.

"First of all, you haven't seen 'getting upset.' What *does* upset me is that you began this lopsided, unsolicited conversation and I just so happen to like it here. And *a lot* has changed since the eighties. Like hairdos, for instance. And we all have cell phones now. Even entertainment has changed. Cities have changed. People have changed. And not everyone can stay up all night long anymore because cocaine has changed."

"See, you're not having a good time. It's not the way Vegas used to be," he interrupted.

"You're right. I'm *not* having a good time. Discussing what Vegas *used* to be like with some stranger is not fun. You sound like a bitter divorcée. I don't care, Ernie. [now speaking with my hands] Can you do me *one* favor? Just one."

"What?" He whimpered, as I squeezed his man balls into minced Raisinets in my mind.

"Stop talking. Especially if you're going to sit there. [it had started to fill up] And *please* don't talk to anyone else in here about Vegas or blackjack. You're a super shitty downpour when you do. It's pathetic."

"Okay. I'm sorry. I'm very sorry. You go back to playing. And good luck. I wish you all the best of luck. Here…" He held his fourth double shot of Crown up to the ice water in my hand and clinked it into my lap and down my leg, reaching at my crotch with a napkin.

"I can wipe it off, Ernie. Just leave me alone," I turned around. And then kinda giggled.

Ernie moved a few stools down, still in earshot so I could eavesdrop on his next idiotic conversation with a new girl. One that hinged on an entirely different chorus. I didn't care. It was finally time to find somewhere near the stage to *stand*, my favorite. We had two perfectly good hours to get the best seats, but needed to suffer through both acts of the unimportance of being Ernie, rushing to lose more money on a game I liked playing wrong.

I've been asked what gay bars are like in Vegas, as if I'm an expert. As if I actually go to bars or clubs of any nature. I'm usually way too full for that. But what I can tell you—compared to Atlanta, New York, West

Hollywood, and San Fran—there really aren't too many establishments designed exclusively for pure gay whoopee and glee. Besides, this is Vegas. *Las* Vegas. We have flamingos, magicians, and people who dress like Diana Ross as a legitimate day job. *Gay* doesn't lasso a prosaic flamboyant wow factor around here. Everyone is everywhere.

And in a town bulging with well-paid impersonators and acclaimed entertainers of all kinds, we were curious how the best queens would captivate the attention of their cultured audiences. It was critical to my research, Ernie or not. And I haven't seen a million drag shows, but it's close. Most of the time, you have a good idea what to expect. Cher, Tina, Liza, Bette, Madonna, Gaga, Beyoncé, Gloria Gaynor, even The Weather Girls and Priscilla Queen of the Desert. Sequins, more sequins, and big, crinkly wigs. Bigger everythings, always.

But this time, our Marilyn was Manson and the lively Ms. Hannigan was no more or less compassionate about little girls and dark liquor than she was thirty years ago. We weren't expecting the Little Mermaid, either, who furthered the momentum with leading creativity, props, and theatrics. Dare we forget entertainment is competitive around here. These guys weren't just masquerading around a fat, frumpy turnstile for Tootsies; they were working. And we weren't just watching men watch men dressed as women mouthing along to a greatest gay hits album, scanning the crowd for the next hand holding a creased bill.

We watched Dolly Parton do her medley and Dolly watched his-her own fake boobs flop around like tetherballs. We also watched Ernie watch Dolly's tetherballs, home to a cleavage vast enough for Ernie to add a thick wad of small bills. Which, of course, was just before he slapped him-her on the rump. His friend, *she* was gay alright. And it was midnight, roughly the time Ernie no longer had a problem with Vegas.

My Vegas.

COME ALL YEE FAITHFUL HAWS

Years ago, Driver surprised me with a spa weekend getaway for my birthday. One that would have been noticeably incomplete without a suddenly surprising accumulation of horse poop and latigo.

No one would have ever believed that at the same time we were retreating at Pura Vida Spa in Dahlonega, a rodeo would be unpacking their patriotic plaid and festal fringe just a few miles over past the yonder. The only thing I was fairly certain of when pulling up to the vested guy at an orange cone was that we would be parking in a pile of dirt and it was going to take more than a paper program to find the tent pouring Clicquot. But good thing for me, I toted my fifteen-year-old shitkickers to the secluded wellness resort despite the sticky layer of summertide for that just-in-case situation. You should have seen me, I blended right in.

But that's all just background data for the cow parts to follow.

The first time I saw those extraordinary words, or name, we were waiting in a long line for lunch at the Bonnie Springs Ranch restaurant. I believe they even call it the Bonnie Springs Ranch Restaurant. The al fresco property is a charismatic and chummy stuck-in-time western town that was once a mining settlement and stopping point for travelers and clanky wagon trains. It's an attraction that was unveiled for commercial use in 1952 to heighten tourism after the Hoover Dam was completed, when the city feared there would be nothing else to do around here. Also enjoyed by locals, Bonnie Springs beams with bucolic shacks and shanties, musical revues, a hands-on zoo, and assorted shoot-outsy performances. It reminds me of Old Tucson Studios—only smaller, not as Hollywood, and rumored to be a little haunted.

We stood in the restaurant with half of our bodies in the long rustic lodgey bar and the other half in the large lodgey dining room. It's totally lodgey, just the way I like it. I readjusted myself at a precocious rate so my hair and camera bag weren't completely blocking the narrow path where patrons needed to get to the hostess stand. To do that, I scrunched my face against the paneled wall and it was there I noticed a sign bearing the angelic amalgamation, "Helldorado Days." I refused to read any further, frantic I hadn't invented the term myself. And by the time we were seated, there was only a flicker of wonder if it/they was/were truly such a thing. Or succession of things. I knew it could only be one of three very erudite and pedantic guesses anyway: a tribute concert-slash-reward vacation for Cadillac's top used El Dorado sales people, a one-off cover band for Spanish explorers cuckoo for Coronado, or Eagles-themed speed dating sessions that backhandedly mock "Desperado." It was definitely something related to music, like Woodstock or Lollapalooza. Or Burning Man, something that can't even be explained by people who attend Burning Man. So more than likely, it was a musical.

Then a few weeks later, I heard "it" was coming to town. And *it* had nothing to do with any of my tentative guesses after all. Instead, it's the annual Wrangler symposium that was introduced by Clyde Zerby in 1934—the perfect time, occasion, and opportunity for the positioning and promotion when thrill-seekers were flocking to examine construction of the highly-anticipated dam between Arizona and Nevada. The event was suspended for several years in the 1990s when attendance was lagging and megaresorts were enough espousal for Vegas, but it was revived in 2005 for the centennial celebration as a genuine reminder of the city's wild western roots. Nowadays, Helldorado hosts a professional rodeo, parade, and a carnival with all the fixings, feed, and fodder that renders the onlooker grinning and mesmerized. And we sure as hell weren't going to miss it.

Below is an extract from the letter I wrote to our most fanciful cowboy County Commissioner…

I couldn't let another day pass without extending my pure delight in the chance to unofficially meet you this past Sunday night at the rodeo. We did not shake hands, nor did we exchange hellos or distant waves. In a last-minute decision, the other half and I wanted to see what Helldorado was all about. Whatever *it* was. We eased into the festivities by first having our tarot cards read, browsing games and rides in the Midway, and then finally clunked up the stairs as a bevy of auctioneer-speed, horse-related announcements were made from the playful master of ceremonies. We sat down on the front row of the first set of bleachers closest to the gates where the participants were corralled, my eyes were as wide as tractor tires.

I can't say I've tackled too many rodeos in my day. And I don't think Tournament of Kings at Excalibur really counts. But I took Sunday seriously. We settled down just in time for the steer wrestling portion of the evening's production. I certainly didn't know it would entail full-sized men leaping into mid-air from the comforts of a trusty steed, launching their person onto darting cattle, trying to fold one another into the ground for the best time.

But what I found impressive was that the guy whose picture I've seen on outdoor billboards, the guy with a classic cocktail name—he was there, too. In fact, a sponsor of the entire steer wrestling group's entry fee, as well as a contestant himself. A public official not afraid to get bounced around, one with a memorable smile who can laugh with the crowd, one who knows what he loves and wants to share it with the community. And in that very instant, my re-election vote was sealed.

Mr. Tom Collins indeed wrote me a personal note back, on his own stationery and everything. I didn't even care that he spelled my name wrong, everyone does. The only thing I forgot to tell him was how much I love gauchos and roughriders. I love the spurs, the unfaded jeans, the shiny belt buckles, the pretty painted ponies, and the women they bring with 'em. Even their obnoxious red hats and super short shorts.

Stefany Holmes

I never said it was my *first* rodeo.

ON THE FLIGHT SIDE

The history of September 13 for Las Vegas boasts of nominal delight in the way of kitten kisses and caramel sunshine. Instead, it's a rather depressing legacy thus far. To date, the only two things that have been significant enough to be published in the monthly almanac have been the unfortunate strep throat death of attorney Harley Harmon's 29-year-old wife, Leona, in 1921, and the poignant demise of rapper Tupac Shakur, who was shot near the Strip in 1996.

I know, kinda shuts down a conversation. *Click.*

That's why I decided to create an interlude with colored pencils so the world could deflect these untoward circumstances, simultaneously boosting the dreary documentation of this superstitiously numbered day. And my drawings, of course, are always an inspiration.

Truth is, there's a lot Vegas has to be joyful about, year round. There's fresh air, little traffic, loads to do, breathtaking vistas, remarkable mountainous contrasts, minimal (if any) precipitation, and fewer entitlement issues than I found when I lived somewhere with a higher pollen count, heavy auto pollution, and frequent asphyxiations from humidity. Not that I feel compelled to compare or anything.

Right now, I'm talking aviation—Wright Brothers, Amelia Earhart kind of stuff.

There's no question, Las Vegas' McCarran International Airport is a funfest. It's recognized as such by any surveyed traveler who's ever been through. It's mesmerizing, surprising, and frictionless. A fact most appreciated if you know anything about Atlanta's Hartsfield-Jackson International plaza of purgatory. Hartsfield's some-5.8 million square feet of overcrowded terminal and concourse sits on close to five thousand acres—which includes, but is not limited to—five runways and a cargo ramp. It's the busiest airport in the world and produces roughly fifty-seven tons of trash every year. Which is not a carbon footprint, but a carbon body double for a dozen dinosaurs.

The only problem McCarran has is its name. No one knows who or where McCarran is, especially if they've drifted over from Topeka or Tokyo. While influential Democratic Senator Pat McCarran penned the Civil Aeronautics Act of 1938, it's been argued that not everyone is aware of this trivia. Past authorities believed the name would just usher (now 40 million annual) tourists effortlessly into the arms of southern Nevada's most sparkling port without question or concern. Which is quite the opposite from Hartsfield-Jackson, a facility that has numerous names, but most don't even know what they are. The abridged and banal version is simply "Atlanta."

Atlanta handles about eight thousand passengers each hour and I can say from experience, it's no picnic. I've unexpectedly run into friends and family at that very airdrome because someone you know will always be there, if not, *everyone* you know—even if you don't know it. Inside, it's a loud, confusing, spread-out sector of competing scents and smells from food, folks, and feet. All are assembled together in a huge, airtight capsule buried in Coca-Cola spills and radioactive gadgets. Though you can get to any destination from there—usually directly—the full-blown process of making a departure from Atlanta exists to intentionally shave off several days of your sanity, as well as your projected lifespan. It can be a poopfest.

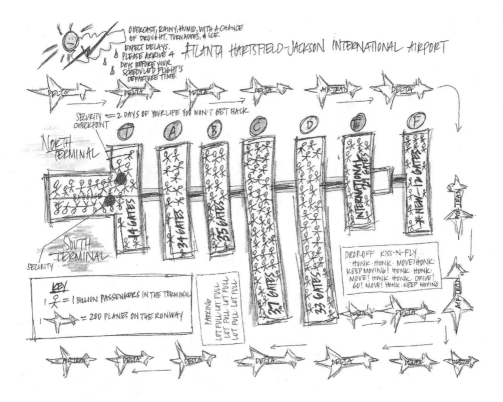

I've even caught the shoe-shiners looking miserable, who, in most of my fantasies, should be caroling barbershop quartet types. The happiest population consists of the Delta folks peddling Amex cards. And if the black-ceilinged smoking lounges aren't enough to make a lifer beg for a Chantix prescription, not much will. Each passenger can enjoy all of the aforementioned features to the fullest before having the chance to relax on the tarmac for an hour or so waiting to take off. Sometimes you'll even have air in the cabin.

There, I've also been harassed for MARTA money at baggage claim from someone who presented no detectable signs of ever being on a plane, but could have ended up at the airport after passing out on the train. And a man once followed me up the escalator kissing my forearm the entire time because I gave him directions to the next terminal. He had brown teeth and smelled like a podiatrist's office, but his chivalrous "Thank you" was a standout.

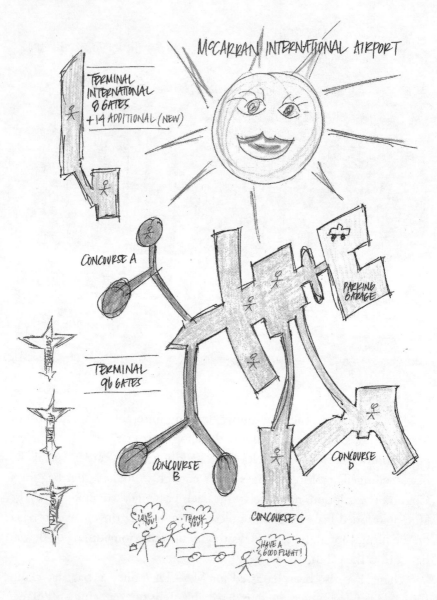

McCarran (above), on the other hand, is like a Tootsie Pop. It's layered with sweet sugary wellness, a soft center, and a happy ending. As of this printing, it's just under half of Atlanta's physical size and still manages with four runways and two terminal buildings. It ranks an admirable 19th in the world for passenger traffic and has approximately the same number of slot machines as Hartsfield has toilets: 1,200. And every takeoff and landing offers unmatched views of the Strip, not a smoggy glance at College Park and the asphalt roof of a Ramada Inn.

But rest assured, they both offer plenty of licks.

HERE COMES TROUBLE

Nancy Birnbaum and I have a lot in common.

I think she's been tailing me for decades, I just didn't know it. Get this: I'm from Sarasota, she's lived there. She was born in New York, I love it there. She was raised in New Jersey, I've been to the Newark airport five times. I lived in Atlanta, she's lived there. I moved to Vegas, she moved to Vegas. *I know!* People probably think I taught her how to count cards. Which would explain why she's so good at poker. (I'm a *really* good counter.)

Nancy and I have shared more residential area codes than I have with anyone else I know. And out of all those serendipitous ports of potential introduction, we didn't meet until Las Vegas. It took a mutual friend from Atlanta, Lori, to introduce us via text. Of course, I got in touch with Nancy right away. For one, I'm not exactly shy. And for two, I needed to meet a professional poker player. I planned to have her teach me everything I should know about poker the moment I would actually become interested in learning. Though I'd need to be ready, poker takes smarts. And patience. Those qualities are usually selective for me.

Nancy wins all the time. She's what they call a "circuit grinder," someone who plays for hours and hours and hours. Something about the word *grinder* evokes all sorts of images, none of which I would pin on poker. Being the 2012-2013 top female with the most cashes and earnings, I assume absolute world domination comes with the job. She's the only woman in WSOP with three circuit rings and a pendant, which is like a medallion (I asked). This also means we're both fond of jewelry.

Obviously, I inquired if she likes to wear all of her prizes while playing and she revealed that "it depends." Typically, she doesn't want her opponents to know how good she is by blinding them with her in-yo-face-rub-it-in championship bling. Wise woman, no wonder she wins so much. She did let me try on one of her rings and its dimensions eclipsed my Yurman in no time flat. The brass knuckle combination made me look like an up-and-coming rapper, I was pleased. This particular finger trinket is easily the size of a gold, bejeweled two-slot toaster and, in a pinch, would leave a dent just as big on someone's cheek or hollow-core hallway door.

Nancy is the owner of the US Women's Poker Academy and their website reveals she "honed her skill of reading people and developed a solid winning strategy." For the life of me, I couldn't get her to explain, detail, share, or outline this strategy. Instead, she read me like bedtime story all through lunch. She read my face, the expressions linked to my face, my body language, my level of hunger, and my hair, of which she asked if it was a hair piece or Bumpit. I think she even read my mind, something I usually only pay psychics to do. Therefore, she should have known my hair was (and still is) real.

Nancy's known in the industry as "Trouble," and truth be known, I've been called that a time or two myself. *You see, there are more similarities than I know what to do with!*

Double Trouble

She's also the team pro for Blue Shark Optics sunglasses and Go Deep gear clothing line. These are really big deals, my non-grinding friends. Speaking of, I should probably be a team pro for PetSmart and Windex. I tried on a pair of her signature edition shades and looked like the most badass human-sized blonde insect in the restaurant. The frames actually looked pretty good on me, considering they were fairly proportionate to physical size of my enormous head (home of the gigantic brain). Someone like me, born without a poker face altogether, should probably own a pair to don even in situations rather common.

For the record, the only card games I know how to play are UNO and Old Maid. And I'd probably have to get on the Internet to estimate with trends and fads the last time I played either of those. The first thing I learned was that poker is played with only two cards—which had me baffled and confused for the rest of my day. For our interview, I drafted a few questions as I wanted to showcase my journalistic zest in yet another brilliant configuration.

What got you into poker?

I was with BMW for twenty-five years and started playing home games in Atlanta. When I moved to Siesta Key, I began selling real estate and playing blackjack at Tampa's Hard Rock Hotel & Casino in 2006. I got addicted to poker by playing small table buy-ins *(sounds like furniture shopping to me!)* and lost a lot. I'm completely self-taught and learned winning from losing.

Where are your favorite places to play poker in Vegas?

I like the Wynn, Aria, and the Venetian *(these are also some of the nicest)* because of their customer service and the action; there's always a game going.

My favorite card is either the queen of diamonds or the queen of hearts. Do you have a favorite card?

A winning hand. *(I let that slide.)*

I know most players wear sunglasses, but what's up with the headphones? Seems like cheating, or something.

People usually listen to music. For momentum, distraction, adrenaline. *(Music is for dancing, not cards!)*

With all of my talking, we ran out of time. The following are a few of the questions I didn't get a chance to ask, so I answered them myself, as myself.

Do you (usually) know when to hold 'em?

Yes, and I'm usually holding a bunch of 'em. Or, my bra does it for me.

Fold 'em?

Nope. That's why I could never work at GAP.

Walk away?

I power walk, everywhere. I'm fast, too, even with the leg weights.

Know when to run?

I try very hard to never, ever run. I had to do it a few years ago and almost lost my legs to the ground. It's definitely not like riding a bike.

Is there really enough time for countin' when the dealin's done?

For those of us who have excellent time management, yes. For those who don't, you better drive it like you stole it and have a really good tax accountant.

Does No Limit Hold 'Em have any boundaries?

I don't understand the question, but I think this has to do with relationships. And snuggling. Or suffocation. Save it for Dr. Phil.

Do you read Hustler? I think that's about poker.

Everyone knows I don't like to read. Does it have any pictures?

DISTINCTLY VEGAS: A LEARNING CURVE

QUEEN OF TARTS

One hundred and eighty-two cards. And hardly a duplicate—I counted.

The closing sum actually began several hours *after* I turned numerous assertive and highly-experienced sales representatives away. Finally, I just gave in to see how many I could collect in one unforgiving, unapologetic stint on the Strip. It's an enthralling exhibition, really. Both of my back pockets were full, all side slots in my purse were crowded, and my bare hands were no longer functional trying to keep the inventory filed neatly between all ten digits. I would reach frenetically for other storage units anywhere on my person when I had time, avoiding paper cuts and the undertow of skinny jeans and striped knee socks stopping short to slurp on their yard-sized souvenir drink.

It's no secret that I'm a big recycling and repurposing advocate, but many times, I'm just regifting. It's definitely not cheap to print the marketing materials in which I'm referring, most of which finish their fate speckled about Las Vegas Boulevard and its surrounding perpendiculars. And then some employed someone is tasked with shoveling up the disregarded rectangular confetti from sidewalks and side streets before sunrise, day after day after day. That's why I stick a few in every outbound care package just to cross-pollinate the country. Rumor also suggests they may be nearing extinction. Therefore, they are keepsakes, for Pete's sake.

There's an art, or a science, to the manner in which these cards are dealt. One of vigorous practice and exact charm. Sorted into stacks of approximately four in a deck— the street hawker, typically found wearing a vivid and printed "GIRLS GIRLS GIRLS" tee—flicks them hastily, but with due concentration and focus. The clipping flutter imitates the sound of a baseball card sandwiched between bicycle spokes, followed by a quick tap on the top of the mother stack to regroup all the face cards for a repeat shuffle. Loaded hands dart out like ghouls in a haunted house at every passer-by on every corner—young or old, male or female, gay or straight, married or single, tall or short, slender or stout. They do not discriminate or make assumptions as to who may be a party most interested, slightly fascinated, impartial, sober, or diligently oblivious.

I don't know why they bleep out the boobies on some of these things; we know they're there. And what they are. I don't think anyone would team up with such a profession if they weren't willing to get stark naked in the first place. I would never tolerate someone superimposing a pair of cartoon twinkle stars on my perky hooters, ever. We all know *those* aren't real.

And as much as I would like to share my examples of the life-like illustrations, I cannot. And not just because my mom is reading, but because I am not a pimp. Or a madam. Nor do I have a license or am in any way affiliated with their gainful merchandising. So, I'm only going to describe a few that are rated G, for my younger readers.

This is a photo of the complete hand I was dealt (from a safe distance), as arranged by my horny cat, Hobo.

Mya: Full Service

I need to know what "Discreet Billing" means. Does it come up on corporate or joint AmEx statements as the Pampered Chef Pizza Stone or is she a gas station? And that might just be a water weenie in her hand.

Andrea: $125

"No Hidden Fees" translates into what? Per hour, per day, per pound? In some places, that's a furnished apartment. For a whole week, with a kitchenette. Besides, she doesn't look like an Andrea. She looks like a Peggy. Or a Doug.

Irresistable Ivy: Call for Special Powers

These are totally rad. Dads probably collect them. They should come with a stale, hardened stick of powdery bubble gum and a plastic sleeve to preserve their mint condition. I only need four more to complete the Sexy Supergirls set. I wonder if they misspelled "Irresist*a*ble" on purpose. I'm most curious if her special powers are just as contagious as poison ivy, sumac, or poison oak. Now I'm done wondering.

Seductive Cat, 6 of 6

Hmm. I see no tail, nor do I see any whiskers, so there's no way she can be a cat? Pees on walls, sleeps all day, and has the ability to leap kitchen cabinets in a single bound? Seductive, indeed.

The most original (so they said) idea I found for my cards won superior praise at the hair salon when I decided to take a few of the girls along to my first appointment. I had never met the stylist and I wasn't concerned about making an impression one way or another. "So what are we doing today?" I was glad she asked, whipping out four escort cards with great hair extensions. Oddly enough, I was the *only* gal who had ever brought them in as visual aids. Made me a wee bit apprehensive, but then they brought over some wine.

"I really like the shade of Casey's one highlight, but don't want to be as light as Kira. Feel like I've been a Chevelle for two years now, so I'm leaning toward Ashlynn." Whatever her response, she definitely agreed. But the problem now, I can't ever wear my undersized crimson bikini when

I'm watering the plants because my neighbors would no longer believe I was retired. They would think I was Ashlynn the escort, who has a heart of gold and fees that exceed an arm and a leg. We also have the same earrings, so when I've got those on, I need to be even more careful where I rig up my two-piece.

Overall, I'm quite pleased with the ways I've been able to utilize my cards, but I don't want to overlook my potential. I might actually redeal them myself on an empty corner in the suburbs or make baby crib mobiles with wire coat hangers, spun wool, and a hole puncher. I see no reason to avoid Christmas ornaments and spring couture, either. Though maybe I'll just keep them in a glass jar on the kitchen counter and ask visitors to guess how many are in there. Then I will decoupage them on a lunch box for whomever comes closest. Because you know no one could ever actually win that shit.

Or, I'll just think of something corny to do with them.

POKER IN THE FACE

We usually don't realize it at the moment.

Even if we do, we definitely don't care. Nor do we want to. We never want to be reminded that our cravings, when at their most exacerbated, are usually harmful to our health. And our welfare. And our relationships. And our careers. And our financial affairs. Because nothing matters less. And nothing matters more. It's an addiction.

A habit. A secret. A vice. Or vice-versa.

It's a crippling routine that batters the sufferer with shameless and shameful thoughts and fears in the same swallow as the fleeting and forbidden pleasure that propped us up and told us to glom on in the first place. To watch. To listen. To wait. To change. Possibly before someone finally said to snap the sweet cuckoo out of it, you dicknose.

Though as much as we joke, it's really not that funny. And as many times as we send sniggers out to sea in distraction, we end up reeling over an issue that could someday render individuals and families hopeless. Because addictions are serious. And so am I.

But, sometimes we have to make fun of ourselves when we can and know that for nearly every recognized dependency, there *is* help. And every casino in Las Vegas permanently stocks slick pamphlets that identify the symptoms and warning signs for an affliction quite native to Nevada, where gambling and pawn shops are simultaneously persuasive and prevalent. Let it also be known that despite the gaudy glitz and over-exaggeration it's known for, the Vegas operation is a very self-aware and considerate

173

machine. One that enjoys accommodating the community and all of its inhabitants, in sickness and in health.

If you've never been to Vegas, or haven't been past the Strip—you should know gaming appliances are everywhere, not just on Las Vegas Boulevard and Fremont Street. Or in the widespread neighborhood casinos, which are also everywhere. They are like churches in the South; you can't turn around without tripping over one. You can find them in grocery stores, gas stations, restaurants, bars, saloons, lounges, truck stops, even the airport. And anywhere there's a flat surface, service for anyone twenty-one years of age, and some form of liquor license. In fact, I'm pretty sure there is at least one video poker or slot machine per every bar stool in the valley. I love the local lexicon and how staff members always wish you "Good luck." It's part of the scenery and lifestyle, like saying "Thank you" or "See you soon." Or "Bless her heart" and "Y'all."

You can also bet on just about anything, as long as there is an opponent for the team or person you wish to wager on. As long as there are odds. Football, basketball, soccer, baseball, horses, dogs, boxing, golf, hockey, race cars, professional, college, major league, and I assume tennis, Jai Alai, bowling, and probably cheerleading, soapbox derby, Chutes and Ladders, and mudwrestling. Not to mention pie-eating and ping-pong. Each division with a format, a spread, options, parlays, and propositions— none of which I understand or care about. But the Sports Books in some of these casinos can be mesmerizing, even for those who think competitions are a snooze. It's still easy to ogle over the expensive appointments and general human behavior of the male species.

I have no idea why it's called the "Sports Book" in a casino, but I have a suspicion it originates from the word *bookie*. Though it's definitely not a book. Or anything that resembles a book. It's not something you read or buy and discuss in a meditative setting, nor is it a spiral-bound smattering of consolidated text you can hold in the palm of your hand. It's a room, often a very large open or closed area where projector screens and/or a gabillion flat screen televisions hug the largest load-bearing wall, while endless, quick-ticking scoreboards of bright electronic red, green, and yellow-ish statistics blink as if they've all got gnats in their eyes.

Games, matches, play-offs, and recaps are all broadcast depending on the season, time of day, possibly the interest of the crowd. A bunch of men hover around their individual cubicles or lazy leather recliners punching on something that places or changes their bets, cheering like grunting bears, and wiping beer from their table trays and arm rests with their shirt tails—usually knee-length polyester jerseys with someone else's name and number on the back.

No estrogen detected.

Vegas is the only place you can bet on whatever you want, whenever you want. (Though I'm still in search of a lively pool for the Oscars.) I believe you can even bet on how many times a superstitious pitcher adjusts his cup and steps over a chalk line. That's why if you have a gambling compulsion and reside in Las Vegas, you have to become agoraphobic. It's like having a sweet tooth and living in a sugar cube igloo with milk chocolate mortar and donuts for doorknobs. A luxurious landscape lined with peppermint bark and Pop Rocks, a mantel of Milanos, Jelly Belly Jacuzzi tubs, and Pixie Stix for pets. You're screwed.

And now that I live in America's fine Sin Bin, I can articulately understand that no one is immune to this problem. So I wanted to ask myself the same set of tough questions each piece of obtainable literature poses. Just to be sure, one way or another.

Have you ever lost time from work due to gambling? No. I have only lost time from the drinking associated with gambling. But that doesn't really apply to work, or at least mine.

Has gambling ever made your home life unhappy? No. I don't gamble at home.

Has gambling affected your reputation? Nobody knows me here. I'm still trying to get one.

Have you ever felt guilty after gambling? Guilty about what?

Have you ever gambled to get money to help pay your debts or solve financial problems? No. I would never rely on my gambling skills to pay for anything.

Has gambling caused you to be less ambitious or efficient? Heavens no. I'm an excellent multi-tasker. In fact, I'm gambling right now.

After losing, do you feel you must gamble as soon as possible to win back your losses? That is officially referred to as "chasing." And, no. I'm not competitive enough to care that I always lose.

After winning, do you have a strong urge to return and win some more? No. I'm usually pretty busy after I do anything.

Have you ever gambled until your last dollar was gone? Every time. But it's never *my* last dollar.

Have you ever borrowed to finance your gambling? Borrowed what? I'm sure I just bought it, whatever it was. Especially if I had a coupon.

Have you ever sold anything to finance your gambling? No. I really like all my things.

Are you reluctant to use 'gambling money' for normal expenses? No. Usually just when it's for my *abnormal* expenses. Like gambling.

Has gambling ever made you careless of the welfare of yourself and your family? I think that would mean I cared about gambling in the first place. So, no.

Have you ever gambled longer than you had planned? I never plan to gamble.

Have you ever gambled to escape worry or trouble? No. I worry that I can't even gamble to escape troubled people.

Have you ever committed, or considered committing, an illegal act to finance gambling? Only when I've gambled in places where gambling is illegal.

Has gambling caused you to have difficulty sleeping? Not unless someone from Security wakes me up. But I don't like to play when I'm asleep anyway.

Do arguments, disappointments, or frustrations cause you to gamble? No. That is the worst way to make up. Or celebrate.

Have you ever had the urge to celebrate any good fortune with a few hours of gambling? I would argue that that would be frustrating. And disappointing.

I don't like the last question, but the answer is no. No, I've never considered anything as a result of my gambling. Not even gambling.

Gambling can be a very serious concern, one never to be taken lightly. Many of the remarks within this essay are ridiculous and intended for amusement. Please exercise responsible participation and discretion in gaming, and beyond. 1-800-522-4700 Gambler's Anonymous Helpline

THE NAME GAME

They're comprised of everything I had never expected. The whole hodgepodge of them, everywhere you go—at any time, day or night. You can find them anywhere, and there are seas of them. Bands of them. Lands of them. Lots of them.

I'm referring to slot machines.

There's something for everyone, really. Perhaps you have a favorite wild, domestic, fantastical, or extinct animal. Or you're a collector/hoarder of standard or peculiar baubles. Maybe you're fanatical about exotic destinations or follow a beloved television cast. The options and opportunities for frivolous frolic unravel to no end just like any other ritzy addiction. They are arranged in straight lines and planted across swirly, printed spews of carpet, manned by women and men wearing embroidered shirts who come running when you set the blinking, pulsating, or solid lights on top of your box aglow with the push of a button—accidentally or on purpose.

If you're anything like me, you don't play games or gamble because you keep close tabs on statistics, trends, payout, or popularity. You probably don't win much, either. That's because you bet for the name, the colors, the theme song, the juju, or the outfit. And you don't even like gambling anyway. This non-strategy started with greyhounds when I traipsed into the track during high school. The numbers were stupefying; it was only natural that I would put my money, all ten dollars of it, on Cool Blonde. Literally, the underdog, but she was the prettiest, by far. I'd simply prefer to wager on something aesthetically appealing, regardless of return. Because there usually isn't ever one of those. (All of my friends are good looking, too, while we're on the subject.)

That's all just to say that when it comes to slot machines, I play only one. Or, *can* play only one, as you know—Pharaoh's Fortune. And I'm glad it doesn't have to race other machines because I think it only walks. Like an Egyptian.

Be advised, nothing jabs the draft from my sails quicker than when some tourist has packed her track-suited ass in my respective Pharaoh's chair and continues to sit there for as long as *I* normally would while Driver loops from game to game, beer after beer. I grow so distraught, I almost care that I've been delayed in throwing money away. But in truth, I just end up with nothing to do inside the confines of a casino, having to pay full price for tepid wine.

So, once upon a time when the pharaoh was giving my fortune to someone else, I decided to browse the latest bumper crop of slotty boxes. I realized these machines are truly granted some prolific names, some sure fit for sharing.

Betti the Yetti

First of all, there's a typo. To my knowledge, an Abominable Snowman, Bigfoot, or a Sasquatch would be a *Yeti*. (With one t.) And they are beasts not often glamorized as females with bouffant hairdos. Pass.

Buffalo

Charging herds of large animals that don't typically thrive in the desert. I don't presume this game is interesting or educational. Or quiet.

Big Ben
At first, I thought this read "Ric Den."
Think I'd rather spend my money at a game called Harrod's.

Dirty Dancing
Plays "Hungry Eyes" and includes a vibrating chair. Though no
one should ever put Baby in a corner, placement for this tall,
expensive system should be reconsidered. I tried to play, spilled
my drink when the seat started dancing, lost five dollars.
It was not *the time of my life.*

Helen of Troy
Nice to finally put the face with a name. But I think
"a thousand ships" is a slight exaggeration.

Kitty Glitter
This would be my name to be if I was a stripper. Machine
makers are fascinated with every species of feline. All of
these various games purr or meow, so calamitous.
Besides, no one should ever take advantage of
the word *glitter* without using any.

Magic Mermaid
Just like kittens, gaming aficionados also have a fondness
for mystical maritime sea maidens with tails. There are
schools of mermaid games, but very little splash.
And there's no Darryl Hannah.

Enchanted Unicorn

This time, a horned horse. There are many
variations of unicorn games as well.
I would have loved this one. In 1982.

Pegasus

The winged horse. Almost as believable as
what you can win on penny slots.

Rich Girl

What you'll never become playing this one.

Ruby Magic
Save your clams for Ruby the psychic tarot card reader instead.
You do not win rubies.
Or headbands.

Samurai Secrets
Tried to play. Noisy and hard to understand.
Dangerous language barrier.
And there is no secret.

Secrets of the Forest
More red-tape secrets. Pixies and nymphs.
Iridescent winged miniature women stuck inside a box, not a forest.

Sex and the City
I can't help but wonder... was winning *Big* really worth it?

Lago di Amore
Lake of Love, how romantic. Champagne not included. Skip.

Kenny Rogers: The Gambler
Celebrity endorsements mean *everything*. This is
the only one that makes any damn sense.

You're probably not supposed to take pictures of the machines, but I told anyone who asked that I was an official game-namer from Georgia doing research to see what titles hadn't yet been used.

Jimmy Crack Corn will debut this fall.

BINGOLOGY 101

I'd actually like to call it "a total mindf#ck."

Because it's not just a game, it's another dimension. And it's not just a pastime; it's a way of life. It's not even one lone barrel bursting with numbers made to match grid-like charts splayed out on unadorned tables. It's a creed with corresponding codes and laws and values and it's the fastest race any one person can dole out while sitting on his or her ass. It's an open sprint to an invisible finish line for prizes designated for the inordinate amount of time spent searching, stamping, and surfing across anesthetizing sets of lightweight, disposable paper cards. It's an alternate language. Like slang. A full-fledged "No Trespassing" zone for people who don't know (or care) anything about bingo. But if you're trying to learn, everyone inside is pretty pleasant. They're like New Yorkers and Parisians. People willing to help if you ask, but they aren't going to leap into your lap with peach cobbler and a puppy because you're staring cross-eyed at a map.

Bingo is popular in Las Vegas. At least, it seems to be. It's the only place I've ever played as a grown-up, and probably ever will. There are about twenty parlors around town, which sounds like a lot, but none of them are on the Strip. They have been arranged in our neighborhood casinos, where the locals go. And the most serious locals can usually be caught wearing and carrying promotional apparel and gear from the very same casino they're sitting in. Items and collectibles they've earned and accumulated from players club points, weekday drawings, happenstance giveaways, bonus somethings, or just waiting in line. The fashions are, in a word, adorable.

And it's not a cliché: bingo really is an institution for owners of nappy-headed troll dolls who can chain-smoke, converse with others about lap-band surgery, *and* swiftly detect featured numbers on a fragile paper matrix. All with a surreptitious level of suggested library silence and stoicism. It's essentially a cult—less the trench coats, stringy black hair, and lyric-free soundtrack. But there are still tattoos. So I guess it's more like a gang for people without any weapons. A secret society for the anti-society type. And I'm not planning my initiation party just yet. Not ready.

All the magic happens in a room with fluorescent lighting brighter than any three KMarts put together. The space is stocked with hundreds of 80 ml colored ink tubes arranged in a vending machine just as you'd find cheese crackers and Bugles. The squishy foam-tipped tubes are called daubers and before playing, I didn't know that. I had no reason to know that. Before that day, I had only used highlighters, red pens, and urine to mark things. Furthermore, I had only played bingo prior to my tenth birthday and we used little TUMS-sized pucks to set on top of our numbers. I remember some of the other students (boys only) thought they could cheat by writing down which numbers had previously won. People who do that with lottery numbers aren't even that hopeful. Or stupid.

I hadn't put much thought into the folks I believed might occupy the proper bingo category, other than the people from that *Roseanne* episode. I assumed the clientele was mainly women, some with flammable hair—and I was right—but that was the extent of my belief system. I would have never thought they would be folks with Olympic levels of competitive lust, though never seen stretching out or warming up. I only envisioned people who spent a lot of time answering the phone for their jobs, and as a trade-off, got to call radio shows to win free tickets for things. Those, to me, are very viable signs that someone can multi-task with non-life-threatening duties.

All I know for sure is that I can daub fifty times faster than Driver and still manage to do some cursory staring. Watching Driver daub is like watching Danielson try to catch flies with a pair of chopsticks. So it goes without saying that Driver needed a lot more help than I did from the nice woman sitting across the table. It was a benefit to us that she had nine fewer cards than we did and a small electronic thing that found the numbers for her. The use of her device left plenty of time to text, file her nails, and tutor a few babes in the woods. We decided to buy in bulk—the multi-pack tablet with twelve cards per page. *Twelve.* And they call numbers every ten seconds. No repeats. No do-overs. No thank you.

Ridiculous.

I really don't know how anyone can smoke and play bingo at the same time. I can't even play bingo at the same time I'm playing bingo. The hall was smokier than the casino itself. Lit cigarettes were either permanently tacked to someone's lip or had been abandoned in a black plastic ashtray burning down to the filter in one long, persevering Marge Simpson-hair-shaped ash. Things move so fast in there, I missed the drink order. Guess they don't want people getting drunk. Could you imagine the retaliation against the "No repeats" regulation from a bunch of dipsomaniacs with daubers? It would be anarchy, turning into a Jackson Pollock painting by first light. Only with more dots.

In bingo, there are also all these terms you're supposed to understand as they relate to whatever game is being played. I never knew there were different kinds of games *within* bingo. I thought you just tried to get five in a row, any kind of row, forming a straight line. Which is hard, yet boring, enough. And it's not like they have the rules (or any rules) posted anywhere. You're just supposed to know what to do, like with toilet paper and petroleum jelly. Basically, a barista person announces the name of the game as if it's an auction, which is impossible to understand when you don't even know what you were playing just before it changed. The patterns are unlimited, which doesn't help, either.

Our nearby bingo hall also runs a pretty spectacular closed-captioned feed of the numbers being selected. It's a regular television screen with a woman's airbrushed acrylics turning ping-pong balls over like the Lotto drawing. It's what commercials for nail salons would look like if they were ever to produce one. I'm not sure if it's a live broadcast or if that woman is really somewhere in the room, or if she's really a woman at all, but it's a striking demonstration if you make the time to watch. Only you can't, because you're playing! There's also the big board where you can check which numbers have already been called. Trust me, it's easier to read the *Wall Street Journal* from a zipline through the New York Stock Exchange wearing a microscope and horse hood than part with a quick glance while daubing. Your brain can literally just shut down, stop dead in its tracks, and spread out on the ground like a cat on a leash. But you're too confused to cry and bingo is too macho anyway.

There's a whole vernacular for bingo. *Bingo lingo*. It's an entirely separate vocabulary unshared with the mainstream bipedal civilization. The "Bingonese," as I call them, speak of things like: Doubles and Triples, Hardways and Rainbow Packs, Postage Stamp Patterns and Crazy Kites, even Blackouts and Coveralls. None of which have any business getting hopped up inside a game that doesn't even use athletic equipment or participate in an annual Pride parade. Coveralls are outer garments dreamed up for extensive manual labor, not sitting.

But it's safe to say all those things may or may not be used during Drag Queen Bingo, something that only happens in and around major metropolitan areas and select hootenannies. And because I like balls so much, I still can't pick a favorite between ball lifters, ball runways, and ball shooters—components I assume demand and embrace blowers, six-packs, and validation. But no matter what happens, my heart is with the ball gate. Always will be.

Fortunately, when the other games move too slowly, the pros cling to Quickies, Speedgames, Speed Bingo, Instant Bingo, and Bonanza Bingo.

Or they're just too lazy to spend the time actually playing bingo. There's also Basket Bingo, Auto Purchase, and Lucky Jars—things that have nothing to do with crafts or cars, but are somehow associated with this same tabletop, numbered-but-not-mathematical activity. Something that should never be confused with keno, which is bingo-*like*, but I'm not sure would ever include catch-ups, chat rooms, callers, and throwaway flimsies—subjects that should remain in their own online community anyway, where the hardcores go for bingo at talked-about hours.

Above all, I appreciate the special sing-songy, rhymey way the more enthusiastic (paid) callers announce everything. Many of the references are British and hint with riddles or what shapes the numbers make; the rest of them just sound like short stories that babies would read from an upside-down book. For instance, the number eight (8), which can be embellished by any, all, or a combination of the following: *Garden State – Golden Gate – At the gate – Harry Tate – One fat lady – She's always late – Sexy Kate – Is she in yet – Wow, I could have had a B8.* And trust me, I know you're curious… Harry Tate was an English comedian. His real name was Ronald Macdonald Hutchinson, which was just not as funny.

The pageantry for thirty gets inside you just the same. (30) *Burlington Bertie – Dirty Gertie – Speed Limit – Blind 30 – Flirty Thirty – Your face is dirty – Tomato Ball.* This goes on for all ninety numbers, but those two could change the world.

In gambling terminology, Burlington Bertie represents the fractional odds of 10/3, more commonly referred to as "one hundred to thirty." Though what's more interesting, "Burlington Bertie" is also a music hall song composed by Harry B. Norris in 1900 and sung by Vesta Tilley. It concerns an aristocratic young idler who pursues a life of leisure in the West End of London. I like her already, and not just because she loves champagne. Here's a smidgen from Norris' turn-of-the-century sensation:

> *I'm Burlington Bertie I rise at ten-thirty*
> *And saunter along Temple Bar*
> *As round there I skip - I keep shouting "Pip Pip!"*
> *And the darn'd fools think I'm in my car*

This prompted me to begin my own theme song. I don't plan to use it during a bingo match or anything, so I've avoided heavy use of cadence and couplets.

I'm Las Vegas Lucy I wake when it's convenient
And here everything is open 'round the clock
The sun is always shining - My fat ass is always dining
And I've got the Osmonds and Elvis on my block
They speak of slots being looser but who are we kidding
I'm too busy being leisurely to care
So there
"Pip Pip!"

NEED TO BE SCENE

Though it may come as a real bombshell, I don't go to clubs. I don't even go *out* to clubs, for that matter. That's why I love giving recommendations, especially in a place like Vegas. The indisputable destination for uninterrupted indulgence, where nightlife runs on a continual loop tucked neatly inside a flickering on-call ward that seizes even fewer winks than the Big Apple. It's a highly-skilled, multi-tiered playground swarming with brazen cleavage and more bartenders than all the mall Santas in Canada.

I can't heave Las Vegas over my shoulders in conscientious endorsement without mentioning the millions of dollars that go into the after-dark darlings of design, drink, and dance. I've combined published lists, zesty advertisements, photo slide shows, and trustworthy reviews of notable hot spots to develop my own field guide to help you folks decide. Because opinionated appraisals are always the most helpful, in my opinion.

But first, there are some things you need to know before you get in line, anywhere.

One. These nightclubs are serious about codes of dress, unlike the rest of Vegas that knows you're a tourist because you've visibly packed for comfort, head to toe. You won't get away with white sneakers, baseball caps, flip-flops, athletic wear, jerseys, bare feet, baggy pants, sandals, white t-shirts, and wife beaters, so don't plan your get-up around any of those non-article articles. Also, some of the establishments don't even allow hats in general, so be cognizant of whatever arrangement you've got going on under that fedora.

Two. Not all of these clubs are open every night. Most are closed Sunday and Monday, but some are even closed five nights a week. That's how *exclusive* they are. Many of them don't unlock their doors until 9 or 10 p.m. and there is often a cover charge, one usually higher for men. Most times, local ladies get in free. (That's my category, which makes me a slightly cheaper date.) You can reserve a table in advance, as well as order "bottle service" for your table or private room. Otherwise, you stand—this is much cheaper. Bottle service basically means you and your group buy the booze and the mixers in advance, and you don't ever have to walk up to the bar. This $350+ fee also includes your own waitress, so then all you really have to do is sit. I think the waitress is also supposed to watch your drinks while you dance, but I'm not sure. I would need mine to watch everything because Driver doesn't always like to hold my purse, particularly the little zebra one with the cute green sash.

Three. Depending on the occasion, there is sometimes a host. This may be someone whose last name is Kardashian, or someone who has married or dated a Kardashian. "Industry Night" refers to various midweek eves when hospitality staffers converge on certain clubs during their nights off, and those designated spaces tend to draw in larger crowds. You might even experience a champagne fire drill (some will include ponchos) or confetti cannon, depending on where you land. And many of the clubs have resident Mega-DJ's who spin from extravagant booths. It's totally mega.

Now that you have a sturdy enough substructure of sophistication, here are some (definitely not all) of the venues in alphabetical order.

The Bank. I thought this was the **Bellagio**'s Credit Union, too, but there is no free checking. Though chances are, you're going to *break* The Bank or *owe* The Bank, and if you get lucky, you can *thank* The Bank. I like expensive names for things.

Chateau Nightclub & Gardens. This manor house is part of the ornate real estate portfolio at **Paris** and has been voted "Best View" by local magazine *Seven*. The elevated terrace is *tres parfait* and their marketing materials look like fine clothing ads from a Neiman Marcus catalog. Ooh la la, it's *not* Sassoon.

Crown Nightclub. Think tiaras and rhinestones. And royal people. This gem at **Rio** has touted lustful things like Karaoke XXX and Latin Libido Night. *Arriba!*

Foundation Room. I know it sounds like a cosmetic studio or war room for construction projects, but it's not. I had trouble understanding exactly where to find this one, which is probably the point. Apparently, it's inside the House of Blues at the top of **Mandalay Bay**. Get better directions from someone wearing makeup right now, not their jammies.

Ghostbar. As you know, I've actually been to this indoor-outdoor setting at the **Palms** where you can see the entire city from fifty-five floors up in the air. I even sat at a table reserved for someone else, probably a ghost.

Gilley's. I've been to this one, too. It's both a restaurant and a country bar at **Treasure Island**, complete with a mechanical bull and line dancing. Even packs heat with live cowboy crooners. It's where we crashed that poor guy's sixtieth, when it felt like *my* birthday.

Hakkasan. This 80 thousand square foot dynamo at the **MGM Grand** is fairly new and boasts the latest and greatest of everything. I feel completely drunk and buried alive just reading all the details.

HAZE. I want this one to be bursting with purple foamy drinks and fluorescent pink chimpanzees. This somewhat psychedelic swirly place is inside **Aria** and has previously been voted by *Seven* as the "Best Place to see a Performance." Wonder if they care who's...

Hyde. I was hoping this was a small dude ranch inside the **Bellagio**, complete with cow skins, longhorns, and leather chaps. Looks gorgeous, so I'm sure it lures gorgeous people. They also serve food and have forty VIP tables, for forty very important groups of gorgeous rancheros.

LAVO. Hotter than lava, I've been there. It's a club inside the **Palazzo**, but I've only dined at the ristorante downstairs. I hear it's a great place for brunch, too, so it may as well be a cruise ship.

LAX. Not to be confused with the airport in Southern California, this two-story doozie at the **Luxor** is likely packed full of people lollygagging and dilly-dallying around in their dress-up clothes.

Marquee Nightclub & Dayclub. This wad of eye candy inside the **Cosmopolitan** has featured celebrity karaoke and a Boom Box Room. I don't know if celebrities are/were actually singing or ordinary people are just singing famous people's songs, but remember, it's still lip-syncing.

MOON Nightclub. This is a really smart name because the moon comes out at night, during its same hours of operation. It's where all the astronauts and astrologers hang out. It's on the top floor of the Fantasy

Tower at the **Palms** and its retractable roof makes things so much easier. Bring your telescope.

1 OAK Nightclub. There's only one oak tree in Las Vegas, and it's inside the **Mirage**. Though it's just 1 Oak, it's actually two rooms. Big ones, I presume. It's occupies the same space as the former Jet Club, in case you can't find that one either.

PBR Rock Bar. As in Pabst's Blue Ribbon, the beer. A huge pewter bull tears through the building's façade in the Miracle Mile shops at **Planet Hollywood**. The website for this Bar & Grill mentions Beer Pong, Jack Daniels, Budweiser, and events that include "Championships." My kind of place. *Not.* But it does have a mechanical bull!

8 ½ Ultra Lounge & Piranha Nightclub. I don't know if you have to address this paradise **on Paradise** by its full name, but I would, just to be polite. It's been voted "Best gay nightclub experience" by *Seven* mag. But this is Vegas, anything goes. And people leave it here anyway, twenty bucks is twenty bucks.

Playboy Club. They say playing blackjack in the Playboy Party Pit at the **Palms** with a bunny dealer is one of the *must-do's* in Las Vegas. Hugh Hefner as himself, as a club. A buffet of bunny ears and bow ties. I'd say bring your Easter basket, but it closed in 2012.

PURE Nightclub. This is where all the vestal virgins go. Inside **Caesar's Palace**, there's lots of white stuff with crisp, straight lines and slick surfaces. Driver has actually taken clients there and raves about the 14 thousand square foot terrace with brilliant views. Driver must be a virgin.

Rain Nightclub. I picture umbrellas and storms of men precipitating from the ceiling to a very slippery floor at the **Palms**. It's on the casino level and also hosts concerts, but it's only open Friday and Saturday nights. When it *pours*.

Rhumbar. You can find this haven for all types of rum at the **Mirage**. Pluck a cigar from the humidor and step outside on the patio to smoke it. You might even be able to see the nightly volcano shows from there. It's a grand production. I can see parts of it from my upstairs toilette.

Savile Row. Also a line of suits and shoes you can find at Sears, but in Vegas, it's a small speakeasy located just off LAX at the **Luxor**. Per their website, it's inspired by the infamous street in London. I recommend you chat only with a British accent because it's described as a "made-to-measure" experience that always uses "reliable discretion." Sounds like my last bra fitting.

Surrender. Even the 'S' in their signage is a slithery serpent that cradles an Adam and Eve red apple, so you know this place is very tempting. Adjacent to the swanky European pools and cabanas at Steve Wynn's **Encore Beach Club**, this stunning joint effort was called "The Total Package" by *Seven* mag.

TAO. This **Venetian** wonder in the Grand Canal Shoppes is also a bistro. Their website had me at "banquettes featuring secured purse drawers." Poor Driver would have nothing to do.

TRYST. Romp around this **Wynn** dandy and fall in love at first sight, or just for the night. This mouthwatering and plush passion pallet is only open Thursday through Saturday, so plan your affairs accordingly.

Vanity Nightclub. The joists at this **Hard Rock Café** canteen are probably reinforced with gigantic mirrors and Post-It Note affirmations. With fifty VIP booths, there are plenty of places for very important vain people to sit. Because making vain people stand would not be pretty.

VooDoo. Fifty-one stories in the sky at **Rio**, this is *the* place to tinker with shrunken heads and special dolls. When up this high on Flamingo Road, it's another setting for great Strip vistas. One of the two floors is actually a steakhouse, so come all *sorts* of hungry!

XS Nightclub. This **Encore** watering hole is sure to inspire overindulgence and more than enough of everything necessary. Their *Seven*-celebrated DJ booth sits in the middle of the club and is surrounded by several floor-to-ceiling LED screens. It's very, very, very, very, very, very excessive.

I know. Vegas is an endless wet t-shirt wife swap indecent proposal wedding keg stand Jäger toga party bachelorette contest with wings, wheels, and smoke, where everyone comes to sign their names with maraschino cherry fingers and donate brain cells to the Las Vegas economy. That's why it all has to stay here when you leave.

It's also why you'll be back.

All product or company names that may be mentioned within are tradenames, trademarks, or registered trademarks of their respective owners. Given Las Vegas' ever-changing lineup, some of these details may no longer be current or exact. Be sure to consult the most up-to-the-minute oracles for all activities and installations when visiting. Have fun and play safely!

LIVING IN SIN: REGULAR LIFE

A THOUSAND CALORIES

Boxer: "Sorry about that [hanging up the phone]. How can I help you?"

Which is such a dumb question. What *else* could he help me with? I didn't walk in there for (or with) a bunny hutch, a chronic migraine, or a pap smear.

Me: "Well, I just moved here and working out is perfectly awful. But this kickboxing thing looks fun, even though there's nobody in here [scanning the empty gym]. I need to get in shape; lots to eat in Vegas."

Boxer: "That's so strange; we just had two other people come in and say the same thing."

Me: "Did they spot you from the Dairy Queen patio, too?"

Boxer: "You know, they didn't say." [*very* serious]

Me: "So how does this work? When are you busy because I don't want to be the fat new girl with a bunch of fitness freaks. Is there like a beginner class?"

Boxer: "Don't worry, everyone is like you. The trainer is always the most fit in the class."

Me: "So everyone is fat? Or is that your nice way of telling me *I'm* fat?"

Boxer: [silent male facial non-response to "Honey, does this make my ass look big?"]

Me: "Alright, so where does the trainer stand and is there music? This party better have music. At least a DJ or something."

Boxer: "Follow me, I'll show you."

Me: "You can just point. I wasn't planning on *any* exercise today."

Boxer: "The instructors move around. They do a good job keeping an eye on everybody and making sure everyone is getting pushed to their max. Every class is the same because there aren't any levels. It doesn't sound like you want to learn to fight, but it's amazing what you'll pick up. We kick your butt for an hour and you'll burn about one thousand calories each time."

Me: "Do you know how many Cosmos that would be? Just roughly."

Me, again: "Okay. So how do the gloves work?"

Boxer: "You mean—?"

Me: "I mean, I know how they work, but do I rent them, buy them, what? For some reason, I just thought I'd be kicking, but you have gloves in here."

Boxer: "You buy the gear. I don't think you want to share anyone else's sweat."

Me: "Yeah, that's disgusting. Didn't think about that. How much are they? And what do you mean by *gear*? More than gloves? Like what, a helmet or something?"

Boxer: "Eighty-four."

Me: "For boxing gloves? Can't I just get some at Target?"

Boxer: "Well, you can, but these are leather. Those would be vinyl."

Me: "Oh, right. Vinyl makes people look fatter."

I was then faced with the decision as to what color gloves I should acquire before the first class. For eighty-four dollars. Their gift shop offers red, white, blue, black, and pink. No way was I getting red because those seem to be everywhere, on every boxer I've ever seen, which is probably two. I didn't want blue because they would bring out my eyes and Latisse would harass me into being an eyelash model. I *love* white leather, but was concerned all the dirt and animal hair would show and I definitely could not wear them to a barbeque. So that left black and pink.

Down to those, I googled Larry Holmes to see what color he wears, or wore. In the first image, he was wearing black, but when I clicked further through his website he had red ones and was also selling used bar equipment. I then googled heavyweight champions from 1960 to present. I didn't recognize any of the names until somewhere in the mid-80s. I eliminated Mike Tyson solely based on his reputation for being a jackass. (Though I do hear his one-man show isn't half-bad.) I considered George

Foreman because we have one of those grills, but Evander Holyfield is so handsome. In all of their photos, they were in business suits so I stopped caring about why I was even wondering.

Pink. *Pink?* Wasn't sure how that would sound, other than assured they were lady glovettes. My athletic days are a bit hazy, but I know we didn't have special "girl colors" back then. I would have gone that route if I knew they were making a contribution to breast cancer awareness, but didn't see any brochures for that, though in the gym's brochure, the female centerfold was wearing all pink. She was no fatty, must be an instructor. That's when I knew I would risk being mistaken for a trainer if I got pink gloves. I also noticed a jump rope was mentioned in the pamphlet. Jumping rope is stupid.

I decided to go with black. Every fighter needs a nickname and I can do more with that in a riddle. Especially in Las Vegas, where every known weight class comes to contend at the MGM. I could be Jumpin' Blackjack Flash. Or Black Bruty. Or, if I played my cards right, Black Eye Correction Serum.

POW-ZAH! Float like a lemon twist and sting like a Bellini.

COULD YA BE MORE PACIFIC?

There are so many barefaced differences when considering general lifestyles and backdrops on the east and west coasts. There's landscape, climate, transportation, attitude, topography, religion, language, architecture—you get it. But there is one semi-inconvenient distinction between the opposite sides of the United States. And *it* is something often lost or forgotten about in the mix of commerce, New York City, where they built the president's house, and television programming.

And that is *time.*

The father of all moments, eras, and accumulations in our history and horizon that we employ to understand, seek, and document what fills *it.* Time is the only real way we can track, trace, and record what has passed and what is still to come. And when things did—or will—happen next, first, last, runner-up, or never.

Time is precious, especially in the morning. And especially to me, in the morning.

As a touching reflection of my feelings on the subject, I remixed Cyndi Lauper's 1984 number one ballad, "Time After Time." Should you be unfamiliar with this tender chart-topper, please refer to your Sony Walkman or lavender Casio cassette recorder for arrangement and lyrics.

On the count of three, pretend you're me and sing like you're performing in front of mirrored closet doors while standing on your twin trundle bed in Converse high-tops and lots of jelly bracelets.

Lying in my bed I hear the phone ring
I haven't hit the 'snooze'
I'm not up, from dreaming yet
Please wait 'til noon
News Flash - Time Zones
I'm three hours behind
It's called Ge-og-ra-phy—

Time after…
Sometimes, when you text me—
I want to punch your head
You keep calling to me, I don't care
about what you've said
Then you say—"Uh Oh"
"She's three hours behind"—
hasn't opened the blinds

Chorus:
If you're up, you can look
at the clock on your wall, at any time
If you call, I won't answer—when there it's 9
I'm three hours behind

After your breakfast fades
and happy hour is on the way
That's when I'm waking up—
don't worry, I am A-okay
Z's happen, I'd like all mine
Still three hours behind—

Chorus:
If you've lost…
It's hell no, not Hel-lo—
Please be kind, my big hand rewinds

Chorus:
If you've lost your Eastern mind

I'm three hours behind
1-2-3 hours behind
Three
hours
behind

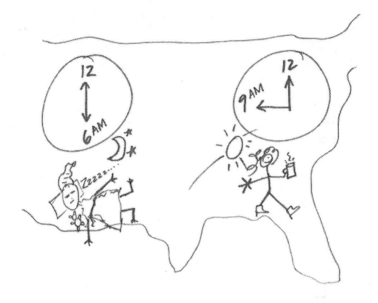

ONE HUNDRED PLUS

(First summer in Las Vegas)

If this were the case in Atlanta, there would be nothing left of me but a modicum of blonde hair, dental records, an underwire, and a pair of ruby red slippers. And some jewelry. All staggering around in a millpond of clammy, swampy goo where I was last seen cavorting sometime after dawn.

But there *is* a difference, and one of distinguished note.

It's interesting to be out and about, mixing with the masses in a new city, advancing into the influx of summer amidst what geography identifies as "the desert"—often associated with cacti and camels. Both require little water, and have an amazing facility in which to store it. Camels have humps and cacti have paddles. And now I'm distracted, but it had something to do with the natives wanting to prepare me for the heat.

I love the heat. And I love to be outside. I don't even mind a little easygoing perspiration and/or premium in-depth sweating. But when temps ascend anywhere above 90 degrees in Atlanta, it may as well be 9,000. And you may as well be treading in a vat of enraged glass smoldering in its liquid state. The humidity follows you like an unemployed shadow, stuck like rubber cement to your caboose, the nape of your neck, and the small of your back. Even tattoos and freckles protest in despair. It's not unlike wearing a black plastic Hefty bag or a Mylar bodysuit on your cut-rate vacation to an armpit. Even envelopes will seal themselves if not chaperoned.

Georgia knows no such thing as a *dry* heat. Or temps that climb so high, windshields just crack and plants singe before your very eyes. Here, there's a level of the sun's brightness so vigorous and inescapable, "The City in a Forest" could never fully comprehend what the absence of all shade yields. Conversely, the average Las Vegan has probably never heard of Quikrete. Or sump pumps and encephalitis, for that matter. They've probably never seen knee-high steam swell from pavement or listened to the testy snapping of a bug light, either.

On lazy days in Atlanta, I changed my outfit three times and did more laundry between June and September than the Waltons did in eight winters combined. You can knock the thermostat down to -4 degrees for relief, but end up with the flu when you go outside to check the mail. That is, if you can actually find the mailbox because your sunglasses have fogged up and the mascara and moisturizer have melted into your eyeballs, stinging like hornets and burning like hell. Even the compressor on your HVAC inevitably gives up and you have to rush order a commercial-grade deep freeze just to live in until the tech can come. He is usually a man wearing a navy romper with dark orange sludge wicking up the shins. He will also complain of the signature sauna conditions, reminding you there is no breeze in your crawlspace. Or attic.

But in Vegas, I can sit under the covered patio and I don't have to be naked or garnished in frozen bags of peas when temperatures skyrocket. I can spray paint my three small patches of grass green at high noon and not even sprout a dewy bead on my upper lip. I don't have to worry about finding a public restroom with a hand dryer for my hair because I no longer arrive anywhere damp. That's why I just smile when locals warn me about the heat, as if Atlanta is somewhere in Nova Scotia.

Then I politely go back to tanning my humps.

SLOT HEARD AROUND THE WORLD

Before we moved to Vegas, I didn't know Driver played poker. Or even liked poker.

The only cards and chips that ever lingered in our joint company had all fatefully fallen as casualties to overstated art projects, stacks of uninhabitable houses, and props for banquet themes and tablescapes. I was grandly unaware it was an interest, a pastime, an escape, or a sport for Driver. But I should have known. I should have just assumed any and all of the above. Because if any twitch from here to there is competitive, could be considered competitive, or has the prospect of being competitive, then it's just one big rabbit hole into the predisposition of a condition Driver faces, just as voraciously. Being inordinately competitive.

Sometimes it's just easier to give in. Especially at a time when my throbbing cerebellum could no longer juggle two things at once. I had lost all focus on the TV show about a meek woman with no prior history of violence who let a Speedo-wearing man she met *in* a public pool convince her to slay his ailing wife while wearing her own husband's Army fatigues. Even more calamitous, most of the suspense following their hackneyed romance took place in her laundry room, where she had just ironed said camouflage uniform. With my concentration evaporating like morning dew, all I could hear were the *ding-ding-ding-ding-ding-ding-ding-ding-ding-ding* cash-out sounds sleeting from Driver's stupid smartphone. In that moment, I would have traded some of my shiniest small appliances to be confounded solely by the riveting re-enactors in that titillating melodrama.

After what must have been an hour, I started asking questions...

Me: "Does it help when you talk to the game?"

Driver: "Well, these people don't know how to play."

Me: "People? What *people*?"

Driver: "The people on Facebook."

Driver participates on Facebook even less frequently than I do. Most days, I think Facebook is as frightening as that anxiety dream about not remembering your high school locker combination. Even well into your thirties. Driver and I aren't even Facebook friends; I see no reason for this to ever change.

I gave it a little more time, to observe and regroup. More dings and dongs and shuffling card noises. More talking to the phone and the "people" inside the phone. More dings, dings, and elongated clinks. Then there were more condescending critiques as to how *it* should be played and what card is needed. More dings. I even knew how much was lost or won and what move or what bet was active. It all sounded horrible, made worse by the narration. More dongs. Aloud. *Loudly.*

Me: "What are you playing?"

Driver: "Poker."

Me: "On Facebook?"

Driver: "Yes." [eyes fastened to the phone]

Me: "So what do they call *that*? FacePoke? PokerFace? Poke-A-Book?" [overcome with laughter at my wit, and sorrow]

Driver: "It's an app."

Me: "Huh? Are you playing with your Facebook friends?"

Driver: "No. I don't know her." [completely serious]

Me: "What's her name? Maybe you *could be* Facebook friends."

Driver: "I've got a full table."

Me: "You should 'friend' all of them. They could be anywhere, you know. And then you could send them a FaceMail when you want to play and you could always play with people who suck. And always win."

Driver: "It's Zynga."

Me: "That's a weird name. Where does *she* live?"

Driver: "It's a thing for all sorts of games. Like Farmville, I think. But I made it an app on the phone because with Facebook you can get more chips for ninety-nine cents to use within twenty-four hours."

I didn't have a response to that. Instead, I took up fictitious occupancy inside a Mentos commercial, where things made more sense. Not only could I have misunderstood that description, I genuinely wasn't interested in adding that kind of invaluable information to my already-vast catalog of things I'll never care about. I then levitated from the sofa, walked into the office, unplugged my laptop, and carried it back into the living room as if it was a stuffed turkey on the platter of my forearms. I staged accent pillows on my legs and under my feet at the coffee table. I opened up a new screen and started laughing. Quietly, I thought.

Driver: "What are you doing?"

Me: "Writing."

Driver: "About what?"

Me: [no response]

Driver, again: *"About what?"* [increased volume and unease]

Me: "That. [pointing with my brow to the phone] Think I'm gonna call it 'Slot Heard around the World.'"

Driver: "But it's poker, not slots."

Me: "Exactly."

[DING]

DIVA LAS VEGAS

I don't know why we didn't win.

I can only make one very humble assumption as to why we were just runners-up. And that is because we were *too* good. We rehearsed for at least three hours the night before *and* we arrived with props. No one else had any friggin' props and it was obvious we were wig, tuxedo shirt, and shoulder pads above the competition.

Driver and I were informed only six days in advance that the weekend's dinner party would include a mandatory, guest-participation-required entertainment theme: "Lip Sync for Your Life - Duets." And I needed to submit our song selection right away. Ironically, a few invitees ended up with unexplained emergencies and bronchitis just before curtain. Coincidence? *I think not.* We had been asked to fake singing, not sickness. And this is Vegas. I thought everyone was in show business. Fine by me... better our chances!

I was certain the invitees would all gravitate toward the short list of distinguished classic duets. You know, the ones you hear at every karaoke bar, wedding reception, dinner cruise, and celebrity impersonator demonstration. Songs known and sung by three-year-olds and octogenarians alike. Something by Sonny & Cher, The Captain & Tennille, Meatloaf, or from the *Grease* soundtrack. But I was determined to tackle something a little more obscure, though still a familiar chart-topper. We were also the only white couple left after the cancellations, so we needed to redeem the rhythm of our race. And I knew just how to do it.

To many, it's known that Driver can be a very good sport when it comes to these things. I call them "projects." There's usually a nice balance between us because I take music, dance, and costume personally, while Driver does not like to lose. So what one may lack in desire to play make-believe will eventually find ancillary incentive in friendly rivalry. Our combined talents ultimately manifest a surefire warranty to kick tush in jovial group activities against those we know or whom we've never met. Together, we make a really good two-person pyramid.

It took me four seconds to decide on our number. I only had to run through the song to make fully sure there was enough involvement in the arrangement to be considered true duet material. Then I had to secretly surrender our choice to the hosts, crossing all ten fingers, toes, and eyes that no one else had the same ingenious idea. "Your part is easy," I promised Driver, who seemed concerned as to what we'd not-be-singing for a small audience.

I would need a mic stand, preferably with a cord, but I don't own one. I thought I could disassemble my mannequin and duct-tape a small extension cord to the top of the five-foot pole that holds the bodice, but the stand itself is rather heavy. And during wine, probably quite cumbersome. Driver told me to get a hairbrush and I was devastated by such disregard.

"Um, *no*. She always uses a microphone on a stand for this one. Lots of arm movement," I asserted. Besides, this was not headlining at a slumber party.

"Well, how 'bout a broom? Lighter than that damn mannequin," Driver suggested.

"Well, I wouldn't be taking the body, but you just gave me an idea." I leaped into the laundry room.

It was a recent gift from Driver—a "Housewarming," if you will. I guess I thought it was a little too fancy, or the gesture was just a little too *NINETEEN FORTIES*, to ever pry from the package.

As you can see, this invention by Quickie is praised for its cobweb removal tactics. I had never once made mention of needing to eliminate webs, anywhere in Carpet Kingdom. But I did mention that all 672,000 blind slats were covered in a chalky layer of sandy dust that probably wasn't going to vanish all by itself. Days later, I was presented with this instrument, backed by a smile that belongs on a poster in an illegal dental office. It was the solution to all of *my* domestic anguish. I'm sure you can imagine the details of my thank-you note.

Dress Rehearsal, Take One...

Me: "Alright, I'm gonna be up here doing this like this. You hang back there with the guitar. Here, wear these sunglasses. Know the words, right? You don't have many. I'm gonna need a lot of room up here, so be careful."

Driver: "Yeah. Is that all I'm doing?"

Me: "You want more?"

Driver: "I don't care. I'm gonna be doing my big wheels anyway."

Me: "Okay, change of plans then. This is good. It's a long song, so the more going on, the better. When the music picks up, lose the guitar and the glasses. When I drop *back* to spin around, you're gonna pull *up* and spin around with me. In unison. Two rotations on the right, two on the left. To the music. Arms and fists up like this, keep 'em level." [I demonstrate as I describe]

Driver: "You are *so* bossy."

Me: "You want to win, don't you?"

Driver: "Where did I put my beer?"

Me: "Which one?"

Driver: "What is *tane*?"

Me: "Seriously, *mechanico*? Oc-*TANE*."

Driver: "Oh."

Me: "You ready? Remember, when in doubt, just shimmy. You're an Ikette after we spin around together, so you gotta think like one."

Driver: "Anything else?"

I, Tina: *"...This is the way we do... 'Proud Mary.'"*

Ike: *"Ro – llin' – on – the – riiii-verrrrr..."*

After the first take...

Me: "That was so-so. We need to do it again. A few times."

Ike: "Naw, naw, you listen heh, Anna Mae."

Me: "Perfect. Stay in character. Let's take it from the top."

Driver: "This is ridiculous."

Me: "Shimmy."

CINCO DE MAYO

Once it started getting the kind of balmy your cleavage wants to scorn, I decided to follow up with Nick. I hadn't heard from him in nine days and began to worry he had melted or evaporated trying to walk to the house. Or worse, he'd dropped my next refrigerator magnet down a storm drain. (He and Ralph were in a flattering battle for my amour.) So, I called.

"I at auction. Still try buy car. No forget you. Promise call tomorrow. Can you hear auction? It close thirty minutes. If no car today, maybe tomorrow. But I call, okay?"

I was too busy cackling in sheer stupefaction to ask, "Well, how the hell did you get to the auction? Please have that person, place, or thing deposit you here. *Pronto.*" I didn't know why he couldn't just walk over; magnets aren't *that* heavy.

It was believed the bipedal Nick was the last person to have relations with the HVAC system at Carpet Kingdom. That is, aside from the previous people's dogs that chewed through the external hoses, wiring, and other unexplained insulation on the side of the house. And if they weren't dogs, they were javelinas. I don't know many winter white poodles that would have survived without permanent damage from such a supercharged necktie party. The mangled mesh of voltaic strands would just bow and flounder in the vindictive winds, serving as the single-most leading waste of black electrical tape I had ever laid eyes on. (If these eyes could talk.)

Delicious.

In the misadventure of my comprehensive system failure, I had forgotten about any and all Cinco de Mayo celebrations available for consumption. Until later that night. It's an event many folks take quite seriously around here, but decidedly, I'm better at Hallmark holidays than circling the fifth of May on my calendar every year.

I watched a little CNN, performed a few dutiful beauty rituals, flung open the bedroom windows, and lay down for a nice long nocturnal siesta. Driver was already passed out and snoring like a Snapper lawnmower, no idea who the Nick was I had been bitching about. All seemed pretty normal, for the most part.

Da-da-da-da-la-la-la-la-qui-qui-qui-qui-arriba-arriba-dee-dee-dee-dee-aye-aye-aye-aye-woooooooooooo! Yah-yah-yah-yah-qui-qui-qui-tongue roll-tongue roll-yaye-yaye-yaye! Caramba.

(Repeat. Repeat. Repeat. Repeat. Repeat. Repeat. Repeat. Repeat. Each time, louder.)

It's so quiet in the desert at night, even silence and restraint carries and echoes over the barren landscape like a stray pup barking in an airplane lavatory. I couldn't tell if the mariachi band and its respective cheering section were actually inside the neighborhood or just leaf-blowing with Cha-Cha instruments around the corner. Nonetheless, it was a bubbly celebration of Corona and his counterparts at someone's converted cantina in Margaritaville. My head was exploding, Anderson Cooper was just mouthing words onscreen, and I had no one else to ask if the convalescence of caterwauling was driving them batshit crazy, too.

Because of Nick's fruitless auction achievements, we would have smoldered to ash had I closed the windows. I was in a pickle how best to survive. So, as an undefeated, enterprising, and neighborly gesture, I sprang from my carrycot, shoved citrus in my satchel, and shot down to my casbah for an early grand opening with all surplus Jewish beauty products in tow. Two hours later, I returned home with a dented Pringles can full of pesos, the perfect everyday sombrero, a temporary tattoo, and someone's studded bolero jacket.

Not only do I have my main muchacho to thank for a prosperous evening and some new amigos, but the way I felt the next morning.

Sicko de Mayo.

DRIVE-BY BIRDIE

Exactly forty minutes before Sherri arrived for the weekend, Driver returned home from another drab business meeting less the sporty blazer and donning slight concern as evidenced by the weird face. Just out of the shower, my wet hair was swept up in a towel and I was headed back upstairs for the blow dryer.

Driver: "We've had some developments. I need to tell you something."

Me: "Did you lose your job?" [expressed with authentic panic]

Driver: "Oh, no. *No*. But it happened on the way home." [appearing relieved that *that* was the most of my concerns]

Me: "Okay, well go. Quickly. Time. Sherri." [tapping the invisible watch on my wrist]

Driver: "I made a deal with a homeless man on Flamingo."

Me: "Is he in the car?"

Driver: "No, but I gave him twenty dollars for what he was carrying."

Me: "And I guess *it* is in the car?"

Driver: "Yes."

Me: "Is it alive?" [really just looking for the full summary and not spotty monosyllabic responses]

Driver: "Yes."

Me: "Is it on four legs?"

Driver: "No. It is not on four legs, but it *is* alive."

Me: "Well, then you probably don't need to leave it in the car."

Driver went back outside and I raced to the closest window to peek. I spied a narrow-wired cage bobbling out of the passenger seat. A white one. And I heard a series of chirps. Piercing, shrilly chirps, like the low-battery signal a smoke alarm makes. But I couldn't see how big or what color it was. Or if there was more than one of them. I just knew it better be a bird. The grungy coop clapped the granite island countertop (that I had just cleaned) and I stared deeply at the contents as if looking into a microscope while wearing bifocals and a bulky ten-gallon topper.

Me: "Is it a Cockatiel? Or a Cockatoo? Or a *quail?*"

Driver: "Cockatiel."

Me: "How do you know he was homeless?"

Driver: "Well, I didn't ask, but he was kinda dirty."

Me: "Maybe he wanted the bird? Did you *steal* his bird?"

Driver: "He wouldn't let me have it at first. But then he wanted the money more than the bird."

Me: "So this man, who you assume was homeless, was just walking around with a bird, in a cage? On Flamingo?"

Driver: "He said he found it after that bad storm."

Me: "So this man, who you assume doesn't have a home, found a bird? And has been carrying it around for a week?"

Driver: "Yep. He found it under a tree."

Me: "So this man, who we assume has no home of his own, just so happened to have a cage? For a bird."

Driver: "He said he got the cage from a friend."

Me: "So he has a friend with bird cages, but no extra bedrooms? Did you ask his name?"

Driver: "The man or the bird?"

Me: [turning to the bird] "Hello, Mr. Winkies. Are you a boy or a girl? Can you talk? You look like you've been shot in the tail. Who has all your feathers?"

Driver: "Mr. Winkies? *Really?*"

Me: "You got any better ideas?"

Driver: "Just not that."

Me: "Hi, Mr. Winkies. Are you hungry?"

Me: [asking Driver] "Well. Let's get Mr. Winkies some food. Can it eat what Titus eats?"

Driver: "I have a bag of food, actually."

Me: "He came with food?"

Driver: "Just a small Ziploc."

Me: "He came with a *Ziploc*? Name brand?"

Driver: "Looks like wild bird seed."

Me: "Wild is right. Why does this always happen to us?"

Driver: "It just didn't seem like the best conditions for the bird."

Me: "I'm glad you stopped. Even Oprah would agree he wasn't living his 'best life.'"

Meanwhile, Sedona was standing on her hind legs at human height pressing her cavernous mouth against the Cockatiel confines, while George barked her undersized head off from the ground. The tile floor accentuated the volume and the quaking between my ears.

Driver: "Think I'm gonna take him upstairs so these guys don't freak him out."

Me: "I'll be up in a minute, Mr. Winkies."

Me, again: [Driver twisting up the stairwell] "What about Flamingo?"

Driver: "Like for a name?"

Me: "No, like for our next pet. *Yeah*. It's a *bird*, isn't it? Just seems a little uncanny that you picked up a *bird* on a street with a bird *name*."

Driver: "Well, it's better than Mr. Winkies." [fading off into the master bedroom]

I threw the clothes from the washer into the dryer and headed upstairs, hearing avian relocation sounds the closer I got to the bathroom.

Me: "Really? Did you have to put him right next to my Sonicare?"

Driver: "Oh. Sorry. There's just more room on your side."

Of course there is, I made sure of that. I have four cabinets, Driver has one. I have more products. Along with every lotion, cream, deodorant, and shave gel we could possibly need through the end of Y3K.

After Mr. Flamingo Winkies tolerated the sounds and swirls of the blow dryer two feet beyond his crate, I knew he hadn't spent too much time schlepping the streets of Las Vegas with his recent rescuer. Reportedly, a man Driver said resembled a short, blue-eyed Jesus with a duffle bag, cargo shorts, and hiking boots.

Just before Sherri arrived, we moved the new bird into the bedroom closet because the cats kept pasting themselves to the cage like state-shaped decals on a creaky RV. Driver was sure to clear off all the items from the top of my shoe shelf so he could have a nice sunny spot in front of the window. The closet is actually the size of my first apartment in Atlanta, so worry not, his conditions were more than acceptable. And Titus, just so you know, is a talking African Grey parrot. He's in his mid-twenties; they live for at least eighty years.

Driver: "I want to make sure he's not sick before we move him into Titus' room."

Me: "How will we know if he's sick? Face down on the bottom or something?"

Driver: "Something like that. Or if he's sneezing. Could have bird mites. We'll just see how the weekend goes."

Me: "Are we gonna get sick if he's sick? What if he has avian influenza or something? I don't want bird mites. Or lice. Or *any* airborne bird disease for that matter."

Driver: "He can't get us sick."

Me: "What about our clothes? I feel itchy."

Driver: "No."

Me: "Do you know if it's a boy or a girl?"

Driver: "No."

Me: "I thought you knew everything about birds?"

Driver: "Well, they can lay eggs."

Me: "Even if they haven't done it?"

Driver: "Yes. Nothing in them though."

Me: "Then how come Titus doesn't lay eggs?"

Driver: "Because Titus is a male."

Me: "Whatever."

Me, again: "So, if Mr. Winkies lays eggs, then we know it's a Mrs. Winkies?"

Driver: "Correct."

Me: "I think it's a boy. Will his feathers grow back?"

Driver: "Yes. I really don't want to call him Mr. Winkies."

Me: "Mrs.?"

Driver: "No."

No decent names came to us over the weekend, but we did realize the bird was way too loud and made *lots* of noise. Especially at sunrise, but pretty much all day long. Driver said it was a sign of happiness, but we probably didn't keep him *that* happy. Three days later, after Sherri left, we needed to redirect our focus to Sir Madame Flamingo Winkies. A better name, a new cage, some millet, and a transition strategy. The pet store only had a hunter green cage and I hate that color, but it was larger than his original casa-not-so-blanca and I knew he wouldn't care.

We set up camp in the master closet while cats and dogs whined, scratched, and whinnied through the door, under the door, and at the door. I took a few moments to do some overdue garment rearranging and we opened up the cage, assuming he would fly right out. But he just looked at us like we were two morons sitting on the floor of a walk-in closet. *His* walk-in closet.

Me: "He looks like a showgirl with those yellow feathers on his head. Do we know any famous showgirls?"

Driver: "Kevin is still the hottest showgirl we've seen."

Me: "That reminds me, we need to see *Jubilee*. Wanna call him Kevin?"

Driver: "Heeeeeeey Kevin."

CHIRP – CHIRP – CHIRP – CHIRP

Me: "Or, what if we named him Sherri?"

Driver: "Okay. But what if it's a boy?"

Me: "Well, I wouldn't want to call him Sherri if he wasn't. And he doesn't have opposable thumbs. Sherri has that weird trigger thumb thing, so it's kinda the same."

Driver: [turning to Kevin] "Heeeeeeey Sherri."

[CHIRP – CHIRP – CHIRP – CHIRP]

Me: "Alright, are you just gonna grab Sherri and put him in the new cage, or what?"

Driver: "We can't scare Sherri. We have to let him get to know us first."

Me: "How long will that take? It's starting to feel like Busch Gardens in here."

Driver: "Maybe tomorrow."

[9:15 p.m. the next day, driving home from Bingo City]

Me: "Okay, what are we going to do about that bird?"

Driver: "What if we named him That Bird?"

Me: [testing it out] "Hello, this is That Bird. I don't mind it."

Driver: "We'll sit in the closet again tonight and get That Bird in his new cage. I promise."

Me: "Bingo is fun, I'm glad we went. Moves so fast. Maybe we didn't need to start with twelve cards per page. We would have been lost without that woman. She was so nice. Did you see that lady at the end with all the rubber penis figures lined up? For luck, I guess."

Driver: "*No!* Did you get a picture?"

Me: "Couldn't. I noticed after we got going."

[After a small moment of silence, we both began to sing, "B-I-N-G-O, B-I-N-G-O, B-I-N-G-O…"]

Driver: "And *BINGO* was his *name-o!*"

Me: "Chirp!"

GUM DROPS

Sure they have them in Atlanta, but they aren't very good.

I think the Georgia Department of Transportation is all too consumed with "other" projects to be worried about a pedestrian's first-hand right to walk safely in the shadows and margins of inconsolable, oncoming traffic. But in Las Vegas, I've noticed a few unsubtle distinctions between the designated footpaths in both cities. Obviously, Atlanta is an older, more established city and I no longer dwell in any of its hundred-year-old neighborhoods. But I'm an enormous proponent of the sidewalk and a highly-seasoned and fully-equipped expert in walkway evaluation, bearing many a two-legged errand, regularly.

I won't lie. It's unbelievable just how level and clear the fashionable tracks are in a city so sinful. I took countless topples over the mangled planes possibly once disrupted by poorly-hidden carcasses in my very own frontage—both sober and schnockered, in full daylight. I slammed smack-down into the water meter cavity climbing out of cars, cabs, and grocery carts more times than I can remember. So I'm certainly not going to take this refreshing masonry for granted. But, I will say, you do notice even a minuscule blemish juxtaposed against such splendor. Stands out like a teardrop tattoo on a soccer mom.

It's an image that can only be rightfully described in refined poetic meter…

Sidewalk, sidewalk, so lovely and true

uncracked and completely even; my, you must be new
Crafted from concrete, not asphalt or brick
my high heels don't catch and my laces don't stick
I don't tumble amidst your crumbles
I don't cave in your enclaves
I glide naturally over your surface
for you are not choppy or unpaved
In Atlanta, you were rubble
where I'd rather amble in the road
But here you are pristine
and I have yet to chip a toe
You are not a threat for trip-and-falls
and I haven't once yet spilled my drink
I no longer require knee pads
just to glide without a blink
There's truly something to be said
about the little things that please
So why someone would deface you
fills me largely with unease
I know you can't defend yourself
or throw it back into their face
But these hideous wads of bubble gum
deserve a very different place
Just wait until I meet a fresh glob
with my sneaker or some other
I'll fling it back into their Mustang
and end up disappointing my own mother
So, stupid people who toss your gum
rethink this form of disgrace
Keep that crap in your mouth
or don't put it in your face
Because these sidewalks are exquisite
they did no such wrong to you
If you must dispose, stick it up your nose
so I can enjoy the view

Neat.

FIGHT CLUB

We were just two laps into the warm-up and all I could think about was lobbing a Celebrex down my throat.

Out of the clear blue, my knee parts felt like jankety antique table legs balancing a Steinway Louis XV with a rhinoceros on top. Bone bearing down on bone, I was surprised they weren't clicking aloud and unapologetically disturbing the synchronized vibrations of my focused fellow classmates.

There were only eight of us and I wrongly ended up behind Teacher for the opening drills. These included, but were not limited to, lots of sprinty, runny, lungey, sidey, leggy, lifty, shuffley things. Like agile pachyderms, the group weaved up and down the four aisles of full body-length punching bags for about ten minutes, and like clockwork I checked the time, *every time*, to confirm that only ten minutes had passed. Then everyone took their places for more overly-demanding jumpy, pushy-uppy, squatty, mountain-climby things closer to the floor.

My general fondness is starting off last in line for these psycho cardio maneuvers, in case I need to cut corners or not leave the winded Driver in plumes of my undulating dust. But sometimes, Teach ends up right behind me when I do that and the whole premeditated plan backfires like a Ford Pinto.

Driver couldn't join me for class on this particular day, something about a conference call. All I knew was that I would be getting skinny and Driver would be getting very, very fat.

Twenty-three minutes in, I forgot about my knees because I had wrapped my wrists so tightly, I was beginning to lose circulation in my soon-to-be Smurf arms. Long before I morphed into Black Bruty, overnight kickboxing sensation, I wasn't aware the proper pugilist needed to bind each hand and every knuckle with fourteen feet of stretchy Ace bandaging for support, a task that effectively slashes nine years off your autobiography. Fortunately, these elastic coils are free of charge when you spend the easy eighty-four bucks for gloves. I had chosen black wraps while Driver plucked the creepy white ones with skulls. They are really intimidating, especially when the wearer is hunched over and panting like a Saint Bernard.

To make each session's sixty minutes soar like a paper airplane through a wet vac, I try to think of trucker names for the pupils around me. This is not easy to do; there's a lot of instruction and you're supposed to keep your eyes and other body parts on the bag. That's why I go during the day, so I'm not girdled by Ultimate Fighting Champions and lingerie models who typically attend the evening or early bird curriculums. Same sequences, just more interest. And dedication.

It was actually the guy with canary yellow wrist wraps, Kelly green boxing gloves, and an unmanageable burping shtick that aroused my imagination's maiden craving for The Rename Game. He would, obviously, live on to be John Deere, though I would never see him again. I suspect he is a farmer and busy in the fields most days, regurgitating coleslaw and tuna fish sandwiches while embossing his initials in the land with an RC12 Series Row Crop Tiller. Just like an Aerosmith video, only without the skinny-dipping and teen stars.

However, I do concede, the sputtering sounds of indigestion were almost a lullaby compared to Kung-fu Man Chu's stirring verbal eruptions. Talk about distracting. It was hard enough keeping the mascara out of my eyes when I couldn't get to my fingers inside the gloves. I even checked for nunchucks because every time he made contact with the bag, a tremendous grunt would supervene. My private Pavlovian response to every groan was *"BONZAI!"* It motivated me, though, specifically when we had to race around and strike every bag with fists and shins and whatever else hadn't fallen off and died on the floor. I was really just running from him, a real-life ninja. Haven't seen him again, either; he probably saw Driver's skulls. So scary.

I didn't let on, but I grew a little melancholy when the clone of Serena Williams rolled in, dimming all of me with her marble stature. Sheer, natural, and manufactured strength unmistakable, she was a walking advertisement for overachievements in physical fitness. Though it was her first time, I knew she would still trample over us like Pamplona. Easily four feet taller than me, just in legs, her kicks marked the bag at the level of my head. If she were to miss, I would need an orthodontist. And since we'd been coached to pretend that our opponent (disguised as a suspended sack) is our "own size," I renewed my vow to always pick on people much smaller than me. However, I was relieved halfway in when Serena asked how I was able to keep going, and I answered honestly. "Girl, you gotta pace yourself. This is not the kind of place you want to give a hundred percent."

But nothing boosted the certainty of my own prowess more than when Agador Spartacus refused to participate in the kicking circuit. Blah blah blah about being a hairdresser *and* a dancer. I would have ticked through every other occupation in the *Yellow Pages* before I would have guessed either of those. He couldn't use his hands *or* his feet because it would shatter one, if not both, of his implausible professions. He needs to take up a sport that won't devastate the dexterity wedded to his livelihood. Like Checkers or staring contests. The gym is for dangerous boxers, not whiny barberinas. You either pay to rot in agony like everyone else, or you don't.

Which brings me to Jessica, the teacher who takes mere mortals from fluffy to fit in one thousand calories burned per session, however many times a day. She's a real doozie. A young Jillian Michaels with an accent over the invisible body fat. At least, I *hope* she's younger than me, by forty years. She can do things with her body that she actually thinks we flabbies can do. Therefore, Jessica is probably a robot. She knows I love to hate coming to class. She also knows I hate jumping jacks, sit-ups, and anything that involves squatting. But I adore everything else. Except the leap frog things, the crunchy things, and push-ups with the gloves on. My hands always slide out from under me and I end up disguised as an easel with Berber-shaped rugburn splotches on my forehead. I also hate too many repetitions of anything. That's too many. But I love how skinny I look when it's over.

Then we go to lunch. A big, fat one.

TRICK MY BOO

I did everything I could to coordinate the perfect All Hallows' Eve experiment. Right down to the actual participation part.

For our first year in Vegas, I needed to conduct my potential suck-fest test on a timid and understated level. One that wouldn't trigger any of my dormant phobias spawned by past first-hand experiences as getting back on the Halloween steed did not come with conviviality. I would brace myself for the worst. It was a trial that would either suggest or deny, for better or worse, what the contemporary holiday module looked like with a two thousand-mile change in backdrop, neighborhood, and approach. I wasn't up for fishing faux spider webs through the red agave, spooning dry ice from skeleton pelvises, painting my face a secondary color, or semi-altering my hair-do into a shape too complex to reclaim. But I did clip coupons for candy, heave home a damaged pumpkin, pick up some glow sticks, and sent Driver out for champagne.

I didn't flesh out an aggressive carving plan, but I did whittle a pernicious grin, strain the seeds to bake, and pull out a Viking helmet with horns. A lacking default item, I know, but one scraped from a compartment of the costume trunk reserved for gratuitous attempts and last-minute gestures. Besides, I maintained faith the kids would be more concerned with fisting my Fun Size™ than grading my garb. Driver downloaded a very unspooky playlist and we parked in two of those horrible folding chairs in the driveway. Chairs I was certain were in the trash when we left Atlanta, but were later identified as someone's rickety recovery from hoarding.

I asked the gaybors in advance if many of the kids trick-or-treated. I had only met President James and some of his stewards, a few strays, and that unexpected passel of matching children who would occasionally ride their mini-horse past the house. Therefore, I wasn't sure what other gems the community had stashed away, ready for release. The guys told me traffic, if any, would be light, that most of them go to the mall since the subdivision is gated and fairly small. When they saw us building our bizarre campsite under the portico, they advised us to turn *all* the lights on, everywhere. Then they went back inside and killed all of theirs, brainwashing their house into a pitch black and undetected fortress of invisible lines and sightless formations.

We just sat there, in those repugnant chairs. And waited. The sun had almost capsized behind the three 360-degree mountain range and we didn't see anyone or anything else with their external fixtures ablaze. We heard nary a faint rumble, heavy footstep, or the words to "Thriller" coming from anywhere other than our dinky portable speaker set. We watched cars returning home from work disappear through the garage doors that would seal behind them. A few of the passengers waved, but most of them just stared.

There I was, puzzled, selfishly hoping my half-assed efforts wouldn't be lost on the dissolution of Halloween in my immediate vicinity. Candy-beseeching, in my particular urban Atlanta areas, began when those who actually went to school, got home from school. Around 3 p.m. And the fanfare would last until you called the cops. Or bought a house in Dunwoody.

Halloween drastically brought a whole new meaning to the words "Trick-or-Treat." More like erased them, because you never heard those words. Not a chance. Instead, you heard a mishmash of the following, whether as a greeting or as a response to my questions and/or concerns…

WE WANT CANDY! You got any candy? Can I pick? I'm Batman. My cousins need some, too. You ain't got none left? Is that all you got? Why you don't got no chocolate? Why you wanme ta dance? I like Snicker. You got those? I'll take a Reese's den. You got two mo? Can I come back? This is my costume. I don't got a costume. If you have any left, can I have it? You got any gum? I'm a witch. Well, then can I come back tomorrow when you got mo? What else you got? That it? My momma, she like Reese's too. CAN-DAY! Is this where you live? I'm a vampire. Don't you got dogs? They bite? Can I see it? Do they eat chocolate? They'll eat me? I don't know what my favorite song is. Can I have a few mo? Are you sure you don't got no mo inside? I'm a ghost. Why do I have ta dance? Yeah, she know where I'm at. I need to get some mo from yo. You stay here all the time? Can I come in? Can I stay, heh?

Keep in mind, only one out of every four hundred children were wearing something that if you had your eyes crossed and closed could have been maybe-related to an actual costume. I also use *children* loosely as well. The ages ranged from anywhere between zero and twenty-five to forty. They were almost all in regular street clothes, and I was usually tossing—when they weren't grabbing—candies into some form of backpack. There were rarely any plastic pumpkin pails with a little bright glow-something inside. Not even a pillow case as a treat bag, which is already bad enough. I learned early on, if you're going to shell out way too much money in the unappreciative promotion of juvenile tooth decay, you better make them work for it.

Hence, the dancing and song-singing. I believe Halloween should be taken very seriously when you're begging complete strangers for candy. And it only happens once a year. So if you refuse to wear a costume, or fashion *anything*, you will be asked to perform. By now, it should probably be a law. Besides, there is nothing in it for childless adults who kindly throw individually-wrapped, unpoisoned treats at adolescents they don't know, especially if the recipients can't even pretend to say "Thank you" with a foamy nose or cape. Do fucking *something*.

It was soon dusk and there was no costume in sight. The neighborhood was even quieter than usual and a sliver of moon just idled in the twilight. We were still sitting in bad chairs.

Me: "What if they don't come?"

Driver: "Well, they might not. Wanna go inside?"

Me: "And do what? I want the kids to see we have candy for them."

Driver: "Okay."

Me: "Can you check the pumpkin? This chair is too low for me to keep getting up and down. Need to make sure the candle is still burning."

Driver: [slowly gets up] "Yeah, it's still on. You didn't give it a nose. How is it supposed to breathe?"

Me: "Pumpkins don't breathe through their noses. And George ate one of his triangle eyes when it flew out on the floor. The whole thing."

Driver: "That dog eats anything."

Me: "No wonder they called her a beagle at the vet."

Driver: "She's a *Chihuahua*."

Me: "I'm just repeating what they said. Vet said his beagle eats everything, too. And that his beagle is also overweight."

Driver: "She's a *Chihuahua*."

Me: "He said his beagle weighs about twenty-four pounds as well. Had to put it on a diet. And that beagles with barrel chests have to be careful with their knees. Oh, she also had to go up to the next weight level dosage for her heartworm pill."

Driver: "Did you tell him she's a *Chihuahua*?"

Me: "I told him you got her in Alabama."

Driver: "She has papers, you know."

Me: "They probably say she's a beagle."

Driver: "You're not nice."

Me: "Kids, *look!* Two of them. Ready??"

Though we had to scream for them to "come over and get some candy," they still count as our first customers. A young male pair loomed up to the driveway with what I thought was a shy limp and misery, but it was actually part of the act. I hadn't anticipated being impressed by any of these bonbon beggars, but they were professionally hemmed into character. One of them was something from either a *Wars* or a *Potter* movie and the other was a caped skeleton with an IV bag full of blood. Fake, I think.

We sat some more. And waited. Then suddenly, there were waves of them. Tiny tribes of fully-clad superheroes and witches, quarterbacks and princesses, Transformers and terrestrials, marching safely and respectfully up to the house. And they weren't yelling. They didn't even have air horns or stolen street signs. Not a single one of them came back for seconds, which means they didn't come back for thirds or fourths, either. I had been conditioned to, as the general rule of house-hopping, "just go back as many times as you want, especially if the house doesn't have any boarded-up windows or anyone napping in the yard."

And they were all wearing costumes. They even had appropriate candy receptacles and they all smiled. They thanked us and they all wished us a "Happy Halloween," reminding me, after so many years, it is supposed to be a *happy* occasion. Some even complimented the house and introduced us to their parents. Many made sure it was okay take more than one piece when we dangled the pail before them. The kids were loquacious and their conversations were wildly coherent. Even the parents were dressed up. We also found an acupuncturist.

There were only two minor instances when I had fumbles. First, when I thought the thirteen-year-old was a grown woman and tot-mom to her sister. Then again when I assumed a little girl was Santa Claus, but she was a pirate. Fortunately, her mother was gracious enough to tell me "she gets that all the time." In my defense, all I could see was crushed red velvet and a belt buckle the size of a license plate. Thanks to the gaybors' blackout, I had no backlighting.

The night's best frock happened on a long-locked gal with golden skin and curls, probably thirteen. Flanked by a trio of girls, she ran up ahead of them. When she crossed over the sidewalk to the driveway, I noticed a lightweight wisp of something streaming from her head and she was holding up her long white dress as not to trip while she sprinted. She arrived gently winded and the few inches of hiked-up garb revealed her sneakers.

Me: "Please tell me you're *The Runaway Bride!*"

Goldie Locks: "Yep. And I gotta go, thank you!"

In that very instant, I started crying. Like full moon PMS crying. I watched her dash to the next house, leaving her friends behind, all with the flip and pouf of unrestricted bliss. It was everything I needed to see for the reversal of what had become unbridled contempt for the colors orange and black. That, along with a dumpster the pig farm had commissioned to recycle jack-o-lanterns for compost. Not only did it renew my sense of Halloween, it rehabilitated my faith in humanity. Now I can peacefully browse tousled pre- and post-Halloween aisles in any given superstore and not start that twitching thing. The twitching thing usually accompanied by rapid eye movement and high blood pressure before it gets really hard to swallow.

But this can't *always* be about me.

October 31 is also Nevada Day, an official state holiday and time-honored tradition hailed with parades, banquets, and jubilees. A date that commemorates the Silver State's admission into the Union in 1864 as number thirty-six. West Virginia and Hawaii are supposedly the only other states that make such a fuss over their birthday, but I can't imagine they throw better parties.

Or get to wear costumes.

YULE SEE

Dear Virginia—

I was just thinking about what we would be doing this time of year in Atlanta. I would possibly be canning the last of my cucumbers, gearing up to complain about the wet wintery weather, and wondering how many days were left until I had to drag all of my sensitive succulents inside. The same inside where the walls were closing in because of all the boxes I had been packing for the five hundred days prior, living the recurring reverie to relocate. Together, we'd be opening boxes. Of wine.

Which reminds me.

I've started decorating for Christmas. You should see my giraffes, so dapper in green plaid. I've also developed a prototype, composed of all repurposed materials, of course. I've decided it's going to be your Christmas present. Because you're not Jewish, and it's red. (Well, *now* it's red.)

I actually began reviewing and rearranging the holiday crap in August, the hottest month in Las Vegas. I thought it would be a great way to spend the afternoon— underneath eleven smelly, taped-up-for-two-years bins labeled "Xmas"—in the garage. I should have never done it after school hours, with the overhead door wide open and the cars pulled out. Because President James decided he should be involved with my meticulous inventory. More like, nosy. Drove right up on one of his bicycles and started touching things. *Every* thing. He didn't know what anything was, so he had to ask. Which, as you know, is a very time-consuming pain in the ass.

Prez dug around in every box that I had just repacked, asking me if things were plastic or glass, seeing if they would bounce, wondering why there were two of some things and eight of another, unrolling strands of Christmas lights to count the bulbs, wondering why the soccer ball was flat (it was a volleyball), curious as to why there were so many animal crates, sitting on the scooter, asking me why I never rode the scooter, asking if he could *have* the scooter, pleading to borrow ten dollars to *buy* the scooter, and asking why I said he needed to ask permission before swinging anyone's golf clubs next to someone's automobile.

He also needed to know the name of every song half a dozen fragile china egg ornaments played. I told him it was elevator music. Then I needed to explain elevator music. And then Muzak, which led to Mozart and Mazel Tov. Topics that more than fizzled with my young audience instantly. It also made me realize you can't just tell an inquisitive mind that something cannot be touched because it's "expensive." That mind will wonder "How much?" And "how many" *that* is, with an increased amount of touching.

I couldn't manage to break down any cardboard boxes without Prez wanting to hold the X-Acto knife. On his leg. On a Santa beard. On a pair of ice skates I thought were lost. Exercises that rendered my tool defective, so he just moved right on to the next thing he saw with a blade. I tried chatting him into pure exhaustion, but it took more out of me. And I certainly couldn't talk him into *leaving*. I asked if he believed in Santa Claus and he said his parents told him there was no such thing. I told him they were wrong and didn't know what they were talking about. And that Santa is actually a woman. That, in fact, *I* was Santa. And that's why we had moved to Vegas, because the North Pole was too cold and he was currently fucking up my workshop. No place for pushy little political hopefuls who can't help but drive Lady Santa batty.

Finally, he left. But only after I white-lied about having a heat conductivity test with a copper cookie cutter. Surprise: I needed to explain what that meant. I warned him he couldn't tell his parents about anything we had discussed or he would only get a lump of coal. Remind me to dress as Santa next Halloween, I might forget. That brings me back to the prototype. I'm (almost) concerned the concept may be too much. It might really take off and then I will have to turn my workshop into a full-scale factory. And, more than likely, I'd need to hire James and Oscar the Veep to do all the work in my garage, never being able to escape the biggest question as to *why I would turn a toilet seat into a Christmas wreath.*

Thanks to James harvesting the seat from the left side of the garage somewhere, I wouldn't have been so efficient with my holiday brooding. I've got the house underway, the place settings accounted for, the cards on order, and most importantly, your Holy Crap Christmas Craft in the hopper. I also have designs for the lid part, but that's more like a Leap Year gift.

You'll notice I still had some jingle bells left over from Miss Titsy Van Karpelstein's 2010 Christmas Dills and some of those jar rings I never knew what to do with. Those would probably explain why my dills made some recipients ill. But the audio on this beauty is incredible. I think you could also use it as a wind chime if you wanted to. It's coming together quite nicely, but I'm far from done. Please advise if you want it to be a little bit kountry, or just keep it klassy. I really want it to be the wreath of your dreams.

So you will always know that, yes Virginia, there *is* a Santa Claus.

TWELVE

Perhaps you, too, might be curious as to when the Twelve Days of Christmas actually begins.

And with some due diligence, you would also learn when it ends. That is, if you have a positive command over first grade math. You may also wonder if there is a true and deeper meaning behind the catchy cumulative chant, or if it's just one of the many holiday theme songs crazy Christian folk roll out every wintery season, regardless of the exact date.

Or perhaps, you already know or never cared.

Every once in a while, I feel decision-makers should hand the song over to Hanukkah because Jewish people have fewer jingles and more days on the menorah to count anyway. I just assumed it was a starry-eyed limerick sung by an amorous gal who would constantly repeat what her sweetheart *sent* her, *gave* her, or *said* to her— depending on the version or your hearing—all twelve days in a row. I'm sure it was first bellowed from a window sill, or the Matterhorn, while everyone within earshot blew fuchsia rose petals through hula hoops and bounced baby ducklings on beach balls. Awash with pride and elation, awestruck parents were woozy planning a shotgun wedding for the hamlet's youngest lovers.

I didn't know the song was originally published in 1780 England, but I did notice his gifts to be rather dated. I was pleased they were creative displays and not so trite and materialistic. Just noisy. Because she, whom I will call Paulette, racks up twenty-three members of the fowl family in the first seven days. All of which are a nice complement to a dozen drummers, an orchestra, and those eight cows the maids have to milk. Smells and bells, not unlike Catholic Mass. Or a Future Farmers of America convention.

I can see how Paulette's seventy-eight presents would be perceived as a bit much by the town two hundred and thirty years ago. I'm sure her broken-record bragging didn't help matters, either. To boot, additional unmentioned and often overlooked expenses include the twelve drum sets, the eleven horns, nine women's dance costumes, as well as the cattle acquisition. Musical instruments, couture, and livestock are *not* cheap, people. Never were.

I also learned the carol is thought to be French (like the hens) in origin. All because of Paulette's particular partridge. The red-legged version was not successfully integrated into British life until the time the song was documented. Since it is believed the song is older than historical records—coupled with the fact that partridge in French is *perdrix* (pronounced per dree)—the line was supposed to be: *A partridge, une perdrix.* From the looks of it, there was never a tree. At least one wearing pears. A produce item really only made popular for the holidays by Harry & David, two wise men I wouldn't be surprised are Jewish. Like Jesus.

The calling birds—the Four Gospels—were intended to be *colly* birds, but no one could hear over the band. And either of the two still sounds better than black birds, which are only baked into pies when singing anyway. Songwriters must have been working around the numbers and not the actual gifts because I would never associate golden rings with the five books of the *Old Testament.* Man's fall from grace sounds like a tragedy, not jewelry.

"Geese a-laying" makes the most sense because so many stories say there were six days of Creation. "Swans a-swimming" fails to remind me of the seven Sacraments, but I'd need to know what the seven gifts of the Holy Spirit were to validate an analogy in the first place. "Maids a-milking" refers to the eight Beatitudes and I don't know what those were, or are, either. But it's definitely a misspelled or made-up word; just look at it. The nine Fruits of the Holy Spirit may very well be pears, but I'm not sure if those are exciting enough to make grown women break into dance.

That's when I decided to ask my mom if she knew any of this stuff and she agreed the song had only one simple purpose. To be sung, in December.

So mark your calendar for December 25 because it's the first day of Christmas. Which, some may argue, is the *only* day of Christmas. And thus, the last day of Christmas is January 6, just in time for the Feast of the Epiphany, whatever that is. But conveniently, there is always plenty of fresh milk, eggs, and live entertainment on hand. True Love's gifts are very giving. And busy.

And since all of mankind knows that no one can improve on a classic (not even me), I wrote a song *on* the twelfth day of Christmas that is sure to get every Jew and gentile off their feet and into the holiday spirit. So, to the tune of Vanilla's 1989 "Ice Ice Baby," a ditty that sampled Queen and David Bowie's 1981 "Under Pressure," I present my very own contribution to tradition.

"12 Dayz of Chrismukkah"
(This one's for you, Gilda Sue)

Yo, Vegas
Let's kick it

No more ice storms [Atlanta]
No more ice storms [Atlanta]

Alright, shop. Decorate and glisten
Bad poetry is back with a brand new edition
The season, greetings me tightly
Flows like a Cosmo, daily and nightly
Is Elvis still alive? Yo, I think so
Who needs the Nutcracker, there are a thousand Cirque shows
Always extreme, my menorah has candles
Light up the tree and tie bows on the animals
Dance. And hang the mistletoe in June
It's never too early to prepare with hot glue
Bellies. Full of fruitcake and jelly
Anything less than twelve is a felony
Love it or leave it, you better count days
Naughty or nice; me and Santa don't play
If there's a holiday, Yo, I'm tryin' it

Check out the sleigh, while my Driver flies it

No more ice storms [Atlanta]
No more ice storms [Atlanta]

Vanilla. Icing on my cookies

So now that the mazel is jumpin'
You either did or didn't learn sumpthin'
Long-winded to the point, to the point I'm makin'
Christmas has a dozen, like breakfast has bacon
Rollin', with my kosher Hos
Behind eight reindeer so the beard can blow
My elves on standby, spinnin' dreidels with the rabbi
Did we fly? Yep. Across a Christmas sky
Kept on, pursuing each and every stop
For all the boys and girls, on every city block
Then we were done, Yo, so I said in Hebrew
To Fashion Show Mall, Saks Fifth Avenue!

HOOD WINKS

No. I wouldn't call it *sentimental.*

Because that would intimate being teary-eyed and weepy, suggesting some kind of longing or pleasant pining for a distant memory or relic that now finds itself, or selves, resting peacefully in a hand-carved hope chest at the foot of an elaborate four-poster bed. One that slings shadows across a rare oriental with a canopy on top. (Canopies make everything so romantic.)

And I wouldn't call it *maudlin*, either. That's essentially just a more dramatic synonym for the aforementioned word.

So maybe it's *reminiscent.* Because that would generally imply that something just came to mind, passing through, ambling along on its self-minding way. When there are no overwhelming feelings or hankerings for emotional outburst that begs for one more chorus or encore.

Kind of like… I saw a beer can and thought of you. Or, that woman named Jan who collects cans.

Because everyone old enough to know knows that if you need to force more brews into the fridge, you need to err on the side of aluminum, not glass. It's much easier to stack, situate, calculate, geometrate, and facilitate with cylinders than you can with longneck bottles. So while unloading a case of beer, I was delivered to a previous time and place—smack dab in the middle of our old Atlanta neighborhood.

Recycling was a hot commodity in that area. It was a way Earth-conscious neighbors looked out for one another, or came together, while trying to keep the combined greenhouse gas emissions to a minimum. There was always someone happy to take anything off your hands that you left unchained to your front porch, in a jiffy. Living with the fear of anything going to a landfill had to be forsaken, once and for all. The object would successfully continue with purpose. Of some kind.

Though it wasn't a justifiable subdivision with gates and guards, walls or dividers, there was still a volunteer association and city guidelines. Regulations mandated that any items for discard could never be placed streetside, at the curb, any earlier than twenty-four hours prior to the scheduled trash collection day. On our street, that was midweek. But it didn't really matter. You could put anything outside—regardless of when it was, what it was, how big it was, how eco-vengeful it was—if you wanted it out of your house. It would disappear. *POOF: Just like that.*

Right now, I feel so compelled to share some examples of the community camaraderie and conveniences. But just a few, the fruits are much too sweet!

Favors. Seven minutes after I set Driver's perfectly good weight bench outside one day, I heard a fellow bellow over the six-foot privacy fence. "Hey. Hey thah. We gonna need the weights, too," chimed the team of two retired (unemployed) men, heaving the mangle of bars and cushioned seat over their shoulders like a boom box. They were not in a truck or van, just on foot, tending to their nine-times-a-day stroll past the house to the inconvenience store, *via the alley.*

Much more than twice I was asked to borrow the hose, which only dragged out the request to use my water. I'd also drop scraps of wood over the fence and all applicable gatherers would inquire about a saw. Like, if they could *have* one. By yelling. But the rotten azure blue Adirondack chair went the fastest. I hadn't even turned to trip over the cracks in the sidewalk when the sonless Sanford pulled up. I was scorned for not providing an even number, or at least *two.* He didn't know where his wife was going to sit and I had a hand in that. Chivalry is not dead at his castle, my lords. It is extinct.

Amenities. Upon our western relocation, I believed I'd miss having a small, unfrequented post office within walking distance of the house. It was so convenient and there was never a wait, primarily because the people in line were usually just getting *a* stamp. Or money order. I felt it was unwise to leave anything in the mailbox, even small parcels I had marked with "Return to Sender." For one, someone stole my red outgoing flag, and two, the box door didn't close. Hung wide open. Sure, I could have gotten an entirely new mailbox, but that would have just brought a brand new wave of attention to my Bed Bath & Beyond coupons. And those are like gold, honey.

I also thought I would miss how consistent our mailman was with his very punctual routine. High noon, every day. I would make a point, whenever humanly possible, to be home so I could immediately run out and clear the contents. The box was Elysian Fields for wasps to congregate because people of all ages would set their lollipop sticks and chicken wing bones in there on their way to visit friends or drug dealers on the other side of the park, *via the alley*. These mail runs had to be swift and focused because there were a few neighbors following my schedule, too. If there was even one slight detour to pick up a Colt 45 bottle in the yard, I'd be contending with several appeals for donations.

Events. Yard sales were always interesting. After my first, I was known as the Yard Sale Lady with the Big Dogs. Fortunately, I've been called worse. Wish they would have called me the *Crazy* Yard Sale Lady and left me alone. But that's what you get for putting glitter on your fluorescent pink signs. People stole those, too; I guess so they wouldn't forget my address. Several of my patrons felt it was okay to just knock on the door because they "didn't have any money" when they were shopping my merchandise, five months prior. I once let a grown man on a women's bicycle put a tape recorder on layaway but still let him take it home without payment. That was the *go-away* program. He did come back to pay, though, in quarters and a few warm crinkly paper bills, demanding batteries and blank tapes because he didn't like to cross big intersections. On his lady bike.

The last yard sale was the most memorable, when preparing for the move. I held this one an entire year before we knew we were going anywhere, but I wanted to be ready. That day, a woman set her eight-month-old grandbaby in Driver's lap and left. We didn't know where she was going or if she was ever coming back. I ended up just *giving* her the antique Radio Flyer trike she wouldn't shut up about because by the time she finally returned, the kid was old enough to ride it. That was all well before the older gent driving a bamboo cane kept shuffling by, coughing up repulsiveness, with both beady eyes drilling holes into an army green futon from somewhere deep inside the storage unit, and Driver's past. By the end of the day it hadn't sold, even at fifteen dollars. Big ticket items like that were generally tougher sales; my shoppers knew how to negotiate. And hover, just like Swisher Sweet smoke. So it was a miracle how he didn't have a limp or need the cane when we told him he could just have it if he had friends to help him haul it off. I guess futons cure polio. He deadlifted it up to his ear, buoyed that thing on his back, and carried it into the sunset. Alone.

Celebrations. It wasn't really a part of town that you could decode the correlating bash or blowout by the shape or color of the balloons tethered to the mailbox. Because they weren't usually balloons. They were more like shoes, dangling from the overhead power lines. Though that man at the end of the street—about ten doors past Boy and Boot's house—did have an astounding inflatable autumnal display strewn about his lawn each year. A pilgrim, an Indian, *and* a turkey. Impressive really, he blew something up for every season. All were the size of those jumpy moonwalk things—which, don't get me wrong, also dotted the neighborhood on special occasions. I called them "Homecomings." This was when someone would be released from prison, free on parole, or returned from some other form of estrangement, and the whole family would unite. Sometimes, they'd have t-shirts made.

Which, in no exact way, brings me back to recycling. Atlanta bins are easily one-third the size of the chest-high tumblers we have in North Las Vegas. And we have two of them, just for recycling. We were lucky in Atlanta, though, to have had two. To have *maintained* two, I should say. An extra was anonymously provided for us because the house was on a corner. And across from a park, abut *an alley*, and at a bus stop. The second wasn't for our benefit; it was additional seating because there weren't any benches. But for that one day a week, they were thrones for the bus people. Or anyone else who needed a break from walking through the park to the inconvenience store, *via the alley*. It was a regular and constant pedestrian process that would transform our dogs into a ferocious Iditarod sled team, training at a nuisance-barking agility course that looped both indoors and out. Driver refused to ever work from home. Even during that gruesome bout with septic shock, still went to the office.

Although Jan the Can and I never met for coffee or sweet tea, I know she meant well. She's the kind of gal you'd want to win the lottery, just to see what she'd do with her jackpot. She would always remember one of our dog's names. "Geow-jah." But she never recognized me, ever. Saw her every day. Think she thought I was eight different people, and we all lived there with Geow-jah. The Can was regularly surprised I would remember her name, but I'm not that amazing. It's just hard to forget a woman named Jan who collects cans. She was always polite on her recycling nights when she would seize the bonanza avenues with her friend, a garbage bag, a plastic cup, and a carton of cigarettes. There was someone constantly on the other end of her cell phone and she would still host conversations with everyone on the street while they held the line.

Like clockwork, she'd ask by howling over the fence if we had any cans, and I, as one of Georgia's handlers, would tell her she could root through the bin. Most times, she would put the top back on while making an unambiguous note that our number of cans was disappointing. And she was sure to tell me, every single one of me. But I couldn't help her. Vodka is only bottled, in glass, and I can't drink it *that* fast anyway. Especially if she's saving her recycling money to buy something outside of walking distance, *via the alley.*

So, no. I wouldn't call it sentimental. But for a long time, I did call it *home.*

DAY TRIPS:
HAVE DRIVER, WILL TRAVEL

SPRING TRAINING

It's beguiling to think a southwestern, subtropical climate slam-bang in the parched Mojave Desert was once a territory lush with wild grasses and a lavish water supply.

No one at show-n-tell these days would ever believe that an area spanning 135.86 square miles—of which less than one percent is now liquid—used to be a fertile port for natural refreshment, rejuvenation, and development. Wetlands, a marsh. Such stats aren't too shabby for a set of coordinates two thousand feet above sea level, proud landlord to almost four thousand hours of sunshine and barely four inches of rain per year.

But when you think about it, Vegas is cradled in a valley—an ideal spot to find water surrounded by the all-encompassing arms of motionless, pastel-colored mountains. It was the epitome of a true oasis, one that provided rest and recuperation for the Paleo-Indians some ten thousand years ago and became home to the Anasazi tribe about the time we swapped BC for AD. And later, it became a significant stop discovered by European Rafael Rivera along the Old Spanish Trail in 1829, a 1,200-mile trade route between New Mexico and Los Angeles. In the 1840s, John C. Fremont—"The Great Pathfinder" who led expeditions and charted topographical reports—arrived when it was still part of Mexico, describing two enticing springs he found in a journal. (To note, he found the springs, not a diary that was leaking.)

So pull up your learning panties—this is important. I'm serious. You're about to get an easy-to-swallow explanation of how Las Vegas was born. And in case you didn't know, Las Vegas is Spanish for "The Meadows."

In 1855, Brigham Young sent a bushel of his zealous missionaries down to convert the Southern Paiute Indians to Mormonism and Vegas became the site of the Mormon Fort. Along a sumptuous creek, it was an appealing locale to plant trees and fashion a Mormon way station to conduct Mormon business and kick up their Mormon knickers halfway between their Salt Lake City headquarters and San Bernardino branch. Needless to say, the Paiutes weren't interested in plural marriage, popular sovereignty, and slavery, so tensions surrounding religion began to seethe. The Indians launched a few teasing raids on the camp and wound up in the Utah War (or Mormon Rebellion) from 1857-8, marking the departure of the Mormon mission. Basically, it was a pretty useless, fourteen-month brawl between the Latter Day Saints and the US Armed Forces. I don't even remember hearing about it or learning about it, but then again, I don't even know what day of the week Latter falls on.

In 1865, miner Octavius Gass purchased the 960-acre Mormon Fort and turned it into a large-scale operational ranch for locals and pioneers. The estate was jazzed up with a blacksmith and small store, a spot where many passing through would leave and retrieve messages imperative. By 1881, Gass had defaulted on a loan and the ranch was passed to cattleman Archibald Stewart and his wife, Helen J. Although Archie perished in an 1884 gunfight, Helen and her family kept the isolated ranch running for many years after his death, despite Archie's failure to leave a will and promise that Vegas was only a temporary stop in their matrimony. At the time of her husband's demise, Helen was pregnant and had to wrestle with probate, as well as champion for permission to sell the property, which she cited as reasons involving the children's education. Today, a portion of that very adobe structure still stands as a Nevada state park at the intersection of Washington Avenue and Las Vegas Boulevard.

The State Land Act of 1885 began doling out sections of this pale brown Orovada soil for $1.25 per acre. (I know, coulda-woulda-shoulda.) Farmers then started to move in after learning there was sufficient water for their fields and orchards from the aquifers, branding agriculture the dominant industry for the next twenty years. By the late 19th century, things were really hopping for the zone that coddled the ruins and remains remembered as the "Lost City," a tract once inhabited by tribes of Native American Indians who were undeniably pushed around and away from their homeland.

But they hadn't seen nothin' yet.

When Helen J. Stewart, "The First Lady of Las Vegas," caught wind of the railroad and land speculation started stirring inflation, she prepared her children and her own property for a sale. In 1902, she signed a contract with Montana senator and entrepreneur William A. Clark, selling the ranch and some water rights to the San Pedro, Los Angeles and Salt Lake Railroad for a slick $55 thousand. Stewart reinvested in nearly another thousand acres as well as a smaller plot adjacent to the family's cemetery named "Four Acres," a plat that was not part of the Clark deal. She lived there for the rest of her life, becoming the first woman to sit on the county school board and on a jury. She was known for her primitive basket collection, her wine, her knowledge of Las Vegas history, as well as her active involvement in what finally grew into a *society*—one that included other women—something she had been longing for since her arrival with Archibald.

Motivated by Clark, the completion of the main railway made The Meadows an ideal outpost to refuel and relax in 1905, an ingredient that officially substantiated Las Vegas as a city. Embracing many conveniences realized by the Gold Rush, this tent town was also the perfect staging point for mining in the surrounding spaces. In only one day, Clark auctioned off 1,200 lots from the Stewart transaction in the downtown area. And in the summer of 1909, William found his name on the map, when the State Legislature formed Clark County.

The railroad yards were built along what was then an unpaved Fremont Street, still a dim lane until the first neon sign was raised at the Oasis Café in 1929. The original Union Pacific Railroad Depot is now home to the Plaza, a treasure that opened in 1971 and punctuates one end of the Fremont Experience. It's been the world's only railroad station located *inside* a hotel-casino. Shocker.

During my regularly scheduled geological pursuits, no stone was unturned. I bumped into an article from Megan Sever published in November 2005's *Geotimes*, one that does a top-notch job explaining many things I had been contemplating. Had I tried to translate the rest without plagiarizing, it would have looked like plagiarism. So below is a paraphrased and palatable quip.

The valley itself is a broad sedimentary basin at the southern end of the Basin bounded by the Spring Mountains and Red Rock Canyon to the west, Frenchman Mountain and Lake Mead to the east, the McCullough Range to the south, and the Sheep and Las Vegas ranges to the north.

All I needed were the names of the mountain ranges so I'd know exactly what I was looking at from all edges of my alluvial deposits. What's even crazier, I had wanted to live at the end of a tectonic province for as long as I can remember. And not just any end, but the *southern* end.

We learned about much of this scientific stuff at the Springs Preserve—180 acres of pure peace, reflection, and magnetism. Some may see it as just an open outdoor area for weddings, eventful activities, and vibrant specimens, but it's truly a spiritual sanctuary, finalized and opened to the public in 2007. Outfitted with galleries, a library, art installations, outdoor amphitheatre, weekly farmers market, Nature Exchange, Desert Living Center, Nevada State Museum, and hands-on Origen Experience— this is a field trip's field trip. One with every means and excuse to absorb the stories of fault lines, rock formations, settler evolution, environmental erosion, the flora, the fauna, and the vegetation indigenous to what went into creating the most frequented sector of the Silver State.

Springs Preserve is a refined and calm diversion from the hyped and stereotyped landmarks of Las Vegas, one that lures you back to center if you let it. An unfettered and nurtured realm of reconnection to the earth and its innate design, all built around the original water source and infrastructure for the city, aptly named the Las Vegas Springs.

Sealed in its most organic shape on South Valley View Boulevard, it's hard to imagine you're in the throes of The Entertainment Capital of the World. It presents a humbling reminder, a basic revelation, and a hard-to-believe reality that this very dollop of geography could once only sling innocent echoes and undulating water into the bold and fine contours of the desert landscape—back when things were untainted by man, machinery, and modernization just a little over a hundred years ago.

Powered by hydrogen and solar resources, the Gardens at Springs Preserve fulfill eight acres of the sprawling LEED-certified campus, grounds that also include several miles of hiking trails and nature walks that weave and wander through the self-sustained set-up just a few miles west of Downtown. From the upstairs Café, guests are exposed to an unmatched vantage point that oversees and observes what fruits the basin bears. The Café balcony offers a perspective of the entire valley so rich and rare; you'll gain a whole new understanding and appreciation for the layout of Las Vegas. It's a venerable vista that triangulates "the birthplace of Las Vegas" at your very feet, while the Strip and Fremont District salute you from ten and two o'clock. On a day dusty or clear, you can see what Las Vegas is made of.

And how it was made.

CLOSE ENCOUNTERS OF
THE NERD KIND

I really don't know where to start.

I guess I could begin with a soupçon from the dialogue before we left the house and a pericope from the conversation on our way home. I've also always just wanted to use those two words in a sentence, even if incorrectly.

[1 p.m.]

Me: "Wonder if there'll be total geeks there?"

Driver: "You mean, besides us?"

[9 p.m.]

Me: "I can't believe we picked those people up off the side of the road."

Driver: "*And* gave them a ride to the airport."

Ever since we tried to go to the Las Vegas 51s baseball game, I had been intent on visiting the elusive Area 51, for which the local minor league team was (re)named. Seems as though most people are somewhat familiar with this reclusive top-secret test and research region about 130 miles north-northwest of Las Vegas, except me.

According to unnamed folks and endless lore, official guardsmen are allegedly authorized to utilize lethal force for nosy rubberneckers and prying eyes that get too close to the unconventional military facility. It's also known as Groom Lake, Dreamland, Paradise Ranch, Watertown Strip, Home Base, and most recently, Homey Airport. (Maybe it really just has fifty-one names.) I had heard all you can see from the distant dirt leading into the base is a "No Trespassing" sign, probably fashioned with barbs and high voltage wires, surveillance cameras, satellites, biometrics, alligators, and gargoyles. But I wouldn't know. Our adventure, planned exclusively around finding all highlighted uber-Trekkie points of interest, was slashed by unforeseen diversions. Diversions that included wildlife photography, landscape memorabilia, potty breaks, the 24-hour Alamo Truck Stop, a shoe in the road, and so on.

We were mesmerized by this shoe and what its story may have been.

Our predicted two-hour excursion unfolded into a four-hour safari to find the small settlement known as Rachel. A town that (per my observation) bears no more than a modest Baptist church and the beloved Little A'Le'Inn. The latter is a double-wide and/or converted trailer with an assortment of other trailerettes to its rear that moonlights as a restaurant-bar-gift shop and lodge for passers-through, passers-by, and avid alienophiles—in no particular order. I don't know if that's really a word, but I do know it's definitely not to be confused with oenophile—a wine connoisseur—which is, furthermore, not to be confused with wino.

This place has incredible props.

You may recognize the name of this locale because it had a generous cameo in the 2011 Universal Pictures movie, *Paul*. We watched it the night before as part of our pre-paranormal pep rally, a quick crash course in quirk. But once there in the flesh, we were told by the three locals and the bartender that it was not the actual setting for the film. Producers, star Jane Lynch, or whomever—only came there, bought a bunch of trinkets, and recreated the set somewhere in New Mexico. I'm guessing Roswell. At least, I think they said New Mexico, could have been Arizona. Do forgive, the A'Le'Inn has a very full bar and did a superhuman job making naïve city folk feel very, very welcomed. They should have shot the movie there, on site, because the original cast is superb.

The other two young guys at the ten-or-so-seater bar were only transitory, breaking from their long and accomplished day of sand-buggying through the wide open *nada* in a rusty jalopy I assumed was only yoked up on a flatbed behind their shiny red pickup because it had been excavated from a junk yard down the road. They were both a good decade younger than me, but I was still flattered when one of them called me a MILF. To my face.

Of course, I introduced us to everyone. All six or so. I was also sure to ask if anyone had any personal experiences with unidentified flying objects while I gummed my delicious grilled turkey sandwich. A quiet gent at the end of the bar started recounting something, but I couldn't hear him. He was confirming wild brushes with otherworldly life forms, so I nodded appropriately when his loose expressions told me to do so while the bartender kept adding more personality to my rocks glass. Another wise elder with a full, thick head of light hair spoke unlike any of the other patrons, especially when he asked for permission to come talk to me. How polite? He asked Driver for the same permission, to come over and talk to me. I told him he would need to wait just a moment while I went to the rest room, which was *not* behind the door labeled "Maliens." *Whoopsie.*

Turns out, Friendly Fred— whose name I, unfortunately, cannot remember—was a native Georgian. Vidalia, to be specific. Interior chatter about the man suggested he was the mayor or something. Or had deep pockets. Or just had a cool house and did a lot of entertaining because he invited us over. I still can't believe we tried to find him. It was probably safer that we didn't, for his sake.

Now I remember, he invented the onion.

On the way home from Rachel, well after sunset and about twenty miles from the house, Driver noticed a couple stranded on the side of the road. Between the gradual slow of the car and the set of eyes to my left peering into the rear-view mirror, I thought we were getting pulled over by the police. And by that time, I was in no shape to explain the cranberry juice on my culottes. Their debilitated vehicle had left the young parents, in from somewhere Utah-based, helpless. They were headed to the big city of Vegas to buy khakis for their kids, something about start of school the next day. As a good MILF, I should have known back-to-school cycles and rituals, but my children only chew and puke up their wooden rulers on the floor.

Six hours they had been there—without water, temps bounding over one hundred degrees, not a single soul had stopped. For the record, this would have never happened to moi. And not just because my mom still pays for my AAA Membership, just because. So, without any advanced notice, Driver jumped out of the car against oncoming traffic to offer roadside assistance. To make myself useful, I offered them beverage service from our scantily-clad cooler. We also provided iPhone chargers, the use of our phones, and Driver almost invited them for a sleepover. Meanwhile, I couldn't shut up. All I kept saying was, "I'm so glad you guys are *normal.*" After about eight times, the female passenger said the same thing to me, but with a more sarcastic inflection over the word *you.* Long story even longer, we drove them thirty miles to the airport so they could at least rent a car at such a late hour. We were pretty sure if they didn't have khakis in their township, they probably didn't have a runway either.

But enough about the strangers, we need to get back to the extraterrestrials.

To me, aliens are kind of like Jesus, though not in a religious sense. I may be alone in this, but I don't know anyone who has ever seen or met Jesus personally. But in our image of him—from our mind's eye, depicted in stained glass sanctuaries, or drawn in illustrations otherwise—he is portrayed as a thirty-something male with long brown hair, full mustache and beard, cloaked in a cascading white robe, often accented with a colored sash, either barefoot or in sandals, and sometimes surrounded by contented sheep. This reflection is a lasting one, generally universal and transcendental.

Similarly, I don't know anyone who has ever met an alien face-to-face, either. Except that sweet guy at the bar whose interview was unintentionally interrupted by the well-mannered onion virtuoso. But our general sketch of the alien typically consists of a jumbo egg-shaped head, football-sized almond eyes, skeletal limbs, and electronic or swishy gestures. Or some variation thereof, depending on their address in outer space. Only with exception to the Great Gazoo from *The Flintstones* do we really prescribe antennas for our fellow Martians, and even those were on his helmet. But when necessary, we are still persuaded to saturate such likenesses with greenish skin so we don't confuse them with anything else. That same kind of automatic response regarding cerebral and commercial assignment of common characteristics for the extraterrestrial is often applied to Jesus Christ as well. It's just what we do.

Scientifically speaking, and as backed by *Paul*, these recurring and identifiable portrayals of aliens (and Jesus) must come from somewhere. Because our brains can't be that smart. Have these two icons actually been seen, heard, or felt? Or, psychologically speaking, are the phenomena just mashed so far into our subconscious, they are exactly what we *expect* to see, think, and feel?

Maybe it's all just a little grey area called *51*.

PEAK SHOW

Mom always told me to just count the trees.

And at an average speed of sixty-five miles per hour, do you know how many trees there are between the central west coast of Florida and the middle of North Carolina? More than any self-respecting fourth-grader should ever know. It didn't take long for Mom to add a key adverb to the end of her lighthearted time-passing plan after I got to about forty-seven. "I meant *quietly*. You should count them *quietly*. You know, to yourself."

I don't remember ever stopping to pee on those junkets, but I do remember the dense population of my father's super-huge American-made company cars that would deliver us there, rain or shine. I was really good at holding it back then. And now I pee all the time, whenever I want. *I love being an adult!* But it should also be known that I don't remember drinking anything on those expeditions, either. I only remember Fruit Roll-Ups, Goldfish, and granola bars, arriving at my grandparents' house parched and bloated, yet welcomed by Speedy's Bar-B-Q and a pretty pink powder room.

Those summer family road trips—probably three—were exactly what I thought about when we made that life-changing left on Kyle Canyon Road. About thirty-five miles northwest of Las Vegas proper, Mount Charleston is an easy getaway from the city heat and all of its sultry seduction and plush production. As you climb through the Spring Mountain range, the towering tree-lined terrain makes you feel nowhere near a desert, nowhere near a city, nowhere near a Cirque show. It's more like Flagstaff or Colorado, or waving a bubble wand inside the watercolor pages of an Olde English fairy tale. The layers of sumptuous wilderness and unsullied forestry stretch out before you like a big screensaver and the environment assumes an entirely different temperament (and temperature) than Las Vegas.

To the surprise of no one, things cool down as you head up, producing what exciting nature types call "climate zones." And because of those, "life zones" consisting of various plant and animal species are formed—six, to be exact. They say it's like traveling through habitats from the desert southwest to the Canadian Arctic. (Once, Tammy and I made it from Niagara Falls to Florida in a day, even with that hinky hold-up at Customs. So anything's possible, I guess.)

I really didn't spend much time in Blue Ridge, geographically Atlanta's closest mountain collection. I didn't need to. After my first fraudulent snow skiing attempt freshman year of college in one of the Virginias, when I was told "lessons are for sissies," I grew coolly disinterested in lofty land stacks frosted in anything white, cold, or slippery. And, when you're from Florida, where the overall topography is wet and nearly concave, it's natural to assume that *any* earthen mass above sea level has been snowed on, to be skied upon. Ultimately, that first swig of wintery ski weather, accidental cliff diving, and bruisy plum-colored kneecaps set the tone for my maximum threshold with chilly hillsides.

So from that journey forward, I wanted my mountains covered only in cocktail umbrellas and coconuts, along a warm wedge of diaphanous water somewhere that looked expensive and was overrun by elevators, room service, and a valet. Sloshing around face down in a dirty Slurpee with a couple of pointy sticks and polar bears wasn't my idea of a vacation, especially after the long-ass drive up there in somebody's dad's conversion van. Mind you, a drive spent devoid of any tree-counting given my windowless rotations on the floor between two captain's chairs.

And *that* college ski trip kinda felt like driving over to Winter Haven for softball tournaments when I was a preteen. But back then, someone's dad *was* driving the van, not someone's boyfriend who wasn't yet old enough to rent from Hertz. And that softball dad would talk to the other van dads on CBs and we all used the nicknames that were ironed on our hat brims as handles. Back then, I was known on the open road as Peanut,

Hollywood, or Attitude Problem. I also remember getting chiggers one year and had to ride home in the way back with all the bat bags. Chiggers are assholes.

Hopefully you can see the van behind my big trophy.

Meanwhile, back in contemporary times Nevada, fresh air and a kicked-open atmosphere accessorize the slow and steady incline up to the Resort at Mount Charleston. Just beyond, the path up to the Mount Charleston Lodge gets a bit trickier, but not really. Just for those of us with traumatic vestibular and inner ear concerns enhanced predominantly while in motion—when *all* motion becomes circular, cyclonic, curly, and feels like a drive-thru car wash. It's a stunning route and a photogenic illustration that transitions from the characteristically coarse burnt orange rock to fuzzy green blotches of scratchier textures that hover over tall formations in the distant shadowy mirages. Mirages that become ancient bristlecone pines the closer you get and the higher you twist through the enchanted forest with lots of campsites and visiting vehicles loaded with Cheetos, coolers, and other substances fit for a forest fire.

We drove through several zones of life and climate to reach the pinnacle; or at least the uppermost height without plowing through the friendly strand of shackles blocking the rest of the road. I believe we had stumbled upon the closed Ski & Snowboard Resort. At almost 12,000 feet, the Charleston Peak is known for its stark white snowcaps visible more than half the year. Snowcaps we can see from the backyard, which, I won't lie, is pretty enviable. Especially when all we could see from our deck in Atlanta were wilty deposits of dog drizzle, a dead and disorderly pecan tree, some droopy power lines, a moldy gap-toothed privacy fence, and the family who would stare back at us through their untreated kitchen and master bedroom windows. The mom had a remarkable lineup of sports bras.

Driver was in heaven contemplating the mere allegory of a solitary woodland living initiative atop Mount Charleston, jeering at adult-sized Lincoln Log cabins built high up on the rock precipice that faces nothing but a large, deep pinyon pine valley occupied by antelope squirrels. To daydream of dangling over the side of a big branchy heap, far from any bandwidth or cell tower, would be a wish come true for my chauffer. Pure agony with a side of sicko for moi. You couldn't get me to make one of those carbonate cliffside cottages my permanent residence if it meant looking like Cindy Crawford and sprouting a brand new superpower. The notion of ever lacing chains around car tires in extended winter months, squatting over a toboggan to hit bottom, navigating with questionable night vision to get to Walmart at 2 a.m. for glitter glue—not an atom inside me could comply with such a lifestyle. It takes a special kind of person to live thumbtacked to the rim of a quarry.

And I'm not her.

In truth, it's really not that high of a mountain. You know, compared to Everest or something. But it's high enough when driving through on an empty stomach, with a lightheaded head and mild curiosity about the sign we passed for English bulldogs.

"You see that sign?" Driver mumbles.

"Huh?" I ask, my zest unconvincing.

"Back there, at that corner. Bulldog puppies."

"I didn't notice a corner. But you know what's funny, just the other day I said to myself, 'I think I would be a bulldog person.' Isn't that weird? Just the other day."

"Weird." Driver, verbose as usual.

The restaurant at the Lodge is a large rustic and relaxed A-frame chalet with a long bar and plentiful panoramic windows that let the view devour you like a late-night pint of Ben & Jerry's Chubby Hubby. Once inside, I felt like I had just suited up for the slopes, bid farewell to my foolish ski troop, and teetered straight over to the grand fireplace for a hot toddy amongst new strangers with brandy. But in reality, I was asking the hostess for a table on the patio, where I could be closer to the majesty of the computer-generated countryside that never fully grinds to a halt. Gazing out over the railing is like watching an infinite spool of three-dimensional pop-up storybook carpet unravel with the momentum of a fat man's free-fall. *BAM*, there's your backdrop.

I sipped my much-anticipated bubbly in prissy bliss with sunny beams of delight warming my ever-demure and dainty features. I could have touched the sun with my fork; we were dining a good 7,700 feet in the air. Bound in a fair-weather scarf, clicking pictures, and listening to a trio of grad school gals discuss the artwork at the Bellagio, I was relieved of any pressure to count 56,600 acres of stationary trees for entertainment.

After lunch, we wound through the village below. The village of just a few hundred happy, self-sufficient, wood-chopping, clean air-breathing, possibly-reclusive mountain people. And bulldogs. Plus one homemade lemonade stand managed by a few little ones, which we were happy to oblige. I gave my cup to Driver, who would recognize the taste of anti-freeze *any* day.

"Where was that sign again?" I queried.

"What sign?" Which should have been a sign.

"Puppies," I reminded.

"Oh, we'll pass it on the way out," said Driver.

Moments later, as we bid the majority of the mountainous area farewell, Driver lumbered slowly over the line to "that corner."

"Are you going to call? Let's go see the puppies. We don't need one, just want to look," I suggested. We got directions and were en route. We barely found the place, but were welcomed by two blue kiddy pools full of puppies stuck to their moms' baggy teats. They were quiet and they were tiny. And though they weren't as cute as I had hoped, I still asked to hold one.

It might be helpful to know, I've always rescued pets. Any familiarity with purebreds and their pricing is lost on me at all times. "So, how much are they?"

"They start around $2,800," she told me, like: Why buy a used Honda when you can have a low-slung show dog.

The response in my head (*"TWENTY-EIGHT HUNDRED DOLLARS. ARE YOU F'ING KIDDING ME?"*) was much different than the one I made with my mouth. "Oh," I calmly gestured, seeking refuge in my reservoir for diplomatic ideas to softly separate myself from the possibility of any transaction. Then, with a melodramatic exhale, I looked the little blob in the face but spoke to the professional dog lady. "I just don't know if I have it in me to do a puppy again," pulling him off my chest and standing up to place him back in the pool.

"Well, I have some older dogs, too," she assures us, like we'd be idiots if we didn't leave with a four-legger.

With that, I seemed to be unwittingly roped back in, "Oh? Well, I don't know how our other dogs will do with an older one. We'll probably need to think about it," certain we were free to make an exit before she wheeled out the one-eyed wonder with beautiful brindle markings and hot pink toe nails. Driver and I looked at each other, looked One-Eye in *the* eye, looked at the breeder, looked back at one another.

And as if to delay the insignificant pageantry of the inevitable, we inquired, "How much?"

Sold.

HUMPTY PAHRUMPTY

They say things have a tendency to come full circle every thirty years or so. But that usually relates to fashion, music, or opinions. You know, entire movements—like bell bottoms, bangs, and Mickey Rourke.

But my full-circle moment was more of a meandering déjà vu that came cart-wheeling back in the form of a feature film after traveling seventy miles west of Vegas through the spiky Joshua trees and wild burros of the Mojave Desert. A movie I recall being way too young to watch, but way too young to understand anyway. It was based on a play that opened on Broadway in 1978, nabbed a few Tony Awards, and landed on the silver screen in 1982. It starred two of my favorite famous people. Well, three, if we count Dom DeLuise. It was also a musical, the only reason I was allowed to watch.

Mom didn't take me to see it in the theater because it was R-Rated, and she's not a trashy woman. But it was still an era innocent enough when the R classification could be arranged for title, innuendo, unnoticeable foul language, fairly discreet adult situations, and repeated use of the word *pecker*. By today's standards, the film would likely secure a welterweight PG nod, if grading on a curve. Instead, Mom and I watched it together when it aired two years later as an ABC Sunday night movie; one of the week's anchoring highlights when it came to modern television programming at the time.

1984 was an election year. Commercials that dotted the two-hour special raved about the Apple IIC personal computer, Dodge Caravan's transportation revolution, *The Fall Guy*, Nuprin, and the soft-spoken words of leadership from our late Ronald Reagan. A pre-K Joey Lawrence informed us of Sprint calling services and Nathan Lane dazzled us with his convincing portrayal of a newlywed husband thankful for his Dinner Classics frozen foods. It was the time well before society took "reality" by its enlarged speckled scrotum, shoved it up our mindless three-headed hinies, and then ate it for a million dollars on camera.

We had heard about Pahrump, both legend and lore. Michael Jackson and Heidi Fleiss have had homes there, and the town even had a bit part in *Rain Man*. It's most commonly known for its two wineries and two brothels. Loosely translated, Pahrump means "water rock," owing to the original artesian wells. Given all the marketing materials and provocative ad campaigns, people assume prostitution is legal in Las Vegas, but it's not. However, Nevada is the only state in which it is a permissible service. In the other forty-nine, it's a misdemeanor.

We weren't planning to visit any brothels, but Mr. Sanders at the winery told us they were right down the road. *Why not?* He suggested we sample Sheri's Ranch because it's more open to hosting the curious general population than the Chicken Ranch. And since he's a handsome, distinguished, upright, and respectable man, I was assured by his endorsement. I assumed it would be like going to Panama City or an at-home water birth.

Sheri's Ranch has a bar like any other—not too big, not too small, maybe a thousand square feet. Nothing fancy, yet very clean. A few booths, a few seats around the bar. Maybe a handful of tall tables, lots of standing room everywhere in between. There was a brass pole bolted to the ceiling and a raised platform near the little cubby with some memorabilia for sale. Some of the ladies sauntered through or occupied stools, watching astutely for suitors. They were almost clothed and seemed quite comfortable. The Madam, or shift manager, paced to and fro, keeping a sharp eye on the girls and the bar, but mainly the clientele. I don't think her name was Sheri, she didn't look like one. More like a Cathy (definitely with a C) or a Roberta. She frequently checked in with the patrons and paired the guests with the gal who would provide their tour. Madam was casually dressed, but don't quote me on the outfit. Driver recalls it was a leopard something. Either way, it wasn't the ensemble I remembered from the movie.

Then again, there's only one Dolly Parton. And not everyone can pull off that many sequins, voluptuous beaded bodices, ten-gallon hats, and plunging necklines with the greatest of sleaze like one of the world's most beloved women. Dipped in Frederick's of Hollywood, Dolly played opposite Burt Reynolds as the sheriff, ruling the roost as Miss Mona Stangley (based on Edna Milton), proprietor and leading lady in *The Best Little Whorehouse in Texas*. Nestled down a gravel road in a large Victorian home, all characters sang and dirty-swing-salsa-country line danced, spoofing and grinding through mildly-suggestive choreographed sex scenes pulsating as if beneath a strobe light. For those who don't know, it's a little *Grease 2* meets *Porky's,* but with more costume changes and better lines. Because it's Dolly Parton!

Also known as the Chicken Ranch, the infamous institution had been keeping the fictitious town of Gilbert (LaGrange in real life) satisfied for several generations over the course of its 130-year tenure. Inspired by a true story, the unnamed Texas brothel earned its alias during Hoover's Depression when gentlemen callers would trade services for livestock and produce in lieu of dinero. Soon enough, the grounds were flanked with Leghorns and Red Island Reds and the gals raised them to subsidize their income and food sources. After mounds of media attention and controversy, the government eventually shut the brothel down in August of 1973, much to the dismay of the prideful town, which is where the movie ends. But in 1975, the rights and forty-one Pahrump acres were purchased, becoming the new home for the Chicken Ranch, reputed as the "Best Little Whorehouse in the West."

I was really hoping there would be a grand stairwell or staircase at Sheri's. A wide open one with a banister for the girls to dismount from, like they did in the movie, the way we did in my sorority house. One year we all went home for Christmas, hell, maybe summer, and the entire first floor had been redecorated upon our return. The theme went from outdated frilly Laura Ashley florals to wallpapered entirely in one deep, dark burgundy hue with an imitation shuttle-woven textured brocade pattern. I'm not sure which was worse. It was like being blindfolded and smuggled inside by a huge Liberace cape. The new wall covering melted into the contrasting maroon carpet, turning the downstairs into an awkward and uneasy solar eclipse in interior design.

(Top to bottom) Emily, Sybil, me, Singer. Notice the floral walls.

What was once a bright and cheery space—albeit too sweet and antebellum for my taste—had transgendered into a dark finished basement with framed print art, commercial kitchen, chandeliers, and large dining room. On overcast days, you'd need a flashlight and a miner's helmet just to get from the junction to the front door. I never knew why it had to be called the "junction," such an industrial term for *hallway*. The renovation was all I could talk about at Rush, considering how much I loved Rush. "I know, looks like a total brothel in here, doesn't it? Don't ever be slutty in your letters. It's bad advertising, wherever you pledge."

Lourdes and me. The new wall covering (far left) that was
not carried all the way upstairs. Bonus information: this
get-up was my go-to for most occasions in college.

Once we got the courage to enter Sheri's, these were my character's lines
(give or take a few syllables). I played the role of inquisitive conquistador
and Driver played the recurring role of Driver.

[To Bartender] Hi. How 'bout a Bud Light and a water? And hmm.
Do you have wine? Then I'll have a cabernet. I know, it's like four hundred
degrees out there. We just came from Sanders Winery, saw all your signs,
heading to the other winery for dinner. Whoops, sorry. Sure, we'll go to
a booth. Any of them? Is it really okay we're here? You're so nice. We'll be
over there. Do we come back up here to order?

[To Madam] Hi. It's nice to meet you, too. Appreciate you having
us. Oh, didn't know we couldn't use our phones, thought that meant no
pictures. It was only a text. We'll turn them off. Maybe after this drink.
Okay, I guess we'll look at a menu. Am kinda hungry. Oh, you've already
picked one out for us? I don't think—. Will our stuff be okay here? Just
walk through there? Are those drapes?

[To Driver] I totally just hung up on Kevin. Guess we need to go in
there if she's waiting. I guess it's a *she*, right?

[To Tour Guide] We've never done this before. The lady suggested the
tour. No, we actually live in Vegas. Cool, then what brought you all the

way out here? Oh, duh. Do your parents know? Do they at least know you're in Nevada? What do they think you do? Sorry, we just had the veggie quesadillas if I have fire breath. Food is really good, wasn't sure what to expect from a "sports bar" [using my quote fingers]. Didn't really plan on dining here. Or being here, for that matter. Can I ask how old you are? Does it feel weird to be wearing that? I mean, because the bar stools are vinyl. I don't even like to sit on vinyl when I'm wearing jeans.

There's a hotel here as well? How much? Is that part of the deal? Separate altogether, got it. Where? Oh, I see. That's a nice pool, even has a waterfall. So you guys can't go into the guest rooms but they can come to yours? Interesting. Oh, where you negotiate, got it. What's the going rate? *How much?* Just for—? Whoa. I was in a sorority, too! Is that your real name? Can you tell me what it is? Governmental?

Do you even need a car here? Kinda feels like a compound. Are you allowed to leave? "Pussy Prison," that's hysterical. I really like the "Condoms are Mandatory" signs. They're everywhere. They sell those in the gift shop? Can't believe there's a gift shop. Like souvenirs or toys?

So this is the Dungeon Room? Dark in here. I love that big chair in the corner. What are those dangly things on the side? Kinda smells like bleach in here, that's good. Or is it chlorine? How many Jacuzzis are in here anyway? A spa? You're kidding. Tennis courts *and* volleyball? Voted "Best Brothel of the Year," I'm not surprised. It's a nice award, looks like real crystal. Does anyone play the piano? Who's Sheri anyway?

Oh, it's your first day back? A sabbatical, that's great. This is where you "line up," in the parlor? What does that mean? So then they pick? This is definitely like a sorority. Are we supposed to tip you?

[To Driver] Shit, I forgot her name. You remember?

[Back to Bartender] What was her name again? Sure, we'll have another round. Do you do that, too? Oh, I bet they do. Probably do okay right where you are. More homes around here than I thought. You from here? We're from Atlanta. No, it's hotter there. What are your busiest days? Even on Christmas? Yeah, we pulled into the other one for a picture but I guess you can't eat or drink there if you're not a sure thing. We'll definitely recommend this place. I'm sorry, tell me your name again.

[More with Madam] It was nice, very informative. She's lovely, very thorough. We should tip her, correct? Do we give it to you or take it over to her? Oh, okay.

[Back to Driver] Why do I have to do it? Yeah I know, but I don't know how much. Okay, here I go. Should I take anything else? I feel so overdressed.

[Back to Tour Guide] Just wanted you to have this for your time. Thank you so much for showing us around. I don't know how much is appropriate. Are we supposed to buy you a drink now? Is that what you're having for dinner? Is it soup? You're a vegan? I'm trying to get off gluten! Do you like that kind? I hope to see you again sometime. I mean, you know what I mean. Oh, online? That's good to know. Can I give you a hug?

[Driver, again] No, I don't know what we talked about. You ready?

VALLEY OF FIRE

About fifty miles northeast of Vegas sits the Valley of Fire, in Overton. It's a breathtaking and more personal scale of the Grand Canyon's textures that can be toured as a motorist or on foot. It's a hiker's delight and photog's fortune. Colors so red and rich, the 360-degree backdrop seen from anywhere in the 4x6-mile basin looks like a Hollywood set or something so phony it should require two valid forms of ID. This precious and commanding phenomenon is almost as moving and emotional as the shapes and structures in Sedona, Arizona.

Dedicated in 1935, this state park spans almost 35,000 acres and derives its name from the great shifting of the sandstone and sand dunes (150 million years ago) that appear to be on fire when reflecting the sun. That's dinosaur days, folks. Ironically, the Anasazi Pueblo peoples were never persecuted for or obsessed with texting, sexting, tweeting, getting (gay) married, saying the Pledge of Allegiance, not saying the Pledge of Allegiance, or tallying their Facebook friends while driving. Nor did they have to remove all clothing to board an airplane or need to conjure up opinions about the old guy from *Duck Dynasty*. They were too busy making baskets and looking for water, farming the fertile Moapa Valley, and chiseling petroglyphs.

Valley of Fire is a place that breeds the kind of serenity and centering I can't quite capture with the most befitting of SAT words. Besides, look how many words I've already used. *I need a break!* So I'll draw you a picture instead. Just make the trip; it's worth it. And take a Subway footlong and some white wine, you can picnic there.

BOULDER DASH

Talk about charming, I have plenty to say.

Boulder City is "A World Away for a Day" and an easy drive from Sin City. It's nearly the only populated area in the Silver State that exists without legalized gambling. However, to appeal and appease, wise urban planners anchored two casinos just outside the city limits on either side. As you probably know, the town was developed in the 1930s to house the hard-working progenitors responsible for making Hoover Dam come true and the vision to preserve it as a wholesome model municipality hasn't wavered or buckled since. That said, should you ever make it to Railroad Pass Hotel & Casino on South Boulder Highway on the way into Boulder City, tell Rosie at the bar and Billy on the piano I sent you. No one forgets these dance moves. Or the hat tricks.

Though don't be fooled or dismayed—"No gaming" doesn't mean "No drinking." I was idiotically fearful in my initial misunderstanding that "No gaming" meant it was a "dry town." Silly me. There would obviously be no Milo's Cellar & Inn if that was still the case.

Depending on the weather, we either dine at the tall center deuce inside or one of the patio tables closest to the main avenue. Inside Milo's, hundreds of wine bottles scale the full heft of the left wall in this enchanting bistro that houses maybe five or six interior tables. The peripheral colors amend themselves on both the sidewalk and within the oaky barreled cave each time the sun dims behind the varied mountains that aren't as close and personal in Las Vegas proper. Milo's feels like a hidden, best-kept-secret grotto somewhere between Siena and Lucca and the Inn's tucked-back courtyard is calmly transcending.

Fortunately for us, Milo's is much closer than Italy. Boulder City is about as delightful as you can get within twenty-five miles southeast of Las Vegas. It's the kind of place I want to ride my no-speed purple beach cruiser with a cat in the basket, yodeling well wishes to local artists, polishing the bronze streetscape sculptures with my grandmother's mink stole, and leaving forget-me-nots on all 16,000 of my neighbors' doorsteps. The town boasts a full handful of antique stores, Grandma Daisy's Ice Cream Parlor, a talking Zoltar fortune-telling box, independent coffee shops, a myriad of low-profile motor lodges, a modest Hoover Dam Museum inside the historic Boulder Dam Hotel, as well as the Boulder Theatre now owned and operated by Desi Arnaz, Jr.

It's a step back in time, at a good time. The people there are warm and welcoming, refreshingly happy. Like eerily happy. *Probably because they can drink.* It's the perfect recess from Las Vegas, an easy escape from busy work schedules and all of my chauffer's diligent, obsessed, and time-consuming Publishers Clearing House submissions that have flooded our mailbox and drained my Latin Music Legends stamp collection. It's why we try to get there as often as possible. But I promise, when that streamered and overexcited knock from the PCH Prize Patrol does happen, not much will change. I plan to just hire someone to pump up my white walls and tighten the horn on my handlebars.

***

If I was to over-share, I would tell you that brilliance almost always strikes when I'm at my most limber. And it's no revelation this genius is handsomely aligned with various hues of dark liquor that conveniently complement any three white sangrias from Milo's. Brown spirits generously submerged into my large Styrofoam cup of stout coffee like an accelerant for arson, whilst propped up just a few doors down at the Boulder Dam Brewing Company on a languid afternoon. It's a formula for greatness that should be bow-tied and backlit. There, my luxurious pony tail has a tendency to flit from side to side as my crystal hair clip shimmers in the bright rays infringing on the pub's interior. The servers pepper me with sparkling compliments about said clip and their flattery makes me flutter my tresses some more. The bar is long, the hops tanks are visible, and the staff is affable. We'll read their trivia cards fanned across the bar and I'll surprise Driver with a few correct answers, especially concerning sports. Each time, I leave smiling and lightheaded, in the mood for antiques, blue marble eggs, and dried sage.

On one particularly notable occasion, after having procured the aforementioned baubles, I asked Driver if we could stop by "the round place" with all the windows and electric beer signs on the main drag. (Between you and me, I think Driver was a little curious about it, too.) As soon as we pulled up, we realized it was attached to the Boulder Inn and Suites. Aptly named the InnerCircle Lounge, we entered quietly with darting heads and cautious eyes. By then, it was dark outside, even darker in there.

Once inside, our peepers had wads to devour. To the right was a meandering game room vaunting of green felt tables and hazy plumes of smoke. To the left was a flat field of charcoal-tinted windows and fewer than five staring faces. Straight ahead was a desolate staircase that definitely went up, not sure about down. Though a hotel, this was clearly a common stoop for locals. And not necessarily folks who live in walking distance, but regulars who are there most evenings visiting the bartender I have a faulty inclination to call Sophie. Several televisions breathe vigor into the matchless ambiance and deeply hypnotize those operating the bar stools. No serious game grumbles or intense roars, just a light mantle of occasional chatter over football plays deemed remarkable or revolting. Guys with beer, sitting there.

The veterans circled around the bar only grew interested in making conversation because they'd never seen us before. And Driver began speaking the loudest to the overhead monitors, nothing of which obscured our presence. That, paired with my wondering aloud why it was so *QUIET*. I asked Sophie if they had any decaf. After all, it was getting late and I didn't need heart palpitations to accompany a long night of twitchy pacing and the bombardment of queries to Driver about the leading signs of cardiac arrest. Sophie graciously obliged by having to run "upstairs" to whip some up, only then learning the glass booze rotunda must be somewhere below the lobby or the kitchen. She trusted all of us to watch over her semi-triangular bar and returned with a tall mug to then line liberally with their finest Irish whiskey. The only insinuation my beverage included coffee was driven by its temperature, in every one of my refills. Her errand upstairs with the mug was quite possibly a rouse to shake things up with the new girl at the Regal Beagle. I knew right away Sophie and I were going to be tight.

Bored to tears listening to the evolving football pontifications, I took note of the quiet woman sitting by herself on my far right. She and Sophie shared a different language and I assumed they were close friends. She was drinking a soda and had a backpack. She was busy, but I didn't know what she was doing. Unaware my head was tilted almost to my shoulder as I observed her, Sophie informed me the woman was deaf. I perked up. Driver lent a swooping glare as if my next step was pouncing onstage at a Kenny G concert. I extended my best you-ain't-seen-nothin'-yet smirk and got up from my stool.

I helped myself over to the seat beside her and let her know I knew sign language. Well, the alphabet. I was giddy to the point of hyper. *Finally, I had someone at that bar to talk to!* Even better, she could read lips. What I learned (once again) about myself was that I cannot move my mouth without volume or sound. And after four quarts of whiskey, I definitely felt speaking louder would be a game-changer. I was almost positive she could hear me.

We talked and talked for hours and hours. Everyone, all five in attendance, heard or saw every word coming out of our lips and hands. Poor Sophie probably had to place an emergency napkin order that week because our written dialogues looked like someone had TP'd the countertop twice and then made a mummy with conversational bullet points and Pictionary portraits. I don't know if that bar ever closes, but the bus line back to Henderson sure did.

At that hour, whichever one it was, Driver wasn't very excited about my offer to give my new friend a lift back to her house. Driver does *not* know sign language—p.s., only a few choice gestures that would soon enough wind up in my personal space. As the translator, I maybe should have sat in the back seat. But as the mentally-impaired person, I sat in the front. And boy was I tired. So tired, I needed to take a nap just moments after we all piled in the car. Fortunately, my friend was able to point the way home.

Driver just had to travel very, very slowly to watch both the road and the arm coming from behind while I was out of commission.

Then, all of a sudden, I was being unkindly jabbed in the shoulder to get out and say goodbye before we pulled into a gas station for a Diet Coke.

I could spend every day basking in Boulder City, peddling around on Purple-Myrtle-Slow-as-a-Turtle and slurping up views of crisp and turquoise Lake Mead. But I choose to cherish it as a place quite sacred. A place I long to miss and a place that must often miss me. Because it's not that *every* day is a holiday here, but sometimes it's nice to go somewhere that reminds me I'm always on vacation.

As having a real job would leave me absolutely no time for all of this "research."

HOT DAM

Thanks to my adulthood dismissal of American history, for all I knew, it could have been erected by a bunch of beavers with discarded toothpicks and smooshed mud pies during the winterization of their territory against the grueling elements and daunting predators that combed the southwest landscape more than eight decades ago. But, that would contend with it being touted as one of the Seven Wonders of the Industrial World.

Unless beavers were already advancing at such a rapid pace that they used popular household vacuums to seize up the Black Canyon of the Colorado River, creating Lake Mead.

I had to see it for myself, beyond the brief and indistinct glance out the passenger side window when we made our initial approach into the Las Vegas city limits. By that point, the thirty-ninth car hour, I was much too dizzy to browse. Or care. So, with my two flat feet on the ground, I would be able to deduce if it was anything other than a muddy mound of twigs and vacuum cleaners all plugged into one big surge protector generating hydroelectric power for Arizona, Nevada, and Southern California.

About a forty-minute drive from Vegas, ours was a particularly windy day. As we hiked up the low-grade incline and made our way to the center of the bridge, I held my shirt down with one hand and buried my Nikon in the other palm. We arrived too late for any tour, but it's a pretty self-explanatory experience. There it was, almost too overwhelming to capture on film, even with a wide angle lens and stunt wire. With over three million cubic yards of pristine off-white concrete in the dam—enough to pave a two-lane highway from California to New York, approximately 2,900 miles, one way—plus another million cubic yards in the power plant and other works. I'm here to say, this art deco arch-gravity dam was definitely not the toil of any beaver family or suction appliance. You heard it here first.

It wasn't always called the Hoover Dam, you know. It was once known as Boulder Dam and there was much controversy surrounding the name and the official dedication, a ceremony to which President Hoover wasn't even invited. *Ouch.* You see, President Coolidge (1923-1929) authorized the Dam in late 1928, President Hoover (1929-1933) ordered work to begin in March 1931 (originally planned for October), and they were all popping their eyeballs out with champagne corks in September 1935 to prepare for the opening in 1936, under President Roosevelt (1933-1945). Per this simple timeline, it's easy to see that ole Herb had very little, if anything, to do with the Dam. He just sat around, resting on his laurels, dealing with the Great Depression or whatever. But they like to name these things after presidents, an exercise that contradicts having temporarily named it Boulder Dam after Boulder City—as you know, the community created to house upwards of five thousand employees and their families to pull off this outlandish historical project. For more than fifteen years, they treated this man-made marvel like an orphan because they couldn't decide what to put on the birth certificate.

The undertaking wrapped eighteen months ahead of schedule, an achievement that cannot even be delivered in contemporary times with all of our technology and astonishing engineering developments. Construction took only five years to complete, half the amount of time it took to find Bin Laden. The total cost was just around $49 million, roughly equivalent to eight fixer-uppers in the Hollywood Hills. Also of interest, there were only two labor strikes, the average summer temperature was 119 degrees, and 112 lives were lost throughout the course of this ambitious endeavor.

So put your turtlenecks, muffs, and long johns on because this will give you chills.

The first man to lose his life on the project was surveyor J.G. Tierney, who drowned on December 20, 1922, while searching the most immaculate site for the dam. Thirteen years to the day later, his son, Patrick W. Tierney, fell from one of the intake towers and died—just months before the grand opening. No one asked, but I think *TIERNEY* sounds like a pretty dam-good name to me.

Maybe *I* should run for president.

VIEW FROM THE PASSENGER SEAT

I'm not sure if it was a wise idea or not for me (us) to watch *Wrong Turn* a few weeks before our cross-country move, but we did. The true account relives the absolute fright and survival skills of one family foursome who took a *guess what?* somewhere in the Oregon mountains. In the dark. In a blizzard. In the middle of nowhere, yet somewhere down a typically closed-off logging road. Driver's ongoing commentary during the show should have been recorded as a gratis lecture series for State Farm insurance.

In case you were wondering, we did survive the five-day drive along I-40's tornado alley from Atlanta, caught on to the most common of KOA rituals by our fourth night in snow-covered Flagstaff, and Driver even showed me how to heat up hot dog buns in the bag they came in over a small charcoal grill. Camping experience accomplished. Quite fortunately, we fell in love at first sight with the as-seen-online-only Spanish colonial in the northern suburbs. What we weren't prepared for, was learning the house came with a Roy, the hanger-onner handy man who just showed up like Schneider and stuck around like smog.

We spent the first night in Carpet Kingdom eating Chinese and sleeping on a quilted pallet on the floor. All animals were piled up around us in front of the gas fireplace you ignite with the flip of a switch, not a cord of wood or petulant pilot light sheathed in decaying brick. We awoke to a blinding sun greeting us from behind a striking perimeter of mountains at 5 a.m., allowing plenty of time to prepare for the Mayflower moving truck that would arrive with all of our worldly possessions four hours later.

And in that matter of time, we lost the cat. *We lost the damn cat.* After finally managing to master the best morning routine to accommodate and drug the feline for long-distance vehicular travel, we got her clear across the country and lost her at our destination in less than twelve hours. I was livid, and certain it was Driver's fault. I dashed outside bellowing for Jillian Junks in my makeshift travel jammies, meeting new neighbors with hasty hair and no bra for the very first time that crisp spring morning. The artwork was soon being uncrated by a stoic two-man crew, the quartet of conversational movers were unloading, and the barrage of "Where would you like this, ma'am?" despite my labels, Post-Its, and other diagrams ricocheting across the flat ecru empty walls. "Where would *you* want a mattress? Probably not my dining room." I had a cat to find, or tears to weep. Roy was there, too.

Then I lost my purse. I had hid it from everyone, including myself. Boxes were being deposited in every free slot on the floor and I was working double-time to unpack as they provided more. Driver was busy asking how best to stay out of my way and assisting with anything else that could be done in between. I've never lived in a home with so many kitchen cabinets; they were everywhere. I could finally put all for-looks-only appliances and had-to-have place settings away somewhere other than the attic or laundry room. And there they were. When tossing my Tupperware cupcake tote into Door #38, my red handbag and tortie kitty were staring back at me from the deep, dark lower shelf with concentrated looks of disenchantment, terror, and agitated impatience. At that moment, everything and everyone was right where they belonged—in our new place, in our new city, diving face first into our new life. All was well in the world.

I told Roy not to let the door hit him in the ass.

***

Turns out, Las Vegas is a place like any other. It's outfitted with real people, children, pets, schools, utility companies, construction workers, mailboxes, art, music, banks, even minivans. It's landlocked like a bunch of other states, has its own politicians, and even has a complete history. What's also true, I didn't catch on fire upon arrival and I've managed just fine without a fog machine or pyrotechnics to blend seamlessly into the city's atmosphere.

The town's normalcy is unexpected. Nothing I've seen or heard has made me clutch my pearls or drop my jaw, so it's either shockingly sedate or my college years really *were* as crazy as everyone thought. Hookers and strippers aren't looped around light poles, men in trench coats aren't flashing you on corners with watches or their privates, and most people who live here don't actually hang out on the Strip. I'm probably one of the few residents who neither works on the Strip nor gambles, but can spend a full day losing all track of time on Las Vegas Boulevard.

It's a spot on the map that makes first and lasting impressions with the attitude of a casino lobby's design, often dressy, gallery-like environments with what may be comparable to the South's version of come-on-in hospitality. Except you can't put your feet on the coffee table or your hand in the ice maker. (Well, it's not encouraged.)

There's no state lottery or professional sports team and I've bumped into more dental offices than churches. The recognizable tract homes are doused in a neutral palate of limited colors not only to merge into the landscape, but to fare decently against the blazing sun's power to fade hues any brighter. Not because locals don't like purple.

Happy Hour around here isn't just a referenced time of day, it really involves drink specials. There's also no such thing as "last call" since most everything is open twenty-four hours. You often hear things like "Today's my Friday" on any given day, instead of "What are you doing this weekend?" I've met the most interesting people at the most peculiar of times at the most spontaneous of venues. And while I don't think I have much of an accent anymore, people still tell me I do. Especially after a few drinks, then I'm totally charming, completely Southern, and have no choice but to overdo it for audiences I have likely courted without their consent.

Also in Vegas, urban planners were miraculously able to find grand inspiration to name streets rather than just reprocessing and perpetuating only one. Granted, they may only be the first names of humans like Wayne and Brenda, but duplicates are rare. I can only imagine the throngs of live *peach trees* that had to die in Atlanta in order to pave all of the streets, roads, avenues, circles, drives, ways, and lanes in their honor. I couldn't even tell you what a peach tree looks like, never saw one.

But I can tell you, I don't miss waking up dressed for sunshine and driving home in a tsunami, dodging falling trees and contemplating the uproar of an ice storm—all before and after weather anchors have told me not to take baths during a severe drought. Nor do I long for mosquitoes or the mushrooms that grow the size of potbelly pigs after each flood and must be kicked over with disposable shoes before someone from the county asks about a building permit. Likewise, I'm not pining for the counterproductive effects of humidity and the inability for spray paint, Wite-Out, and those too-tight jeans to dry naturally within sixty-four hours. And I would be remiss if I didn't mention pollen: the fifth season. Can't say I ever had much use for that chalky yellow mist of allergy-inducing anguish and parading dusty layer of nature's germination process on everything from my car to inside things with childproof caps.

More than anything, I've learned how much I love people who love Vegas. I also love people who don't. But I especially love the ones who have never been, yet carry resolute opinions and steadfast convictions about the city, just like I did. Those are the people I want to climb inside this book, ruminate a little, rub it three times for luck, and realize they've just changed their minds. The tassels are optional.

After all, tomorrow is another day.

ACKNOWLEDGMENTS

For Mom and Mike—there are no words. My attempt will sound clumsy, trite, and insufficient—but I love you, I thank you, I have needed you. You've plied me with love, support, laughter, solace, and have always told me to chase what inflates me with joy and inspiration. Mom, you are the ever-present *wind beneath my wings*, and set the example I wish to one day become. LUM.

For Driver—who got on board with every outrageous idea or event this project required. You humored me, laughed at me, humored me some more, and sometimes (I think) had just as much fun as I did. I will never be able to thank you properly, or enough. But, thank you. You're a really good driver, too. I love you.

For my dear friends within these pages—thank you for letting me exploit you with splashy puddles of genuine fondness. The memories will always be too big for any book. (You know I'm not much of a reader anyway.) Always remember the feathers, the dancing, the drinks, the music, and talking for hours on end. One day—*they say*—we will be old and might not be able to soar from the stages, spring from the banisters, and concoct new routines. But we will always have each other. Please wear sunscreen.

For Leslie Silver, Patricia Zdravkovich, Barbara Hamby, and Hollis Gillespie—all of you amazing instructors and authors through different iterations of my life—have influenced, changed, and challenged the way I write and think. You gave me just enough to let me happen upon, develop, and settle into my voice. I thank you, from the ground up.

For Jami Carpenter, Editor —thank you for believing in my "stories" after only one phone conversation, having ain't never even seen what I writed like. I must be amazing on the phone. Your knowledge of Vegas was necessary and I appreciate you understanding semi-colons give me the shakes.

For Fallon McBride, Graphic Designer—thank you for transforming our twenty-minute dialogue over coffee and a few of my sketches into the very image within my mind's eye ("I'd like it to be me as Miss Piggy as Scarlett O'Hara as a showgirl"), incorporating your own clever style into the cover that fashions the face of this opus. You are so unbelievably efficient, creative, and astute—you blew me away.

For Christal Presley—who paved the book way for me, thank you for letting me pick your brain into tiny little pieces. For Kami Chandler— thank you for our bottomless conversations on creativity and simply knowing we'd both get to each of our *every* wheres. For Lori Perrotti— thank you for the times you've asked to team up with a writing project, leading a long-standing cheer, and just a friendly reminder that you promised to "buy 200" of these.

For Tim and Michele Strickland—thank you for the business opportunity to seize this whole Vegas extravaganza, the belief in Driver's smarts, and let's face it, heeding moi's fervor to relocate. I will forever cherish our night that I almost mud-wrestled that woman, in my dress-up clothes, at Gilley's. I could have taken her, these thighs are like nutcrackers. Michele—you and me—Donny & Marie. *Tick-tock!*

For Fred Jolly and Pete Prioleau—thank you for ushering us into Las Vegas like the big warm hug you remain today. We would have otherwise stumbled a bit to find such an exquisite assembly without your immediate introductions and smattering of love. And to our entire group, each and every visit has been a precious gift. Tremendous blessings you all are.

For Diana deLatour, Evie Frye, and Kirstin Nelson Pilot—thank you for taking the time to read this in its very unframed state and offering honest feedback. You were all equally gentle and kind in your critiques and appraisals, and have been part of very distinct periods in my life thus far. I love that you all said, in your own way, "I actually enjoyed it." *Actually!*

For Tom Gaylord—thank you for suggesting the title after I had been struggling with several I knew would require way too many permissions to use. We shall hoist a glass of something to celebrate. Funny we would meet at a book signing—Oscar Goodman's, of course!

For Margaret Mitchell—thank you for giving the world an incredible piece of literature. With all of my respect and appreciation, thank you for letting me honor a little bit of your creative spirit and permanent legacy. I wanted *you* to have the last words in this book.

For the Mayors Goodman—thank you for having such contagious passion for this great city and making yourselves accessible to the people who thrive within it. You've been the change, made the changes, and reinvented the complexion of Sin City. I'm thrilled to have been here while both of you have been in office and deliriously giddy to have made your acquaintances. The Green Envelope Girl thinks you're super-fly, Carolyn, and YOLO, Oscar. See you at the Plaza, cheers!

For Celine Dion—can we be friends?? Your people can call me directly because I don't have any people for them to call!

For three guys I don't know personally (yet!)—Tony Hsieh of Zappos and the Downtown Project, Pasquale Rotella of Insomniac Events and the Electric Daisy Carnival, and Rehan Choudhry of the Life is Beautiful Festival. You guys have done some amazing things for Vegas and I know I'm not alone in thanking you.

For Bette, Cher, and Tina—you gals are the constant music in the soundtrack of my life. You don't know it, but I thank you often, for all sorts of things. This book should be no exception.

For the City of Atlanta and the City of Las Vegas—you and your residents will always be special, dear, and memorable for me. I am grateful to have incorporated you into my life's repertoire, my experiences, my lessons, and my growth. Atlanta (and the airport), please know, had you not been so rife with variety and animation, you would never be worth writing about.

For my favorite Vegas restaurants—Mount Charleston Lodge, Oscar's Beef Booze Broads, Golden Steer, Thai Basil, Firefly, Triple George Grill, and the Barrymore. You can thank my ongoing appetite and your incredible fare and service for the repeat patronage, and Driver for paying.

For my favorite Atlanta haunts and sensations—Café Intermezzo, Vickery's, Buckhead Diner, Anis, Universal Joint, Raging Burrito, Eddie's Attic, and Wahoo. You can thank me for not having been in an office all those years and was able to spend copious time on your patios, at your tables, lining your bars, and writing from your booths. I miss you, a lot. I often daydream of magnolias, hydrangeas, dogwoods, and the tulips that begin to rise just after winter. But more than anything, I miss the front porches, the back decks, and the sides of sofas I occupied with dear friends and welcoming personalities, engulfed in deep conversation, comfort food, slick banter, and disorderly laughter. Thanks *y'all*, for being that, and those.

For anyone who reads this book—thank you, very much. Come to Vegas. Bring Chapstick, hydrate, and you wear sunscreen, too.

Love & Light,
Stefany